ISBN: 9781313774864

Published by:
HardPress Publishing
8345 NW 66TH ST #2561
MIAMI FL 33166-2626

Email: info@hardpress.net
Web: http://www.hardpress.net

Date Due

TA EIC EAYTON

MARCUS AURELIUS ANTONINUS
TO HIMSELF

ὁ Ἑρμᾶς δὲ βλέψας εἰς τὸν Μάρκον Σοὶ δέ, εἶπεν,
ὦ Βᾶρε, τί κάλλιστον ἐδόκει τοῦ βίου τέλος εἶναι; καὶ
ὃς ἤρεμα καὶ σωφρόνως Τὸ μιμεῖσθαι, ἔφη, τοὺς θεούς.

JULIANUS, *Caesares*.

Marcus Aurelius Antoninus to Himself: an English Translation with Introductory Study on Stoicism and the Last of the Stoics

BY

GERALD H. RENDALL, M.A., Litt.D.

LATE FELLOW OF TRINITY COLLEGE, CAMBRIDGE

PRINCIPAL AND PROFESSOR OF GREEK

UNIVERSITY COLLEGE, LIVERPOOL

London

MACMILLAN AND CO., Limited

NEW YORK: THE MACMILLAN COMPANY

1898

A.111383

PREFACE

ENGLISH translations of Marcus Aurelius abound, from that of Meric Casaubon in 1634, to that of George Long first published in 1862. The choicest, alike in form and contents, is the Foulis Press edition executed by James Moor and Francis Hutcheson ; and it better deserved reproduction than the looser version by Jeremy Collier. But none, in point of scholarship, reaches the level of modern requirement. In this last quarter of the century, the poets, historians, and philosophers of Greece have, one after another, been given to English readers with scholarly precision and in becoming dress. And it seemed worth while to do the same for Marcus Aurelius. For purposes of education, the classical writers justly enjoy more vogue, and are better suited to train taste, intellect, and imagination ;

but by direct and permanent appeal to heart and
conscience, without support from prescription or
conventions, Marcus holds his own and lives.
Translations, essays, and the records of biographies
all testify how simple and learned alike fall under
his spell, and find in his *Thoughts* material that
gives support to duty, courage under disappointment, consolation in sorrow, and calm amid the
bustle of life.   To Renan, they are 'the most
human of all books ; ' ' the gospel that will never
grow old.'   To Myers ' the life of Marcus ' —
and the *Thoughts*, they only, are the life—' will
remain for ever the normal high-water mark
of the unassisted virtue of man.'   To Matthew
Arnold ' the acquaintance of a man like Marcus
Aurelius is an imperishable benefit ; ' as ' the
especial friend and comforter of clear-headed and
scrupulous, yet pure-hearted and upward-striving
men, in those ages most especially that walk by
sight not by faith, but yet have no open vision.'

In dealing with a writer such as this, in
whom matter and mood are the things of prime
importance, a translator's first duty is to make his
English natural, clear, and readable ; and, subject
always to this demand, to reproduce, as far as

may be, the manner, tone, and accent of the
original. These are a part of idiosyncrasy; they
give reality and life to this self-revelation of a
soul. And in spite of certain obvious defects and
obscurities of style, the task is not impossible.
That the style is crabbed [1] is in large measure
true ; but by no means, that ' it lacks physiognomy.' [1] Marcus wrote in Greek, because
Greek in the second century, as Latin in the
Middle Ages, was the natural medium of philosophy and the language of his teachers. He
acquired it as a foreign tongue, after his entrance
upon manhood, and moves in it with some constraint and difficulty. Latinisms of syntax as
well as of vocabulary are not infrequent ; and
even the habit of Greek composition strikes one
as newly acquired and practised. As the work
progresses, and as the same trains of thought
recur, utterance becomes readier, and he wields
his instrument with more precision and dexterity.
The heavy cramped vocabulary, the deadness
of expression, the formless monotony of clause,
that characterise the first book, give way to
more natural and simple movements ; language,

[1] So M. Arnold.

structure, and thought gain ease and freedom,
almost with each successive book.   The first four
books abound in awkward and difficult Greek ; in
the last four stumbling - blocks are few.   Yet
throughout the style is essentially the same.   Its
' physiognomy ' is unmistakable ; it wins insensibly
upon the reader, and becomes part of a familiar
personality ; the deliberateness, the restraint, the
struggle between natural sentiment and Stoic
' apathy,' are rich in suggestion and appeal ; the
words, as was said truly of St. Paul's, ' have hands
and feet.'   The very sense of effort produces a
certain uncommonness of phrase, such as gives
interest and even distinction to an intelligent
foreigner using a tongue and idiom not wholly
familiar.   Marcus hits off phrases and combinations, which, if not quite felicitous, strike the
mind and stick ; he never becomes rhetorical like
Seneca, or prolix like Epictetus, or glib like
Lucian ; and a certain choiceness of expression
lends impressiveness and charm.   Throughout,
too, it may be said that the poetry of sentiment
is in advance of the poetry of actual phrase.   And
thus upon the whole the *Thoughts* may be numbered among the books, in which a translator

may gain as much or more than he is forced to lose in the process of reproduction. One cannot, without pedantry, reproduce details of mannerism, yet their general effect may remain recognisable.

Harmless *anacolutha*—changes of person, tense, or syntax—I have purposely retained, as proper to a private diary of thoughts. In reproduction of vocabulary, I have been as strict as my command of English allowed, and have been, perhaps, over-scrupulous in careful concordancing of words. Yet this is of no small importance : to the student, as correlating passages of kindred thought or phrase, to the general reader, as preserving a real and often telling trait of mind and manner. Though strict consistency is unattainable in the change from one language to another, at least the most characteristic repetitions are retained. Stoic terminology in this matter presents some special difficulties ; it reached Marcus in a late scholastic phase, and English does not always possess or admit a scholastic counterpart ; of this the theory of Pneuma and pneumatic currents may serve as an example. Sometimes the scholastic term has passed through and gradually outgrown scholastic precision and severity. In such cases I have selected some term (or terms) of general, rather than technical significance, rendering ὑπόληψις, for instance, throughout, by 'view' or 'assumption;' φαντασία by 'impression' or 'regard.' For the characteristic τὸ ἡγεμονικόν, after repeated trials, I could find no standing equivalent, and in place of translation have reluctantly fallen back on the imperfect paraphrase 'Inner Self.' As a mere convention, and to save tedious iteration of phrase, I have written Nature with a capital, where it represents ἡ φύσις τῶν ὅλων (or τοῦ ὅλου) in the original.

The Introduction, the scope and intention of which is explained at the outset, is strictly supplementary to the Translation; full references are supplied to the work itself, but I have abstained from adding references to other writers, ancient or modern. Where much is matter of controversy, the statement of conclusions must necessarily seem at times dogmatic and unguarded, but any student of Stoicism will perceive how much I owe to specialists like Stein, Hirzel, and Bonhöffer, and to historians of philosophy such as Zeller, Windelband, and many others.

In choice of readings I have not followed any single text, but adopted that which most commended itself to my judgment. Stich's *Teubner* edition gives all important MSS. variants, and the emendations of previous editors and critics. Others come from various sources, and most of those due to myself are discussed in *The Journal of Philology*, vol. xxiii. 116 pp.; those which materially affect translation are printed in an Appendix at the end.

I tender grateful thanks to Mr. R. D. Hicks, Fellow of Trinity College, Cambridge, for minute and friendly pains expended upon the Translation, and to Professor A. C. Bradley for valuable hints and suggestions for the improvement of the Introduction.

CONTENTS

INTRODUCTORY ESSAY

ON

STOICISM AND THE LAST OF THE STOICS

THE aim of this Introduction is not to give a complete or balanced exposition of Stoicism as a whole, but to consider so much of it as remains implicit or explicit in the words of Marcus Antoninus, so that the reader of the *Thoughts*, in approaching the 'dogmas' and the formulas which they contain, may have in mind their origin, their meaning, their development, and their eventual content for Marcus and his contemporaries. For this end portions of Stoic doctrine may be ignored, or touched but lightly : Stoic developments of logic and of grammar may pass unheeded ; physics and physiology will concern us only in their ethical connexions ; and some sides of epistemology may be disregarded. Upon the other hand special factors, which asserted or reasserted themselves in the Roman phase of Stoicism, will receive consideration in excess of their real importance to philosophy at large, or even to Stoicism as a system. In physics the revival of Heraclitean formulas, in ethics of Socratic aphorisms is

b

marked; in psychology a new, or at least modified, physiological basis was furnished by the medico-physical speculations of the Pneumatists; in epistemology, Epictetus becomes of no less importance than Cleanthes. Thus the treatment of Stoicism will be selective, intended to supply so much of history and exposition as a careful reader may desire for comprehension of his author. The treatment of the subject is neither strictly chronological, nor strictly systematic. As each topic comes under consideration, I have felt free to follow it to its particular destination in the pages of Marcus, or merely to allot its place in the general *corpus* of doctrine, which he received as Stoic dogma.

I.—Origins of Stoicism

Of all ancient philosophies Stoicism is the most historical. The person of the founder is but a term in a continuous series of thought. The system of Plato or of Aristotle bears the sharp impress of a single mind, apprehending and affirming a new synthesis of truth; the office of disciples was to preserve and transmit thoughts, which in their fulness they grasped imperfectly. Emphatically, the disciple was less than the master. But Stoicism was the product of many minds, not one : the function of Zeno was to combine far more than to originate; his individual contribution to philosophic thought was small, and to some extent tentative. The unification of the system and its logical completion was largely the work of successors, Cleanthes and Chrysippus, so that the proverb said truly, 'Had there been no Chrysippus, there would

history of stoicism resembles that of a religion rather than a speculative system
⤷ permanent unity; combining seeming opposites into a solid platform; deep and conscious
⤷ derived from opposite types and schools of thought.

I   ORIGINS OF STOICISM   xv

have been no Porch.' And this power of development and adaptation was inherent in the system. Founded in the fourth century B.C., it was a quick and growing creed in the second century A.D.; living, it survived transplantation from the Greek world to the Roman, from the school and the cloister to the Senate and the throne; dying, it bequeathed no small part of its disciplines, its dogmas, and its phraseology to the Christianity by which it was ingathered.[1] In these respects its history resembles that of a religion rather than a speculative system; while its range, from Socrates to M. Antoninus, covers almost all that was permanent in the ancient culture, and even survived the wreck of European Paganism.

From the first its hold upon the past was deep and conscious: its evolution is a striking instance how human thought, convinced by slow experience, secures gradual advance, by combining seeming opposites into a solid platform for new effort. Supervening at the moment when the *original* forces of Greek thought fell back exhausted, Stoicism constructed an impressive and, to some extent, a permanent unity out of factors derived from opposite types and schools of thought, and so evolved moral and social conceptions that have become an heirloom of Western civilisation, and are embedded in the inmost structure of the Christian state. In this sense it is the most 'historical' of ancient philosophies in cast and in expression; and M. Aurelius is only partially intelligible, without some knowledge of

---

[1] "The basis of Christian society is not Christian, but Roman and Stoical" (Hatch, *Hibbert Lectures* on 'The Influence of Greek Ideas and Usages upon the Christian Church,' p. 170).

the various deposits of Greek thought, which find a
place in his philosophy, and which form a combination
of dexterous and surprising intricacy.

Early in the sixth century B.C., when Greek thought
thrilled into sudden interest in the causes and origin of
things, the first question to rouse and baffle intellectual
curiosity was, naturally enough, the make and nature of
the external world. What was it made of? How did
it come into being? and continue to exist? What was
its 'nature'? These were the questions which first
troubled the waters of Western thought, and aroused
the speculative curiosity and imagination of the Ionian
philosophers. Behind the countless variety of things lay
an irresistible suggestion of order and of unity, which,
amid the infinite diversity of phenomena, seemed to
connect the phases of matter, and to shape the round of
being, in alternations of succession and recurrence, within
the limits of some fixed mould, or subject to the operations of some unifying power such as inhabits and directs
the individual organism. What was the fixed something
that underlay the phases of transformation? The
earliest guess attributed the unity to oneness of *material*,
and looked for some elemental stuff that might be
regarded as the common cause and basis of existent
things. The study of phenomena showed everywhere
the passage from form to form, the processes of birth,
change, decay, and reconstruction, nothing anywhere
coming out of nothing, or passing from being back into
nothingness. What was the fixed One among the
moving Many? The great visible unities, earth, sea,
and sky—the solid, the fluid, and the gaseous—were

the great visible unities — earth (solid), sea (fluid), sky (gaseous)

Thales - water - prime unit of nature, of material being

Anaximenes - air - spirit, breath of life, quantitative infinity

Fire - generative heat, ductile energies, incomparable mobility; truest source and rep. of nature's one inherent life

tried in turn by the Ionian physicists. Thales selected Water, the most versatile of substances, and the most variable in form, as the prime unit of 'nature,' that is of material being. Anaximenes gave the preference to Air, which thought and language had so long associated with the spirit and breath of life, and which alone met the demand for quantitative infinity Others turned to Fire, and contemplating its generative heat, its ductile energies, its incomparable mobility, found in it the truest source and representative of nature's one inherent life. Theory directed and quickened observation, and foundations of science were laid in the observation of the celestial bodies, and in the study of rarefaction, condensation, liquefaction, congelation, and other natural processes : but for the understanding of Stoicism the main outcome is the fixed determination to derive the world of matter, in spite of superficial appearances, from a *single* source of being. And the Stoics, in their more mature endeavour to explain the Universe on a monistic basis, pay tribute to these early cosmologists in freely employing such terms as Air, Breath, Fire, to denote that elemental substance or spirit which pervades and underlies all things that are.

Nature defied these efforts to reduce its contents to a single physical term, and the death-blow to such endeavours was given by the genius of Heraclitus. He propounded a more intelligible reconciliation between the Many of sense and the One of thought. To him the shifting panorama did not suggest kaleidoscopic states of rest, succeeding one another as a series of abrupt and stationary rearrangements. Being seemed rather

Stoicism to understand — fixed determination to derive the world of matter, in spite of superficial appearances, from a single source of being

Air, Breath, Fire — elemental substances, spirit, that pervade and underly all things that are

the expression of a moving power, not of separable
substance or identity, but manifested only in the passage
of continuous phenomena. The many are the moving
realisation of the eternal One. 'Being' was always
'becoming'—not a state but a process, not rest but
motion—and its true image was the flame which in
kindling extinguishes, and in extinguishing kindles that
which is its fuel. 'All things are in flow'[1] was the
central and lasting summary of his teaching, which
eventually supplied the basis of Stoic physics, and
became the key to ethics, history, and life. 'Being is
a river in continual flow, its action for ever changing,
its causes infinite in variation'[2]; and in the pages of
Marcus no figures are more recurrent than the Heraclitean metaphors of the 'river,'[3] the 'flame,'[4] and the
'upward and downward path'[5] of the elements of being.
To Heraclitus himself, except in so far as he was
content to let figure usurp the place of fact, 'the ever-
living fire' remained material, akin (though more in
virtue than in kind) to the visible fire 'that burns and
crackles,' that uses all substances for fuel, but in con-
suming re-endows with new forms and properties and
use, the effective instrument or medium by whose
operative power 'the death of earth is the birth of
water, the death of water the birth of air, the death of

---

[1] πάντα ρεῖ, quoted or illustrated, ii. 3, 17 ; iv. 3, 36 ; v. 10, 13 ;
vi. 4, 15, 17 ; vii. 25 ; ix. 19, 28 ; x. 7, and many more. For the
ethical place accorded to Heraclitus, cf. iv. 46 ; vi. 42, 47 ; viii. 3.
[2] v. 23.
[3] ii. 17 ; iv. 43 ; v. 23 ; vi. 15, 37 ; vii. 19 ; ix. 28, 29 ; xii. 3, etc.
[4] iv. 1, 19 ; viii. 20 ; x. 31.   [5] iv. 46 ; vi. 17, 46 ; vii. 1 ; ix. 28.

air fire, and so conversely'[1] by return along 'the downward path.' This 'plastic fire' operates in man as a
kindling movement of inherent life, an inhaling and
exhaling heat or breath or spirit, which at once conducts
and reveals the processes of life ; and on the larger scale
of the universe it is the quickening cosmic flow which
constitutes a world-order out of the consumption and
replenishment of interchanging opposites—moist and
dry, soft and hard, dark and light, hot and cold. As
an inner life or reason of phenomena, as supplying the
power and determining the mode of their expression, as
the instrument of rectification or balance between con-
tending opposites, as the unseen operative and directive
power, it may be spoken of as Reason or Justice or
Destiny or God. Thus in their inmost being 'gods
and men are one.'

In language of this kind scientific intuition outran the
power and even the desire of exact analysis. Grappling
with a new and complex order of truths, as fascinating
as they were baffling to scientific apprehension, Heraclitus found in metaphor and figure the fittest expression for ideas which eluded experimental or observational
proof. His genius for analogy and aphorism, and in
particular his predilection for moralising physical processes—so natural to early speculation, extricating itself
from mythological modes of thought—anticipated later
conceptions of philosophy, and oracular ambiguity of
form gave to his *dicta* a compass and a pregnancy
which captivated and inspired the imagination of successors ; his forecasts seemed a divination, and 'the

[1] iv. 46.

dark' philosopher was ranked first among the prophets of science. As interpretation of phenomena advanced along the lines which he first opened up, the figures he had used seemed at each step more pregnant with suggestion, and the master's authority is claimed for applications and affirmations which lay far beyond his own materialistic horizon. His two cardinal contribu--tions to physics were, his resolution of mechanical change into continuous dynamical progress, and, as its consequent, the idea of an unbroken sequence of successions, constituting an invariable cosmic march or rhythm of events, which might be personified as an unalterable cosmic will or destiny (δίκη, λόγος, εἱμαρμένη), or generalised into an abstract uniformity of natural law. He himself persistently interpreted it as the expression of an *ethical* order ; and his followers, the school of Ephesus, continued to be the avowed and scornful antagonists of all who remained content with bare materialistic Sensationism.

The Stoics, largely for this reason, based their physics upon Heraclitean formulas, and constantly assume his authority for their own developed conceptions of the *anima mundi*, of Pantheistic immanence, of cosmic cycles of being,[1] and of the periodic conflagration [2] of the world. Marcus Aurelius himself, perhaps more than any Stoic writer, exemplifies the tendency to fasten almost superstitiously on allegorical intentions in the master's words. Heraclitus, with bold materialism, had ascribed the tottering gait and reason of the drunkard to the *damping* effect of liquor on the inner fire of consciousness, and this is

---

[1] v. 13, 32 ; vi. 37 ; ix. 28 ; xi. 1.   [2] iii. 3 ; x. 7

moralised to signify the aberrations of the mind callous
to the promptings of the Universal Reason. The human
speech or thought which Heraclitus pronounced common
to all is magnified into the directive Reason immanent
in all things, and the material oppositions on which
Heraclitus loved to dwell become a figure of the ultimate
opposition, which subordinates sense, impulse, and all
other powers of man to the prevailing mastery of
Reason. The charge of 'misunderstanding familiar
things' which Heraclitus levels against his contemporaries is moralised into man's estrangement from the
compelling dictates of Nature, and his persistent variance
with the besetting Reason that directs the universe.
In the same spirit Heraclitus' treatment of sleep as
the abeyance of all active consciousness is turned[1]
into a declaration and example of man's unconscious
cooperation with the Order of the world, even when
he least designs or actively promotes it.

In studying the early stages of Greek philosophy, the
violent oscillations of opinion remind us vividly how free
the field was for fearless speculation, how unhampered
by settled presuppositions, and how small as yet the
body of ascertained fact, which acted as pendulum to
steady the eccentricities of thought. While at Miletus
and then at Ephesus, philosophy, following the clues of
physical hypothesis, was passing from a mechanical to a
dynamical conception of the world, and gradually shaping
the conviction that the force behind phenomena was
single in kind and uniform in action, in the West the
problem of Being was assailed from a very different side

---

[1] iv. 46 ; vi. 42.

by thinkers of the Eleatic School. Xenophanes, Parmenides, and Zeno, of Elea, with growing insistence
upon dialectic, attacked the problem from the side of
thought and logical predication, and sought to determine the nature of the physical universe from the
implications contained in the simple predicates 'It is'
and 'It is not.' The idea of empty space—a something which is nothing—appeared to involve a contradiction in terms, an attempt to think what is unthink-
able, an assertion that 'What is, is not'; and the denial
of void led logically on to the denial of motion and of
any possible plurality of being. It is needless here to
criticise the method of procedure ; for Stoicism does
not stake its case on pure dialectic, in adopting the
Eleatic inference, and affirming the universe, physical
as well as conceptual, to be a single Being, without
beginning and without end, self-existent and self-limited,
homogeneous and unchangeable in quality—

> A rounded sphere, poised in rotating rest.[1]

In terms of physics the resultant universe must be
a One, a *plenum*, finite, continuous, indivisible, equally
extended and evenly poised in all directions—a perfect
sphere.

For its logic of Being Stoicism reverted to the
Eleatics, as for its physics to Heraclitus ; but the two
demanded reconciliation. On the showing of Heraclitus
true Being realised itself in the world of Becoming, in
the ordered succession of phenomena : but though the
doctrine of Becoming might interpret the transience of

[1] viii. 41 ; xii. 3.   Cf. xi. 12.

phenomena, it could not satisfy that ultimate idea of
Being, which thought required as the antecedent and
necessary presupposition of phenomenal appearances;
true Being, on the showing of the Eleatics, must be one,
eternal, homogeneous.   How was it possible to combine
the idea of this unchangeable and self-existent One
with the plurality, the transience, and the qualitative
variety of phenomenal existences?   If both views expressed a truth, there must be some unchangeable sub-
stratum manifesting itself in and through the diversities
of individual things.

The Atomists attempted to supply an answer, approaching the question from the purely material side.   First,
Empedocles broached the doctrine of the four elements
—earth, water, air, and fire,—somewhat arbitrarily singling
out these four substances, subject to modifications of
density and intermixture for which mere motion might
sufficiently account, as the indestructible homogeneous
elements of all phenomenal things.   This doctrine of
four elements, in so far as it expresses four *states* of
matter—solid, liquid, gaseous, and igneous,—merited
the acceptance which it found from all the schools,
and is freely adopted for purposes of classification by
the Stoics.[1]   But the system of Empedocles, though
containing popular and plausible elements, lacked philosophical consistency.   The selection of four elements
was arbitrary and superficial, and as an enumeration of
primary forms was as provisional as the seventy odd
elements of modern Chemistry; it gave no account of
the ultimate constitution and significance of matter, and

[1] *E.g.* iv. 4; ix. 9; x. 7.

in assuming a plurality of primary elements failed to meet the pressure of Eleatic logic. Moreover in its account of motion it fell back on psychical terms, love and hate, that assumed the indwelling operation of some life-power resident in matter. Thus it was only fitted to be a stepping-stone to the Atomistic doctrine of Leucippus, which received scientific form and completeness from the genius of Democritus.

Empedocles, rationally convinced that nothing could either come into being or pass out of being, constructed his finite universe from a few limited groups of material elements. Democritus pushed the conclusions of his trenchant and rigorous materialism much further, and cut away the remnants of mythological prepossession and phraseology which clung about the system of Empedocles. Repudiating as unreasonable the idea that the same elements can assume different forms, he found his unit of being in the indivisible atom. To the atoms, infinite in number and infinitesimal in size, he attributed none but the primary qualities of solid matter, those which result from its property of filling space, viz., position, shape, arrangement. Only in respect of these is variation possible; and the variety of things represents only that variety of form and combination in the molecules, behind which it is impossible for thought to pass. Democritus did not shrink from the conclusions to which this absolute pluralism committed him. Unlimited void was necessary as the field of action for the innumerable molecules; the free motion of atoms in space was the single (or twofold) presupposition which formed the ultimate demand on reason. All qualitative differences are resolved into forms of quantitative relation or juxta-position. From the uniform action and reaction of moving molecules, without conscious aim or teleological direction, as the purely mechanical result of fixed 'necessities' or laws (inherent in the nature of body and void), worlds make and unmake themselves, and among them our own world came into being, exists, and acts. Movement is a property of molecular matter, which analysis has no warrant for attributing either to inner will or outer impulse; it is impossible to get behind the experiential fact, that atoms move, except when obstructed and brought to rest. Thus Demo-critus, speaking the last word of the Physicist philo-sophers, and anticipating the main positions of modern materialism, assumes (in spite of metaphysical ob-jectors) the existence of void, asserts the sovereignty and uniformity of mechanical law, limits action to cor-poreal substance, discards the assumption of a Cosmos, and denies the exercise of autonomous and intelligent will, immanent or directive, in the conduct of the universe.

Such speculations ran counter to the spirit of the age, and received no serious attention except in the domain of physics. In this province the attitude of Stoics and Epicureans is characteristic. The Epicureans accepted the concourse of atoms and the exclusion of divine action, as relieving life from settled plan or teleological obligation; but at a crucial point, and expressly to secure so-called *freedom* of will, they inter-polated the theory of spontaneous swerving of the atoms, and set aside the universality of law. The Stoics, on

'the other hand, accepted from Democritus just that
which the Epicureans rejected, the conception of
binding inviolable law—'*All things by Law*, saith
the Sage,'[1]—stretching in a chain of causation (physical
and moral), from the beginning of things : but they
deny the blind clash of atoms, as the contradiction of
reason and of providence, and irreconcilable with the
facts of cosmic unity.[2] Dilemmas of logic, the argument
from design, and the occurrence of special providences,
were all brought to bear upon the materialist position ;
but among the later Stoics, as in Marcus, the entire
stress is laid upon the moral argument and the attesta-
tion of man's own consciousness. 'Either an ordered
universe, or else a welter of confusion. Assuredly then
a world-order. Or think you that *order subsisting within
yourself is compatible* with disorder in the All?'[3] 'The
world is either a welter of alternate combination and
dispersion, or a unity of order and providence. If the
former, why crave to linger on in such a random medley
and confusion? why take thought for anything except
the eventual "dust to dust"? . . . But on the other
alternative, I reverence, I stand stedfast, I find heart in
the power that disposes all.'[4] Belief in Cosmos, not in
Chaos, is an intellectual and still more a moral necessity,
out of which reason can only argue itself on pain of self-

[1] vii. 31, with an explicit allusion to the Atomists. Cf. also
x. 25, 33 ; xi. 1. In xii. 14 it is ἀνάγκη εἱμαρμένη, and similarly
viii. 35 ; ix. 28. Elsewhere moralised as the *allotment* of destiny.

[2] iv. 3 ; ix. 28, 39 ; xi. 18 (1).

[3] iv. 27. Cf. ix. 39 ; x. 1.

[4] vi. 10, and cf. iv. 3 ; vii. 75 ; ix. 28 : xii. 14.

confusion ; without it, motive and justification, or rather excuse, for continued existence fails.

Such were the chief phases of pre-Socratic thought, which eventually found coordination in the Stoic scheme ; but before passing to the Socratic period, two minor contributions deserve brief recognition.

Anaxagoras holds a remarkable position in philosophy. He enjoyed extraordinary reputation upon both sides of the Aegean : at Athens the battle for free thought raged round his person, and Lampsacus, the home of his exile, honoured his memory with an altar dedicated to Mind and Truth. He gave impulse to the speculations of Plato, and Aristotle accounted him the first to speak ' soberness among the babblers.' Great rather in promise than achievement, he neither created a school nor made permanent contributions to philosophic method or result. As in person he transported philosophy from the Schools of Ionia to its new home at Athens, so intellectually he represents the transition from physical to metaphysical modes of speculation. Turning his back upon the old Ionian physicists, using at once and superseding the Empedoclean doctrine of elements, he devised a new theory of the constitution of matter and the origination of the world. Matter in origin homogeneous, and containing in every part, however minute, the same constituents or qualities (though not always in the same proportion), was differentiated into kinds by the action of *Nous* (Mind, meaning probably mind-stuff). *Nous* takes the place of the semi-mythological Love and Hate, which figured in the system of Empedocles, and stands outside of matter,

conscious and even supra-sensual, rather than amalga-
mated and infused. 'All things were jumbled together,'
was the summary of his teaching, 'till *Nous* gave order
to the whole.' His doctrine marks a stage of untenable
transition, but is feeling its way to a new and higher
metaphysic, and was potent in fixing and determining
the place of *Nous* in philosophic terminology. There
is no proof that Anaxagoras invented or approached the
thought of incorporeal existence; on the contrary, the
terms he uses are explicitly material; *Nous* is 'thinnest
of all things'; it is 'unmixed'; its action on matter is
still conceived and expressed materially; for the time
had not yet come to broach the question of immaterial
being. Neither was his *Nous* the mind of a divine
creator or upholder of the world, an idea quite foreign
to his point of view; the agency of *Nous* was invoked
only to initiate, not to maintain or to direct motion.
Nor yet again was it a world-soul pantheistically conceived as immanent in all things. Nevertheless, in
isolating *Nous* from all other forms of matter, in making
its activity the originative motor of the Cosmos, in
associating with its essential properties the terrestrial
and, still more impressively, the celestial order, in choos-
ing and emphasising the name that suggested personal
intelligence, he helped to give currency to a term, and
even to conceptions, which from different sides Plato,
Aristotle, and the Stoics adopted and filled with a
new content.

There is one more debt to record, a debt rather of
temper and aim than of direct intellectual obligation.
Pythagoras, it was said, surveying the order of the

universe, first gave the name of _Cosmos_ to the world,
and ascribing the cosmic order to some constraining
power, declared that at the heart of things the quickening
soul and seminal origin of all being was God, the one,
eternal and unchanging. His doctrine of the music of
the spheres and his conception of the soul as a harmony
seem to foreshadow that 'smooth and even flow' of
soul, in which the Stoics found the realisation of man's
Inner Self. And behind the coincidences of mood and
language, they revered in him 'the holy or august
philosopher,'[1] who first taught philosophy as an authoritative 'way of life,' who studying to possess his soul in
peace began each day with litanies and chanting of
ancient hymns, and night and morning prescribed upon
himself and his disciples the rule and exercise of self-
examination,[2] to tune the soul into accord with life.
The revived Pythagorean brotherhood of post-Christian
centuries, adepts bound not so much by tenets of a
common creed as by disciplines of philosophic life,
cherished the true spirit of the master, his rule of silence
and of worship, when they 'bid us every morning lift
our eyes to heaven, to meditate upon the heavenly
bodies pursuing their everlasting round—their order,
their purity, their nakedness. For no star wears a veil.'[3]

[1] vi. 47.   [2] Cf. ii. 1.   [3] xi. 27.

II.—BIRTH OF STOICISM

§ 1. *Debt to Socrates, Cynics, and Megarians*

So far, though the centres of philosophic culture are as
widely separate as Sicily and Asia Minor, the development of thought was in the main lineal and simple.
With the concentration of philosophic interest at Athens,
schools arise, divide, and multiply, and in the clash of
opposing creeds unity of direction disappears.   Socrates,
the foremost pioneer of the new movements of thought
in the fifth century, stands at the head of the great
Delta, through which, by diverging and often interlacing
streams, Greek thought expanded into Oriental and
European Hellenism.   Though Stoicism incorporates
large fragments from Plato and from Aristotle, the direct
line of affiliation is through the Megarians and Cynics,
and the divergence of view is fundamental.

In the Socratic and post-Socratic Schools, Ethics and
Metaphysics become the main determinants.   While in
Ethics, Plato and the Stoics both start from Socratic
premises, and by different routes reach kindred though
not identical results, in metaphysics their solutions stand
fundamentally opposed.   To those who argued that all
known forms of Being were phenomenal and all knowledge of it perceptional, and that such Being and

Knowledge could carry no stamp of permanent validity,
Plato replied with the new and daring metaphysic that
not merely might there be Being without body, but that
for such Being man has appropriate organs of cognition.
Just as Being exists without body, and by its very nature
transcends phenomenal existence, so the knowledge
which apprehends it stands above perception and independent of its subjective disabilities.   Created being is
the product and the correspondent, not the embodiment
of the central 'idea of the good,' which itself immaterial,
uncreate, self-conscious, is eternally engaged in realising,
projecting, sustaining, and surveying the innumerable
utterances of its own activity.   Thus Plato evolved his
transcendental Idealism, and in severer metaphysical
form Aristotle upheld a similar distinction between the
idea and its embodiment, between Being abstract and
potential, and Being realised in actual and concrete
form.   Stoicism took a less adventurous course ; adher-
ing to the traditional axiom that body alone can act
or be acted upon, it was driven to the opposite alternative of monistic Materialism.   It must not then, either
historically or philosophically, be regarded as a reaction
from Platonic metaphysics ; the representatives of relapse must be sought rather in the Academic and Peripatetic schools.   Historically, Stoic descent derives from
Socrates, through Cynic ethics and Megarian logic;
intellectually, the system never passed through Idealism
to Materialism, or through Dualism to Monism.   It ignored
certain contradictions which disconcerted the metaphysical
genius of Plato and of Aristotle, but its interpretation
of the world could claim continuity and independence.

The Sophistic Age, signifying as it does the attainment and realisation of *self-consciousness* in the Greek mind, involved a necessary change in the direction of philosophic interest. For the old problem, What is the make and nature of the world? the less obvious and deeper problem is substituted, What is the make and nature of man? When once questions of the analysis of consciousness were broached, the prime interest inevitably shifted from the object to the subject, and it became imperative to understand the nature, processes, and relations of thought, perception, and emotion, before attempting to deal with their subject-matters and contents. Until the forms of consciousness were to some extent understood and their worth determined, it was useless to discuss its reports, or compare its testimonies. All knowledge might (as Protagoras taught) resolve itself into successive acts of individual perception; inner criteria of truth, reality, and permanence must be established, before philosophy could carry conviction, or even claim a hearing. Physics must wait till psychology could formulate and justify its own validity. To frivolous and irresponsible rhetoricians, ethics, logic, or physics might furnish equally good sport for argument and opportunity for self-display; but to serious thinkers, bent on establishing a stable harmony between thought and life, the moral and psychological issues were supreme. The philosopher claimed distinction from the Sophist.

For this reason Socrates, more resolutely than any of his contemporaries, turned from hypotheses of physics or metaphysics to study the nature of man. Just as the older physicists, convinced of the reality of a cosmic

order in the world of things, set themselves to discover
the underlying source of unity in nature, so Socrates,
convinced of the presence and necessity of moral order
in the domain of human relationships, set himself to
discover the basis upon which it rested, and in seeking
to 'know himself' tapped the sources of moral philosophy.
Assuming that some real discoverable unity must under-
lie the general conception denoted by 'goodness,' and
seeking for its definition and basis, Socrates eventually
found in *knowledge* the only firm foundation for virtue.
Moods, impulses, and passions, by reason of their
individual and subjective quality, could never furnish a
standard of right action. Knowledge, on the other
hand, resting on solid foundations of correspondence
with objective facts, could give consistency to action
and prescribe laws of moral conduct. Right insight
into the conditions and results of action would carry
with it right conduct, for no man perceiving the right
course would deliberately choose and pursue the wrong.
Knowledge of what was good would thus ensure the
exercise of goodness, and just analysis of the contents
of goodness would place them within the reach of all.
Wrong-doing is failure of insight, springing from ignorance
and want of education, a mistake that will correct itself
as soon as the right way is discerned. Supply the
needed insight, and the right course of action will follow,
for what is good is also what is beneficial, and nature
ensures that man will follow what is beneficial to himself.
By the same reasoning the way of goodness is likewise
the way of well-being, in which man finds his happiness.
The teaching of Socrates may be summed up in the

injunction, *Know thyself,* and in the formulas, *Virtue is knowledge—Virtue may be taught*[1]*—No one wilfully goes wrong*[2]*—Virtue results in happiness;* and all these maxims are first principles of Stoic dogma. In respect of all, Stoicism—at least in its later exponents—adheres more closely to the Socratic tradition than any other school; and, alike in temper and interest, Epictetus reproduces the teaching of the master more faithfully than any of his disciples or more immediate successors.

The power of the Socratic conclusions lay in affirming the ultimate harmony of morality with reason, and in vindicating for the results of reason real and authoritative validity. Man's moral sense, the existence of which is irrefragable, demands and certifies the reality of knowledge. The weakness of the affirmations, regarded as a system of ethics,—apart from the confusion of will with knowledge—lay in defective and confused analysis of the contents of 'goodness.' To give positive meaning and efficacy to the dictum, 'Virtue is knowledge,' it was indispensable to define with some precision the subject-matter of the knowledge meant. To explain it as 'knowledge of the good' reduced it to mere tautology, until the contents of 'goodness' were enumerated or defined. According as the idea of pleasure or advantage or prosperity was permitted to preponderate, the maxim could be turned to Hedonistic, Utilitarian, or Eudæmonistic inferences, so that by variety of emphasis broadly contrasted types of ethical

---

[1] Cf. vi. 27; viii. 59; ix. 11; x. 4; xi. 18 (9).

[2] ii. 1; iv. 3; vii. 22, 62, 63; viii. 14; x. 30; xi. 18 (3); xii. 12.

theory could found themselves upon the language and authority of Socrates.

In affirming that Virtue was Knowledge, Socrates proceeded to enlarge the scope of Virtue or Excellence ($\dot{a}\rho\epsilon\tau\dot{\eta}$) to the full range of general conceptions, and in the hands of his greatest disciple it rapidly expanded into a well-proportioned harmony of intellect, emotion, and will. But the Cynics, accepting the formula, pro- ceeded in an opposite direction, and instead of enlarging their idea of Virtue to co-extension with the range of thought, they contracted the sphere of Knowledge to the area of individual activities. Associating knowledge exclusively with practical action and decision, Antisthenes tried to exclude from consideration everything except the problem of personal will effectuating itself in action. Openly scouting Platonic Idealism, and denying moral or logical value to general conceptions, he tried to satisfy the intellectual demand with the barest Nominalism, and even to restrict logic to mere identity of predication. In Physics the harshest materialism, in Ethics the narrowest individualism, were the natural consequents (or perhaps antecedents) of his position. The sole concern of the philosopher became correct adjustment of the individual reason in the practical conduct of life ; and even this reduced morality confined itself within a narrow range of self-regarding virtues. Inasmuch as virtue was an act of will, within the individual control, all wants or desires, whether from within or from without, that lay outside the realisation of the will, were contradictions of virtue which the wise man would not tolerate. Here too an act of will was sufficient for the realisation of virtue and happiness. Outer relationships and inner dissatisfactions were within the province of the will; and all that threatened to contravene or abridge its independence must, in behoof of virtue and happiness be willed away. Wants must be reduced to the dimensions of will. Thus, curtailment of obligations, needs, desires, and affections became the keynote of Cynic morality: ignoring first the claims and then the decencies of social obligation, it promoted insensibility, often of the coarsest kind, to a premier place among the virtues. The demands thus laid on individuality might seem excessive and forbidding; but the strong and racy personality of Diogenes gave vogue to the experiment, and the eccentricities and anti-social bravado of his imitators, by the very violence of the contrast which they offered to the traditions and usages of Greek life, secured notoriety, and even enforced attention and respect. For, in spite of its intellectual and ethical shortcomings, Cynism proclaimed two needed truths in accents of the most arresting and uncompromising kind — (1) the unconditional supremacy of the moral will, in the determination of life; (2) a truth as yet unfamiliar to Greece, the independence and responsibility of *the individual* as the unit of morality.

All that was vital in Cynism was taken up into Stoicism, and coordinated into a more comprehensive scheme of morality and thought; and the Stoic enlargement of its doctrines will be the most instructive commentary upon the principles of the system itself. But before passing to this wider theme, it will be well to anticipate the future of the parent name and sect.

The Cynic tradition, remaining true to its emphasis on practice rather than on theory, survived in more or less close association with the Stoic, and shared its revival under the Roman Empire. There the Cynic profession resumed its protest against worldliness and self-indulgence with so much conviction and success, that charlatans and schemers found it worth while to disguise themselves in its livery, and from Plutarch to Lucian, from Antoninus to Julian, the Cynic figures now as the butt of the satirist, and now as the cynosure of the moralist. To Juvenal, the Stoic differs from the Cynic only by the cut of his cloak. In Marcus Aurelius, as habitually in Epictetus,[1] Diogenes is coupled with Socrates as the pre-eminent and authoritative type of moral courage, rectitude, and tranquillity. Even the sincere Cynic, with his crude and often rampant individualism, was constantly in danger of ignoring social claims, and straining moral independence into mere nonconformist bluff; but in the true Cynic, purged of insincerity and ostentation and intolerance, inured to hard ways and to harsh words, Epictetus[2] recognises still the ideal 'athlete of righteousness,' ready and clean and strong, who, having disciplined all passion and desire, and attained the perfect freedom of the will in harmony with the divine, is able to renounce the allurements of ambition, the distractions of wealth, and the preoccupations

[1] viii. 3; cf. Arr. Epict. 1, 24, 6; 2, 16, 35; 3, 21, 19; 3, 22, 24; 4, 7, 29; 4, 9, 6; 4, 11, 21; and *Ench.* 15.

[2] Arrian, Epict. iii. 22, *On Cynism.*

of married or domestic life, and so to move among his
fellows in fearless isolation, as God's commissioned
messenger for the service and conversion of men,
privileged, through blameless transparency of life, to
become father and brother and friend to the whole
family of human kind.

Thus, though Stoicism widened the basis and the
intellectual outlook of Cynism, it stood faithful to the
tie of descent and the inalienable claim of moral
affinity; and the main dogmas of the Cynic school—
the identification of virtue with knowledge, the autocracy and indivisibility of virtue, and the moral independence of the individual—remained firmly embedded
in the Stoic creed, the central core of its teaching, and
the *raison d'être* of its promulgation.

§ 2. *From Cynism to Stoicism*

The founder of Cynism was Antisthenes, pupil of
Gorgias and Socrates; his disciple Diogenes was its
most effective missionary, and from him the leadership
passed on to Crates. At Athens the two teachers who
most influenced Zeno, the author of Stoicism, were
Crates the Cynic, and Stilpo the Megarian. The latter
brought a new and unexpected element to bear on
Cynism, by grafting upon Cynic morals the system of
pure dialectic associated with the name of Euclides of
Megara.

Just as Antisthenes had narrowed philosophy into
a problem of personal ethics, and dissociated it from
general dialectic, so Euclides, sensitive only to another
side of the Socratic impulse, divorced dialectic from

the corrections of experience and consciousness, and
by processes of pure logic was led to deny the reality
of matter, of motion, of becoming, indeed of everything
except the content of the equation, 'That which is, is.'
Methods closely resembling those of the Eleatics, though
somewhat less material in scope, led him to similar
results, and he imputed to the one abiding reality,
which he called 'the Good,' those attributes which
Parmenides had assigned to real being. Aided by a
brilliant and magnetic personality, Stilpo at Megara
succeeded in fusing this logical conception of the
abiding One with the naturalist morality of the Cynic
school. Such a fusion gave small promise of fertile
result, for the two combined not so much by natural
and organic coherence, as by a rigorous severance of
sphere, which rather excluded contradictions than assured
agreement. Logic was detached from life, and transcendental being was put out of touch with phenomenal
existence ; no reconciliation or communication was
provided between the One or the Good, the finite reason
of man, and the infinite multiplicity of phenomenal
change. Such was the position when Zeno appeared
upon the scene.

Hitherto we have referred only, or chiefly, to ethical
modifications of the extreme Cynic position. But other
elements, not less important, went to the making of
Stoicism as a coherent body of thought. Born at
Citium, and of Phœnician lineage, it seems probable that
Zeno had early imbibed the theistic or monotheistic
conceptions of the East ; the Oriental strain, which re-
appears in almost every representative of the School, can

hardly be accidental, and goes far to prove that Eastern predispositions were latent in the Stoic creed. Early in life he came under the influence of the Heraclitean School of physics, whose traditions kept their hold upon Asiatic Greeks, assimilated as an integral part of his thought the doctrine of physical Flux, and found in it a potential harmony between the materialist individualism of the Cynics, and the Megarian doctrine of the One.

The passage from Cynism to Stoicism, the change of conception or of stress which it involved in the treatment of common terms, best shows the gradual and half-conscious way in which the scheme of Stoicism was evolved. We have seen how, in its definition and pursuit of virtue and of happiness, the Cynics gave unconditional authority to the criteria of individual experience and will. These were direct, imperious, and valid, and this conviction lies at the base of their philosophic creed. 'Life in agreement with Nature' was the summary of their aim, and was a formula well calculated at once to attract and to mislead disciples. For centuries philosophy had been engaged upon the study and explanation of 'nature'; and now that it was looking for some general formula corresponding to the idea of virtue, such as might provide a canon of right living simple, consistent, and authoritative, no prescription could have seemed more apposite or satisfying than that of 'agreement with nature.' It presented, at first sight, such straightforward and self-commending credentials, that practice might well precede discussion, and dispense with scruples of dialectic and analysis. For man, 'nature' meant clearly the functions and processes and sensations which constitute man's life. With these e must put himself in agreement. The intimations of sense and instinct were the sure utterance of nature, convincing and unimpeachable; in agreement with them, virtue and will would find their natural exercise, and attain full and undivided self-realisation. The one sufficient way to happiness lay in obedience to the primary mandates of Nature, as expressed in impulses of appetite, of function, and of natural propensity, and satisfied by inner self-satisfaction of the will. Centring on these, the wise man would refuse to implicate himself in disturbing sensibilities, or in any gratuitous distractions of thought or affection or exterior deference or obligation. Praise, blame, and the whole array of social sanctions were extraneous to the man's own nature, and must not be suffered to impair that unconditional self-assertion and self-mastery which were indispensable to moral independence. Still less could any weight attach to purely external appendages, such as wealth, rank, costume, reputation, or environment. These things are not to be decried as in themselves baneful or undesirable; or to be regarded as temptations, which the wise man must by virtue of his profession eschew; they fall strictly into the same category as their opposites, poverty or squalor or obloquy. The inner satisfaction is found in ignoring, not in mortifying the desires. So far as the Cynic—or the Stoic—is an ascetic, it is by compromise rather than upon principle, a precaution and in some sense a confession of weakness, rather than a counsel of perfection; asceticism is not inculcated as a form of moral

culture, though it may have its uses as a prophylactic.
'The plank-bed and the skin'[1] were parts of 'boyish
aspiration'; the tub of Diogenes was adopted on its
merits—positive and negative, not its discomforts, as a
domicile.   Towards all externals, the philosopher's strict
attitude is nonchalance, the charter of his self-sufficiency.
He does not court pains or privations of any kind as
salutary; he only defies and derides, when he cannot
affect to ignore: if once they presume to influence or
modify the will, they must be annulled.   Apart from
that, they remain, in the strictest sense, indifferent.

Now with much of all this—with the identification
of virtue and happiness, with the supremacy and self-
sufficiency of the moral will, with the oneness and indivisibility of virtue, with the valuation of external
goods, with the cultivation of 'indifference,' and the
contingent claims of self-renunciation—the Stoic was
in complete agreement, and the points of divergence did
not, at first sight, seem practical or of much significance.
They chiefly concerned that 'agreement with nature'
on which the Cynics took their stand.

Zeno, so far as express record goes, seems to have
shrunk from the full formula, regarding it, perhaps, as
perilously wide, and to have phrased his aim as 'life in
agreement,' that is to say, a realised self-consistency of
conduct and aim, attained by settled self-conformity of
the inner will.   Now in this there might seem nothing
alien to the scope of Cynism; the assertion of the
cardinal principle is rendered, if possible, more unconditional than before.   But, as a matter of fact, the insertion

[1] i. 6.

of the term nature had (perhaps undesignedly) tended to narrow the main principle and throw the stress upon a single side, instead of upon the whole, of individuality. The antecedents and associations of the term were (it must be remembered) inalienably material; they concerned the growth and make and substance of the material world, and, as applied to man, tended to confine reference to the like processes, material and animal, observed in him. Will 'in agreement with nature' tended to mean will exercised upon the animal activities; and in suppressing the limitation, Zeno removed a misleading emphasis. He, in effect, recalled attention to those elements in man which stood in less direct relation with the material world. Agreement with one sort and side of man's natural activities could not satisfy the demand for inward self-conformity, which was set up as the moral ideal. For unity of act and disposition, it was essential to coordinate understanding and reflection with sense and impulse and perception, and to integrate rightly-ordered and operative reason with each exercise of virtuous will. This did not involve a reconstruction of the main system. The 'agreement with nature,' the validity of sense-perception, the authority of sensuous impulse, the supremacy of will, the identification of happiness with virtue and its corollary doctrines of imperturbability and things indifferent, all remain untouched; but notwithstanding this, the reinclusion of reason, and of some, at least, of the reactions between man and man, as well as those between man and the material world, in the expression of individuality, enlarged to that extent the area and contents of self-regard, and in so doing produced a corresponding modification in each determination of the will. The characterisation of the Wise Man, and even the valuation of things indifferent, felt the effects of the change.

As apostles of individualism in the sphere of morals, the Cynics had led the way in personifying the moral ideal in the figure of the Wise Man; and it was not unnatural that, in emphasising the salient features, they fell into extravagances that verged on caricature. His end was to be self-sufficing, to assert and to secure for 'nature' its undisturbed prerogatives of independence. By force of will he will put down all foreign disturbers of the peace; as champion of the independence of the primary impulses and instincts, he will resist the intrusions of thought, the distractions of fancy, the clamour and agitation of the affections; deaf to praise or blame or provocations from without, he will remain inflexibly true to self-regard, and give no quarter to competing interests or solicitudes. He will claim full satisfaction for each demand of nature, though he may elect to keep one or another in abeyance rather than involve himself in extraneous and entangling obligations. He will imperturbably coerce feeling and behaviour by restraints of will, and regard everything outside the inner authorisations of his personality as matter of unqualified indifference.

Apart from excess of emphasis and something of wilful paradox, the deformities and eccentricities of the Cynic 'Wise Man' spring chiefly from that narrow and one-sided intolerance, which must result from satisfaction of the self-assertive instincts, when reason is not per-

nitted to insist on considerations of decency and
onsequence. Deaf to the voices of tradition and
ulture, determined to isolate the individual from the
ociety, and to flaunt the superiority of will to outer
ircumstance, the Cynics fell rapidly into the quagmires
f ascetic bravado. Positive value' and professional
clat were attached to abstinences and mortifications,
rhose sole moral justification lay in the reduction of
xternal needs ; the virtues of simplicity and temperance
rere caricatured in exhibitions of mendicancy, dirt, and
oul diet ; all forms of regard for social *convenance*—
elicacy or decency or civility—were ranked as weak
ubservience, as apostasies from idiosyncrasy ; to be
naked and unashamed' became a chief part of vocation,
nd the test of moral independence. From this the
toics were saved. If in fear of moral enervation they
pproved some gratuitous austerities, and if at some
oints they confounded independence of will with
ıppression of sensibility, at least they never interpreted
ıccord with nature' in terms of relapse to animalism,
ıd it was rather from want of humour and good taste
ıat they indulged in academic discussions upon
ınnibalism, irreverence to the remains of the dead,
ımmunity of wives, and such like Cynic banalities,
an with any serious thought of giving them practical
nction or application.

The course of Stoic ethics is, in fact, the progressive
ılargement and clarification of the Cynic ideal of
nduct, under the stress of that larger conception of
ıature,' which was inherent in Stoic monism. The full
ıntent and interpretation of the formula was only

d

gradually realised. Its deeper implications—such, for instance, as the religious significance of pantheistic immanence, the introduction of moral emotion and moral æsthesis into the sphere of natural religion, the ascription of evidential value and meaning to its intuitions, the full recognition of 'the social moment,' and the conception of world-citizenship—unfolded themselves through life even more than through thought, and find their fullest exposition in the pages of the Roman Stoics. 'Return to nature,' so far from implying reversion to animalism, and the reduction of man's needs to the level of the beasts, was found to involve fundamental differentiation of reasoning man from the unreason of the brute or the inertia of matter, to place man on a unique spiritual plane, and eventually to summon him from individual isolation to conscious brotherhood with kind and harmony of will with God. These are the elements of Stoicism which have proved most permanent and universal.

One of the first effects of the reinstatement of reason in its 'natural' place was to reintroduce the whole order of 'things indifferent' to the purview of morals. So long as virtue was solely right condition and exercise of will, acting upon the intimations of instinct and sense, no alternative was possible but absolute acceptance or rejection ; no intermediate course, no parleying or suspension of decision, could be allowed without admitting the fallibility, and surrendering the independent autocracy, of the moral organ. But with the appearance of reason on the scene, with its power of discrimination, of valuation, and, above all, of 'suspense,' the position

nanged. Technically, indeed, the supremacy and inde-
endence of the will was left untouched, and its dis-
egard of things indifferent was as unqualified and
ncompromising as its rejection of things undesirable;
ut reason notwithstanding made allowances which
ne virtuous will could not admit; it established from
s own point of view classifications and degrees of
nerit, it attached conditional values and preferential
laims to recognition, according as things *tended* to
dvance or to retard the life according to nature, and
o reduced the number of things strictly indifferent
o a remnant which stood out of all determining rela-
ion with the will, and to which reason itself could not
scribe such secondary value, positive or negative. In this
ray, a body of scientific casuistry was elaborated, which
lassified things indifferent—whether mental qualities
r emotions, bodily or social conditions, external or
mputed goods, proprieties or defaults of behaviour or
lemeanour—in categories of relative esteem, that went
urther in minuteness and subtlety of discrimination
han in any other school of ancient psychology. These
ould not indeed affect the crowning act, the realisa-
ion of virtue in the will, without thereby losing their
character of 'indifference' and passing into another
category of things, but they could so pave the way to
virtue, and make the approaches easy and insensible,
hat the tiro might by their aid be conducted to the
hreshold of the sanctuary, and, passing by a step
rom the region of folly to the fruition of wisdom, be
numbered among the elect and indefectible.

By these steps Stoicism entirely altered the physiognomy of the 'Wise Man.' Reason, when once its place in Nature was vindicated and re-established, tended to become the dominant partner in each exercise of will. It alone could supply criteria of self-conformity, and interpret and direct the impulses of sense; it alone could justly pit reduction of needs against surrender of independence. Thus on all sides it was necessary to right action, and held, as it were, the casting vote in the adjustments of nature to life. Control came to be regarded as more important than first momentum, and thus the very essence of personality and 'nature' was found to lie in the dominion of reason. Gradually it usurped more than mere directive power, and claimed to decide the prior question of use. It might refuse assent to any line of movement, and pass sentence of inertia on any impulse or emotion. At this point the reversal of original position has become complete. For the 'nature' in which reason at first had no admitted place is now placed wholly at its mercy, and may be set aside as unauthorised, and in conflict with the mandates of the premier authority. Nature has become contrary to nature, and must therefore cease to be. Suppression of the emotions (ἀπάθεια)—a self-determination distinct from the imperturbability secured by disallowance of needs—takes a cardinal place in the Stoic scheme of life. And thus, as we shall see, the idea of personality —of the ultimate unity of the individual will and conscience, of an *Ego* distinct from physical organism and environment — eventually dawns upon Greek thought, and unexpectedly reveals a deeper dualism new to philosophy—that antithesis, namely, of spirit and flesh,

of man and his material embodiment, of moral aim
and realised experience, which conducts to the baffling
problems of determinism and free-will.

It was the work of centuries to unfold the implications thus latent in the formula, 'life in agreement with
nature,' so different from those which it first seemed
to convey. But even at an early stage, and from the
purely psychological side, Cleanthes was amply justified
in replacing the term 'nature' in the symbol of the
School, and adopting the full formula as his definition
of conduct and ideal. Nor, from the Stoic standpoint,
did the adoption involve an ambiguity which has been
sometimes charged against it. It was a cardinal assumption of Stoicism, that nature in man is identical with
the nature of the universe at large, and on that assumption it is meaningless to ask whether Cleanthes meant
to prescribe 'accordance with his own individual nature'
or 'accordance with nature at large.' He would have
repudiated the distinction ; and whatever ethical implications might result, at least they would not depend
on initial ambiguity of term.

III.—Stoic Dogma

§ 1. *Physics and Doctrine of Being*

THE main novelties or extensions of thought by which Zeno effected his new synthesis were (1) the *identification of Reason in Man*—on the one hand *with the Reason of the Eternal One,* on the other *with the principle of existence in all phenomenal things;* and (2) the idea of immanence.

Previous philosophers had from various sides approached the first affirmation, but none had given it the breadth and actuality of meaning which it assumes in the Stoic system. The doctrine of Anaxagoras, alike in the name and conception of *Nous,* supplies a striking anticipation and coincidence. But in the actual exposition of his system *Nous* became little more than a hypothesis to account for the first beginning and existence of the Cosmos. It was assumed as a prime motor, not realised as an efficient cause of being or of action. All intermediate steps, including the origination of life, animal or vegetable, were attributed to mechanical media. Others among the physical philosophers, from Thales to Democritus, had assigned to Mind (in one phase or another) a place among the elements; and at times the thought of a world-soul, of *Nous* on a large scale imposing unity of motion on the celestial spheres, was entertained.   But the conception of its action did not differ from that of other elements; it was regarded as a sort of spiritual *Phlogiston*, possessed of superior mobility, lightness, dryness, heat, or other qualities of the kind.   Neither did it inhere in all matter; whenever it was present, or present in sufficient amount to make its sensible mark, it exhibited its own characteristic qualities, and produced appropriate forms and degrees of intelligence.

In the Stoic system *Nous* is no longer one of the elements, *primus inter pares;* it is *sui generis,* antecedent to matter and the material elements, no longer juxtaposed but omnipresent, the condition and motive cause of every form of being; and by a new dynamical conception it is regarded as *immanent* throughout creation, equally permeating and determining every kind of substance.   The most general and comprehensive names accorded to it are——from the physical side, *Pneuma;* from the psychical, Reason or *Logos;* but, corresponding to the phase which it assumes, it is recognised in relation to the Universe as Nature, World-Soul, Destiny, Fate, Necessity, Providence, God, Zeus; in relation to Man as Soul, Mind, Pneumatic Current, Breath, or Vital Heat; in relation to Matter as Force, Air, Fire, or other modes of motion.   Thus, 'from one point of view, the single element into which the Ionian physicists sought to resolve the material world, is found upon a higher plane; from another, it is comparable, and even at times loosely identified, with that plastic Fire ($\tau\epsilon\chi\nu\iota\kappa\grave{o}\nu$

πῦρ) of Heraclitus, which represented the least material form of being, and in 'the upward and downward flow' mediated the passage of elements from phase to phase. The *modus operandi* was mainly conceived and stated in terms of Heraclitean physics. At the same time, while in respect of material nature and dynamical virtue the Stoic *Pneuma* borrowed largely from the Heraclitean Fire, there yet remains, behind many striking resemblances of function, attribute, and nomenclature, the broad distinction that, while the fire of Heraclitus is itself a phase or mode in the mutations of being, the Fire or Spirit of the Stoics is the indefectible and all-pervasive unit and cause of all Being.

Its nature was material. To the Stoic every form of causation, just as much as every imparted motion, implies bodily action, and cannot be conceived in any other way; so that not only sensation and emotion—as the physical effects of shame, anger, or the like sufficiently demonstrate—but also thoughts and qualities, memories and imaginations, nay, even intellectual abstractions, such as time or parts of time, possess corporeal existence. And thus, in whatever category conceived—corporeal, psychical, or cosmic, whether as Air, Fire, Soul, Destiny, or God—the life-giving 'reason' of things remains always equally and unchangeably material; while, conversely, matter is only and always a mode of spirit, and the material world is not merely comprehended and sustained, but at every moment existent only through the present immanence and virtue of life-giving spirit. Thus the whole conception of being becomes in its essence *dynamical*, and while the Stoic vies with the

Epicurean in resolute materialism, his view opposes the
sharpest contrast to the atomic theory of being espoused
by the Epicureans.　To the Epicureans life is mere
juxtaposition of atoms, which accident has combined,
and some other gust of accident will part ; to the Stoics
every form of being is an expression of the cosmic
power, an energy correlated to all the other manifestations of energy, among which it takes its place.　The
total Universe is God ; and a real and logical, not
merely sentimental, pantheism is attained.　The conception, as will be clear when approached from the
ethical side, at once gives guarantee and consciousness
of power, and also limits the exercise of that power
within the terms of cosmic solidarity.　Will, the expression and the evidence of life, is not, as with
Epicurus, a caprice of swerving atoms, but a part of the
motions of a life larger than itself.

Stoicism was in the first instance content with its
monistic affirmation, and the method or process of
actualisation was not conceived very distinctly.　It was
attributed to certain seminal principles ($\sigma\pi\epsilon\rho\mu\alpha\tau\iota\kappa o\grave{\iota}$
$\lambda\acute{o}\gamma o\iota$), centres or spores as it were of procreative activity,
at which an inner irresistible impulse of the generative
Reason erupted into spontaneous activity and realised
itself in appropriate forms of phenomenal being.　These
'seminal' reasons' do not differ in *substance* from the
central Soul-force, but, as it were, exhibit and centralise
portions of its energy in time and place, and confer
upon the resultant form of being the specific characterisation which constitutes its individuality.　The term
Logos, covering the ideas of Reason, definition, principle,

and the like, was of convenient breadth, and just as the central Reason at large formed the basis and principle of all phenomenal life, and was literally the reason that accounted for and defined its being, so these seminal principles and outputs of Reason were the basis of individual forms of life, and determined the quality and mode of their existence. Marcus Aurelius describes them in the clearest language at his command as 'germs of future existences, through which nature operated the visible cosmic order, assigning to them productive capacities of realisation, change, and phenomenal succession.'[1] In man 'the seminal reason' is not exactly the Ego, but that which determines the quality and character of the Ego, and which at death is re-assumed into the central Reason, a portion of whose energy it expressed for a season in the form of an individual man.[2]

In clearness of conception a marked advance was secured by the doctrine of strain or Tension ($\tau\acute{o}\nu o s$), which Cleanthes and his successors applied to almost every domain of psychical or physical activity. As the source of phenomenal being, the name usually ascribed to the originative power is *Pneuma*.[3] This Pneuma, under certain conditions of spontaneous activity, was supposed to experience a Tension, as the result of which

[1] ix. 1.

[2] iv. 4 and vi. 24, with which compare the precisely parallel vii. 10 and x. 7.

[3] In the translation, I have retained *pneuma* or *pneumatic* in iv. 3, ix. 36, and x. 7 ; but in ii. 2, xii. 30, and uniformly for πνευμάτιον, render 'breath.' In ix. 2 I have preferred 'atmosphere.'

it ' sparked,' as it were, into a new form of activity.[1] To
this continuous and automatic thrill [2] or tension the self-
realisation of the Pneuma is due ; and the phenomenal
self-manifestations of the Pneuma correspond to the
various degrees of tension, under which the Pneuma
precipitates itself as material existence.   They may
be either of the psychical order, such as reason or
instinct, or of the physical, ranging from the rarest
ether to the densest forms of solid matter.

The whole process was conceived in the most rigidly
physical terms, and quantitative as well as qualitative
differences were admitted, and held to affect the resultant
life.   The leading phenomenal variations were differentiated, as corresponding to the various degrees of
tension ; the indwelling Mind of man attesting by its
extreme mobility a high grade of inner tension, and
materialisation becoming grosser with each successive-
relaxation or loss of tension.   At the highest grade of
tension the Pneuma acts as the World-Soul, super-
sensuous and ethereal, occupying the same relation to
the universe as the individual soul to the human organism;
at another grade the Pneuma becomes the indwelling
Mind or Reason, the 'governing element' in man, by
which he enters into conscious relation with cosmic
life, and upon which hangs the whole of personality ;[3] a
lower grade takes us from the rational or logical faculty
of man to the lower psychical life of animals possessed of
instinct, impulse, and gregarious affections, which Marcus

[1] πληγὴ πυρὸς ὁ τόνος ἐστί Cleanthes 76.
[2] vi. 38.
[3] For its functions, and psychological relations, see § 3 and   4.

dignifies with the name of Soul (ψυχή), though devoid
of man's distinguishing characteristic of Mind or Reason.
A yet lower grade manifests itself as that Nature (φύσις)
or power of growth which is the characteristic of vegetable
life, while a yet lower drops from the organic to the
inorganic quality, and effectuates that simple power of
' hold' or cohesion (ἕξις), that physical *state*, which constitutes the unity of stones or other inorganic compounds.
Thus the doctrine accounted for the existence of as
many kinds of being as there might be kinds or degrees
of tension, and enabled the Stoics to retain a reasonable
belief in the doctrine of four elements, while it elucidated
the true significance of the Heraclitean theory of
physical mutation of the elements.

At every grade, the permeation of the Pneuma is
conceived to be co-extensive with the existence it supplies; it has a way and motion of its own,[1] whose effect
is felt dynamically, wherever it is present; it does not
act by mere mechanical juxtaposition of parts, nor even
by chemical combination or fusion, but rather by an
all-pervading flow that permeates the whole being, technically described as universal commixture or interpene-
tration of parts.[2]   The condition of right tension[3] in
the organism, and right admixture[4] in the compound,

---

[1] Hence the language of v. 9, 14; vi. 17; viii. 60; x. 33.

[2] The κρᾶσις δι' ὅλων doctrine, not mechanically tenable, and
at bottom violating the axiom that two bodies cannot occupy the
same space. But it is important for the right understanding of
Stoic pantheism, and was quite as intelligible as subsequent doctrines
of void, phlogiston, ether, etc.

[3] εὐτονία, cf. vi. 30 τὸ εὔτονον καὶ τὸ ὁμαλές.

[4] x. 1 εὐκρασία, and cf. δυσκρασία ix. 2.

gives that balanced adjustment of being which constitutes the state of health, be it moral, physical, climatic, or of any other kind. The Tension doctrine was a philosophic speculation of considerable acuteness and imaginative power, derived from the phenomena of expansion and contraction, especially in their observed connexion with heat and cold, and is a striking forecast of modes and activities of being, which in the phenomena of Electricity and Magnetism and in the properties of Ether have found scientific realisation, such as at once serves to confute and to elucidate the postulates of Stoic physics. In the hands of medical philosophers, investigating the relation of breath and of vital warmth to life, the theory became the accepted basis of physiology and scientific hygiene, and was used to explain the facts of respiration and circulation, the pathology of fever chills and in-flammation, the action of blisters and poultices and cautery, and the every-day phenomena of blushing, pallor, faintness, and sleep. Inhalations of Pneuma from the surrounding atmosphere supplied *Nous* to the new-born infant,[1] and raised it from merely vegetable to human potentialities ; the processes of sense and thought arose through conduction of Pneuma to brain or heart ; painful and pleasurable sensation represented movements of the pneumatic currents running smoothly or roughly [2] in their appointed conduits ; the ' smooth flow '[3] of virtue and contentment had its physical counterpart ; and the function of the arteries, as distinguished from the

[1] Cf. vi. 15, 16 ; x. 7.
[2] Cf. iv. 3 ; v. 26 ; vii. 55 ; x. 8.
[3] Cf. ii. 5 ; iii. 12 ; v. 9, 34 ; x. 6.

veins, was interpreted to be conveyance of the Pneuma. Thus, in one phase at any rate, the Pneuma of the Stoics is the oxygen of modern Chemistry; and the Stoic doctrine of being on the one hand expands into cosmic pantheism, on the other narrows into processes of human physiology.

It is not clear to what exact point Zeno himself carried the mechanical expression of these ideas, or how far he extricated his own thought from the apparently insurmountable dualism implied by matter and force (whether conceived as spiritual or material). But it is indeed needless, even in so important an addition as the theory of 'tension,' to discriminate the precise contributions of successive masters—Zeno, Cleanthes, Chrysippus, or even the later school of medical philosophers—for Stoic teaching crystallised into a body of doctrine, representing the final revision of Zeno's system as supplemented and in details rectified by the severer method of his two great commentators. This body of doctrine formed a permanent deposit of orthodox belief, which pious Stoics accepted with a homage almost as implicit and unquestioning as that which Epicureans rendered to the dogmas of the master; and apart from casual aberrations of individual idiosyncrasy, or from unconscious relaxation of thought or expression, there was no deliberate reconstruction or abandonment of dogma, from the days of the founders to the last deliverances of Marcus Aurelius. For Epictetus 'what Zeno says' is still held to sum up the lore of the philosopher.

§ 2. *Cosmic Pantheism*

The thought of the world as a living organism had early found a place in philosophy, and was indeed the philosophical restatement of that animism, which seems almost the instinctive assumption in man's first guesses at an explanation of phenomena.   It was as natural to attribute personal life to the Universe at large as to Sun and Star, Ocean and River, tree and spring.   But the progress of Greek thought tended to discredit this theory of the universe, and to exclude it from the Schools by substituting either the purely mechanical explanations of the Ionian School, which culminated in the atomic theory of Democritus, or by inferring the existence of a creative power exterior to the action of phenomena. The reversion of Zeno to an explanation, which had virtually fallen out of Greek consideration, suggests importation from without, to which the after-thought of combination with Heraclitean physics, is by no means adverse.   Whatever be the truth of this, it seems clear that Zeno did not *argue up to* monistic or pantheistic belief from Hellenic premises of thought, but that his main affirmation was rather a sudden and daring postulate, assumed as a theory of things, and then gradually substantiated or corroborated, partly by himself and partly by his successors, as the one intelligible reading of phenomena regarded as a whole.

Stoicism was assimilative rather than derivative ; the strength of the system lies in coherence rather than in *à priori* proof, and rests less on central stability than

on skilful combination of auxiliary supports and out-
works.——The monistic core is in constant danger of
falling apart, and needs ingenious buttressing. The
unity of the world was only explicable as the expression
of a single power, and Zeno ventured to assume that
power to be identical with that which declares itself as
consciousness in man. No rival theory could be said to
hold the field, or to give satisfaction to the intellect; and
the general position of the school might be stated thus.
Platonic theory, and still more the rarer metaphysic of
Aristotle, exacted a belief in some immaterial ἀρχή or
beginning, as the first cause of all material existence.
To one disciplined in Cynic or Megarian modes of
thought, the demand was intolerable and even meaningless. There could be neither cause nor being without
body, which alone supplied the capacity for acting or
being acted upon. Whatever the first cause might be,
it certainly could not be incorporeal, transcendent——in
other words non-existent. So far, assuredly Democritus
was right. Upon the other hand, the first cause was
assuredly one, not many. The Democritean theory of
identical mechanical action in an infinite number of
isolated atoms[1] met the problem of existence and of
fixity in things. It had the advantage of the Academic
or the Peripatetic supposition in being compatible with
thought, but it was incompatible with the observed
behaviour and course of things.[2] It involved a contradiction, though not an absolute denial of reason. It
did not attempt to give account of the order and un-

---

[1] Cf. iv. 45.
[2] ix. 39; x. 6; xi. 18.

deniable purpose which the course of physical phenomena everywhere exhibited,[1] and which the ethical needs of man demanded and implied. Though morality, from man to man, might seem individualist, that is to say, atomic, its very existence does in fact presuppose a larger sanction, which alone makes it identical and authoritative—a moral order binding upon individuals, and integrating them into a society. The old sanction of civic obligation had withered in practice and been expunged from theory, but the survival of morality itself confirmed the existence of a basis at once individual and universal. This lay in a common source of energy, not in mere parity of individual impulses. Alike then from the physical and the moral side, it appeared that the cause of being was material and unitary, and common characteristics suggested, if they did not prove, identity of nature. Converging lines of evidence from many sides corroborated and justified acceptance of this supposition. The play of subject upon object, through the various organs of mind and sense; the abounding evidences of mutual adaptation; the vital and emotional *rapport*[2] that exists between ourselves and nature; the subtle 'sympathy of parts'[3] that links together the remotest members of the universe—in heaven, earth, and air; the unwearying courses of the sun; the fateful concurrences and influences of the stars;[4] the evidences of augury and divination; the availing prayers and

[1] iv. 3, 27; vi. 10; vii. 75; x. 28; xii. 14.
[2] Cf. iii. 2; vi. 14, 36; x. 21.
[3] iv. 27; ix. 9; cf. vi. 38; vii. 9.
[4] Cf. vii. 47; xi. 27.

e

observances of countless tribes of men ; these all confirmed and ratified the instinctive intuition that all
world-life was one. Even man's organic frame reproduced on the small scale the giant organism of the
Universe. Man's soul, located at the heart, fed with
inner warmth, receiving, emitting, and directing thence
the multifarious currents of vital energy and consciousness, was but the microcosmic counterpart of the
central Sun,[1] whose life and light-giving beams irradiated
and interpenetrated every part and pore of the cosmic
whole. The soul of man was consubstantial with the
soul of all things, and in human consciousness realised
itself as no blind, atomic, isolated force, but as a
conscious immanent directive energy of life.

Such then was the main synthesis that took
possession of the Stoic mind—the World a complete
and living whole,[2] informed and controlled by one all-
pervasive energy, which 'knew itself'[3] in the consciousness of man—the microcosm, and declared all nature
one, coherent, rational. The processes by which this one
immanent world-soul attained phenomenal differentiation,
the law of its cosmic evolution, the goal of its endeavour,
the meaning and the relations of part to part and part
to whole, were only gradually discerned ; and before

[1] Hence the fanciful seriousness, with which both Epictetus and
M. Aurelius draw moral lessons from the sun.—Cf. vi. 43 ; viii.
57 ; ix. 8 ; xii. 30. The world-soul receives explicit mention, vi.
36 and vii. 75 ; for comparison with man's soul see v. 21 ;
ix. 22.
[2] iv. 40 ; v. 8 ; vi. 9, 38 ; vii. 9 ; ix. 1, 9 ; x. 1.
[3] xi. 1.

entering on these problems it will be well to note the corollaries—for thought and life—that followed from the main position.

The principle of life impregnated all being, every-where; the consequence implied the presence of the cause, and could not exist except as alive by virtue of the inherent quickening energy. Dead matter—that is, matter uninformed with spirit—involved a contradiction of thought; the negation of spirit is nothing less than the denial of existence. The conception of God, as the motive and sustaining power of things, was made to tally with the scheme of monistic materialism; and it needed little violence to language at a time when the material presence of God in phenomena was still among the familiar assumptions of polytheistic belief. It was only necessary to adapt it rigorously to the terms of Stoic thought, and dissociate it from any suggestion of transcendence or immateriality of being. God immanent in the Cosmos, not extraneous or antecedent to it, is revealed as the one omnipresent cause and manifestation of life. Not only is the inherence of God a condition and necessity of being, but God is made commensurate with being : the pantheistic conception of the world is complete and all-inclusive. God acts and inheres in as many forms as the vital energy itself, and must be recognised no less in the physical energies of heat, and breath, and vital currents than in the psychical energies of soul, and mind, and reason, or in the larger moments of cosmic energies, which, as destiny, or providence, or fate, rule the appointment of phenomena, and determine the direction and the order of the evolution of the universe. In this sense, but in this sense only, God was immanent in man, and reveals himself in his most essential form as conscious reason. This tenet decisively differentiates Stoic pantheism from other pantheistic forms of thought. Platonic thought, in referring existence and all activities of thought or consciousness to immanence of the Idea, was in a sense pantheistic; so still more was Aristotelian, in treating form as an effect of the divine reason. But both asserted priority of ontological existence for the divine; and neither admitted the idea of *conscious* pantheism, nor tried to break down the permanent dualism of subject and object, Matter and Form. God was the primary efficient cause of existence, but was implicit as an effect, not immanent as sustaining, energising, self-conscious life. In the Stoic creed God is in no sense transcendent above matter, but immanent and consubstantial: the world is the *substance* of God;[1] Nature is not the creation or the image, but the fulfilment and content of the Divine.

All are but parts of one stupendous Whole,
Whose body Nature is, and God the Soul.

Stoicism, in ascribing phenomena to the action of mind, attached a moral, instead of a merely mechanical, interpretation to each motion of the Universe. It was, alike in whole and part, the expression of purpose working towards a conscious end. 'Necessity' in the physical order, and 'Destiny' in the moral, are reconciled as self-acting 'Providence,' irresistible, rational,

---

[1] οὐσίαν θεοῦ Ζήνων φησι τὸν ὅλον κόσμον καὶ τὸν οὐρανόν.

Diog. L. 7, 148.

and beneficent.[1] Not merely in general scope, but in every detail, its action was teleological. To the consistent pantheist, imperfection in the universe must argue defect or unreason in God; and faith loses every stay unless it can hold that 'the disposing Reason contains no evil, does no evil, and inflicts no injury on anything.'[2] To the perfect rightness of the whole the Stoic clings with immovable conviction. Purpose, design, providence, were everywhere at work, and all lower processes must be interpreted as means towards higher ends[3]—inorganic life subserving the design of organic, vegetable or animal; the vegetable or animal subserving the social and the rational; the physical existing for the intellectual; the part or individual for the whole.[4] Each part—olive or fig-tree, horse or dog[5]—is there to make complete the universal order, of which it forms a transient part. Man is no exception to the rule, but its highest and conscious exemplification. To him, too, the world-order becomes at once a norm and a constraining stress, to which his action must (willingly or unwillingly) accommodate itself. As a norm of action it becomes to his moral sense an outer law, empowered to prescribe authoritative rules of life and obligation, a 'categorical imperative' of duty. 'The good man submits his own judgment to the power that disposes all, as good citizens to the law of the state.'[6]

---

[1] ii. 2, 3; v. 8, 24; viii. 35; xii. 14.
[2] vi. 1; ii. 11, 17; vi. 44; ix. 28, 35; x. 1, 20; xi. 17; xii. 5.
[3] v. 16, 30; vii. 55; xi. 10, 18.
[4] Cf. ii. 3; v. 8, 22; vi. 45, 54; x. 6, 33; xi. 18.
[5] iv. 6, 23, 48; v. 1, 6; viii. 15, 19; x. 8; xii. 16.
[6] Epict. I, 12, 7.

Hence, for the first time in Greek thought, there emerges the idea of duty and of the sense of sin, independent of inner impulses or of human obligation or relationship. Nature, immanent as thought, looks down forbiddingly upon the motions of sense, impulsive and precipitate ; and looks up with guiding and sympathetic reverence to that cosmos of which it is part. Assuming the *rôle* of a constraining power, that as whole to part can overrule the action of the individual to the purposes of the world-order, it erects an outer determinism, beside which man's freedom resolves itself into capacity for conscious cooperation with a power that exceeds and comprehends his own. Man, like the olive, but with consciousness superadded, spends his brief moment according to nature's law, and ' falls ' when it is ripe.'[1] Thus Stoic free-will becomes a selective power[2] of inner self-determination, by which reason or moral will is able to accept or to resist the reactions of sense and impulse and circumstance upon inner disposition. Passive obedience may become active. In the sweep of the great cosmic current, Will can for its season keep personality intact, and may consciously realise and accept the trend of destiny ; but its action is circumscribed to itself ; it cannot shape events, or move or modify things without, or vary by a hair's breadth the course of Necessity. It becomes devout and almost fatalistic resignation—

---

[1] iv. 48.

[2] In the terms of Epictetus a χρῆσις φαντασιῶν. Epict. I, I, 5-7 ; I, 20, 5-7.

Lead me, O Zeus, and lead me, Destiny,
What way soe'er ye have appointed me !
I follow unafraid ; yea though the will
Turn recreant, I needs must follow still.
           CLEANTHES, ap. EPICTETUS, *Encheiridion.*

As a further consequence of this, the declared community of mind between the cosmos and man, and the perception of a single purpose uniting both in common ends, produced a sympathetic sentiment towards nature, unknown before except as some vague, instinctive presage, unauthorised and unexplained. But when nature stood revealed as a sentient being, pulsing and interpenetrated everywhere with the same stream of life as fed man's own, the pathetic fallacy found standing-ground in fact, and became, alike in ethics and in poetry, a new source of imaginative appeal, that, from Cleanthes to Shelley, from Vergil to Wordsworth, has expatiated in the enlarging fervours of the poetry of pantheism.

No system of material monism will permanently satisfy man's intellectual constitution ; it is metaphysically shallow, and fails to meet the necessities or account for the existence of thought ; but the Stoic attempt, noble, far-reaching, and on its own lines exhaustive, not merely held for centuries a more active and commanding sway over the minds and hearts of men than the metaphysics of Plato and Aristotle, not merely interwove itself with Christian discipline and doctrine, and found philosophic reconstruction in Spinoza, but at this day, alike in the poetic and scientific imagination, enjoys a wider currency, and exercises a more invigorative appeal in the field of natural religion than any other extra-Christian interpretation of the universe. And rightly so ; for Stoic Pantheism first gave reasoned form and basis to that imperious instinct of cosmic unity, and likewise of communion between human and divine, which haunts men with persistent power, and which any philosophy aspiring to be permanent must explain and justify. Thus it is no surprise to find the genius of Stoicism perfectly expressed in the lines of one to whom its formal doctrines were a sealed book :—

> O God, within my breast,
> Almighty, ever-present Deity !
> Life, that in me has rest,
> As I—undying life—have power in thee.
>
> .   .   .   .   .   .
>
> With wide-embracing love
> Thy spirit animates eternal years,
> Pervades and broods above,
> Changes, sustains, dissolves, creates, and rears.
>
> Though earth and man were gone,
> And suns and universes ceased to be,
> And thou wert left alone,
> Every existence would exist in thee.
>
> There is not room for Death,
> No atom that his might could render void :
> Thou—Thou art Being, Breath,
> And what Thou art may never be destroyed.[1]

§ 3. *The Soul of Man. Psychology.*

The relation of man to the world gives the key to

---

[1] Emily Brontë, *Poems.*

his inner constitution. Human psychology, which the Stoics diligently elaborated, rests on the pantheistic assumption, which is the keystone of their system. Every manifestation of life derives from the immanent presence of the one world-life. The soul in man, incarnate for a season as a spring of human life, is subsequently reabsorbed into the cosmic spirit from which it emerged as a seminal principle of separate life. Comprising and controlling all the activities of thought, emotion, sense, and life, like the world-soul itself, it may be known by many names. Epictetus, for instance, speaks usually of 'soul'; but Marcus characteristically favours the scholastic designation, which throws chief emphasis upon the directive will, and calls it the *Hegemonic*[1] or Master-Power. The purest expression of soul, the *distinctively* human element, which unites man with the highest in nature, and keeps him 'in touch with god,'[2] is the Reason, Mind, or Understanding (λόγος, νοῦς, διάνοια, λογισμός); the sovereign presence of this element lifts man above every other creature, cements the inalienable brotherhood of kind, and makes conscious conformity to nature his spiritual prerogative and goal. An absolute unity prevails within the dominion of man's self, and the whole is properly described by that which is its highest function and expression; virtue and knowledge are made one, and the contributory activities, which concern the emotions or the appetites or the

---

[1] This I have reluctantly paraphrased in the text, as *Inner Self*, or here and there *Governing Self*; for the World *Hegemonikon* (vi. 36; vii. 75) I have used *Soul*.

[2] xii. 2.

functions of the physical organism, are 'parts' and movements of the same life-force.

Stoic psychology does not base itself on study and observation of psychical processes, so much as on determined vindication of the supremacy of the *Hegemonic* power or will. The unity and the ascendancy of the *Hegemonicon* was held to exclude any psychology such as the Platonic, which accorded distinct and separable status to the rational and the irrational nature, to Reason, Passion, and Desire. The Stoic declined to recognise rival and independent powers, and regarded the emotional or sensuous, as well as the rational and intellectual, activities as '*parts* of the soul.' Physically, they are conceived as currents of the one life-giving Pneuma, acting by different channels upon centres of consciousness, placed in the heart, or by some teachers in the brain. In this way they are incorporated in the one soul-energy, and placed absolutely at the disposition of the directive power. They are set in motion by external stimuli, but in their realisation as physical or psychical activities (πάθη, ὁρμαί, ὀρέξεις) they are actual affections, functions, and 'parts' of the soul itself, and their subordination to the intellectual or reasoning faculty depends upon the fact that their action and indeed existence rests upon 'judgments,' favourable or adverse, and that the supreme judgment-forming power, man's guarantee of freedom, is vested in the reason, and is able to ignore and override the dictates or the protests of emotion, sensibility, or passion. In the case of the animals [1] we see impulse and instinct, unprovided

[1] iii. 16; vi. 16; vii. 55.

with the superior check which puts man on a higher
plane. In man, impulses and affections are not of
necessity irrational; on this point the language of
Chrysippus and others is unmistakable. Strictly speaking, they are in themselves non-rational, but capable
of adoption by the reason, and so of becoming
rationalised. But there is a constant tendency among
the zealots and rhetoricians of the school to press the
verbal antithesis, to decry all forms of emotion as aberrations from right reason, and to exact from the Wise
Man their entire eradication. The question is at
bottom one of terms. It is possible to confine the
terms emotion, desire, and the like to those *unauthorised*
affections and impulses, which are not incorporated by
the directive power and so raised into constituent
parts of virtue or right reason. On that understanding
the doctrine of Apathy (ἀπάθεια) may be pressed without
reserve, and the emotions treated as suspects or detected
criminals ; but the restriction is arbitrary and misleading,
as at variance with psychological fact. The emotions
and affections do not change their nature in receiving
sanction and adoption from the reason and the will ;
and Stoicism lost much in moral efficacy by obscuring
and even denying this psychological fact, and extending
its disapproval of irrational (or unrationalised) emotions
into a wholesale and undiscriminating ban.

Sensation is treated on the same lines ; the five
senses, often grouped as a single faculty of soul, are
thought of as outlying feelers, so to speak, of the Pneuma,
directed from the centre to the surface of the body,
and maintaining communication between the conscious

Pneuma within and cognate manifestations of Pneuma without; the act of consciousness is referred to the interior soul, the sense-organs only providing instruments of communication. The pleasures of sense, just as those of reason in its own department, are due to the smooth or rough flow of the Pneuma-currents[1] in the channels appropriated to their action, though Reason and Will have power to ignore such excitations at their pleasure. In a lower order still, and served by other organs, comes the generative or reproductive faculty, and (without much clearness or coherence of view) the faculty of speech.[2] Throughout, the materiality of the soul is unflinchingly affirmed, and nowhere more unreservedly so (in spite of some incidental laxities of expression) than in Marcus, who, following the medical theorisers of his day, describes the soul as an exhalation of the blood.[3] Death similarly is the 'evaporation'[4] of the immanent Pneuma from the physical organism, prior to its extinction or re-immergence in the world-Pneuma.

The object of these laboured and somewhat barren speculations is plain, namely, the determination to main-

---

[1] See p. lvii. [2] This classification seems referred to in xii. 31.
[3] ἀναθυμίασις ἀφ' αἵματος, v. 33; vi. 15. The principle of evaporation (ἀναθυμίασις) plays a large part in the speculations of the Ionian physicists. To Heraclitus, soul is an exhalation from air, and Cleanthes regards the sun, the *Hegemonikon* of the World, as recruited by exhalation from the sea. The transition from liquid to gaseous is the normal assumption; but the explicit pathological association with the *blood*, as vehicle of vital warmth, was worked out by Diogenes of Apollonia and the medical school. In Marcus it possibly reflects the personal teaching of Galen.
[4] ἐκθυμᾶσθαι, vi. 4.

tain, throughout the spheres of perception, emotion, desire, and reason, the totality of the individual as an organic and inseparable unity. The Stoics did much for the establishment of this conception, and it was unfortunate that they did not grasp it even more completely, in assigning to the different faculties their prerogatives and spheres of exercise. A sounder ethic would have resulted from a more complete analysis and understanding of the nature of will. Here the Stoics—like other schools of antiquity—came short, and were content to rest in psychological abstractions, adopted or devised by their first masters. Instead of investigating the ends of action, and finding in them intrinsic or external criteria to determine the relative value of particular functions and precedence among the faculties, the Stoics selected a single faculty or group of faculties and assigned them exclusive, and more or less arbitrary, dominion over the rest. They were right in declaring the highest and most essential element in man to be the rational, otherwise denominated the social or the universal,[1] as relating man's consciousness to the widest and most comprehensive range of interests. But they erred, partly under the influence of Socratic *dicta*, in identifying this rational faculty too exclusively with the intellectual. That virtue is inseparable from knowledge is true; as virtue passes beyond the instinctive impulses, and widens its range of action and view, the more do perception, insight, and foresight become indispensable. But besides the faculty

---

[1] The habitual terms in M. A. are λογική, *rational*, πολιτική and κοινωνική, *social* (or *unselfish*), and the more unusual καθολική, *catholic* or *universal*, *e.g.* in vi. 14, vii. 64.

of knowing, virtue involves the habit of willing and acting; while it leans on the understanding for guidance, it derives its motive power from desire and will. Analysis may separate the three, and adjudge precedence in time or dignity; but every moral act presupposes not only the knowledge which reveals and defines the end, but also the desire which adopts it, and the will which gives effect to the desire in an act of self-determination. Without desires, which depend for their existence on the affections and emotions, knowledge remains impotent, and loses the motive power which elevates it into virtue. Each exercise of virtue implies an existing basis of character and knowledge, determining itself in a new act of volition. Thus in so far as the Stoics were misled by an unsound psychology into denouncing all emotional activities, and set themselves to 'efface' and 'extinguish' impressions and desires,[1] instead of enforcing the need of selecting, guiding, and utilising them to the best end, they narrowed and weakened the scope of their morality. By suppression of desires, the moral ideal could easily be reduced to that hard and narrow self-consistency, towards which the Stoic type habitually leans, or drill itself or decline into the moral 'apathy' which results from restricting virtue to the sphere of intellectual and unimpassioned self-regard. This is the secret of that 'accent of futility,'

[1] Few maxims recur more frequently in M. A. Cf. *e.g.* v. 2, 36; vi. 13; vii. 17, 29; viii. 29, 47; ix. 7; xi. 16, to which iv. 7 and all its parallels ii. 15; iii. 9; iv. 3, 39; vi. 52; vii. 14, 16; viii. 40; ix. 13; xi. 16, 18; xii. 8, 22, 25, 26 may properly be added.

which marks the thoughts even of a writer so keenly alive to altruistic and social obligation as Marcus Aurelius.

§ 4. *Knowledge and Perception*

Such was the organism of the soul, by means of which perception, judgment, knowledge, and will were effectuated and unified. Knowledge was based upon material sense-perception. Through the senses the mind had contact with external objects, and perception was explained as an 'impression' made upon the soul,[1] or, in more guarded language as a 'modification of the soul,'[2] produced by the impact of types or images of the objects of sense. Perception then is an affection or movement within the soul produced by an impulse from without; but the active and motive power in perception is regarded as proceeding in the main from the thing perceived,[3] not as supplied or emitted by the percipient; the soul is mainly passive, though in the act of perception the response elicited from the percipient implies an answering activity in the percipient's consciousness. The perception itself does not originate in a movement or activity of consciousness, but is rather a result or content of consciousness called into play by an outer force. Sensation entertains the impression, and conscious perception results. Such sense-perceptions are of very different kinds, and vary according to their relation to the object which they reproduce : perceptions frequently

---

[1] τύπωσις ἐν ψυχῇ.   [2] ἑτεροίωσις τῆς ψυχῆς.

[3] Almost all Greek schools, not excluding the Platonic, treat perception and thought as communicated from without.

give imperfect or misleading representations of the objects which they represent, and to this is due that untrustworthiness of the senses which was used by the Sceptics and other schools to undermine the very possibility of certain knowledge. But, according to Stoic belief, there do exist perceptions which, to a healthy consciousness, give so complete and perfect a representation of the object and all its sensuous properties and qualities, 'apprehend' it so fully,[1] and reproduce it so convincingly, that by an inner and self-evidencing virtue they constrain mental assent to the completeness and accuracy of the representation, and furnish a sure basis for knowledge.

It has been usual[2] to restrict these authoritative perceptions to the sphere of sense-impression, and to urge that there was no logical escape from this for the consistent materialist ; but Stoic monism, by its identification of matter with soul, eludes this difficulty, and the organs of sense are not the only possible channels of contact between subject and object, the mind and the external world. The Stoic paradoxes regarding the ' materiality '

---

[1] Hence called φαντασίαι καταληπτικαί. φαντασίαι which I have (almost consistently) rendered ' regards ' or ' impressions ' occurs very frequently in M., and is certainly not restricted to *sense*-impressions.

[2] I have ventured to follow Bonhöffer, who is at issue with most previous interpreters. The discussion hardly falls within the scope of M. Aurelius, and I have therefore been content to summarise results. He refers to the doctrine of ' assent ' or certitude, *e.g.* κατάληψις (iv. 22 ; ix. 6 ;) and συγκατάθεσις (v. 10 ; viii. 7 ; xi. 37), and cf. iii. 9 ; vii. 54, 55—but does not treat the subject systematically.

of virtues, concepts, moral or æsthetic qualities, and such
like, do not involve the corollary, that such qualities or
conceptions admit of sensuous perception only, but on
the contrary themselves imply that, even on the materialistic assumption, mind can come in contact with things
external to itself through other organs than those of
sense.   The fact that virtue or beauty or number or God
is in Stoic phraseology 'a body,' does not preclude it
from being perceived by some other organ of soul than
the five organs of sense.   The reason or understanding,
the psychical as well as the sensuous activities of the
immanent soul, are no less 'bodily' than the senses, and
it seems correct and consistent (in spite of strong counter
assertions) to believe that the Stoics admitted 'perceptions of reason' as well as 'perceptions of sense' to a
place in their theory of knowledge.   Without this admission it is difficult to understand how authority could be
claimed for any abstract conceptions, or for existences
that lie outside the range of sensuous perception.   To
these perceptions of the reason the same note of authority,
varying with the completeness of the apprehension and
representation, will attach as to the perceptions of sense
already discussed.   Thus then the means and bases of
knowledge are twofold, first the organs of sense, secondly
certain organs of apprehension resident in reason and
forming elements in the unique constitution of the
human mind.   These inborn elements of reason have a
specific name (προλήψεις) attached to them, and are a
universal endowment of the mind of man.   They consist
in certain innate ideas (κοιναὶ ἔννοιαι) of moral qualities,
good and bad, becoming and unbecoming, fair and foul,

f

and so forth. They are not indeed consciously realised from the moment of birth, but are nevertheless implicit in thought, and as the seminal reason gradually matures, they become an integral part of the reasoning consciousness. Neither again are they perfect or infallible in exercise, any more than the perceptions of sense ; rather they are general and indeterminate ideas, which need careful comparison and adjustment and development under the guiding disciplines of reason. But in right surroundings, and under just and watchful disciplines, they gradually become clarified and perfected, and lead on to invincible convictions, which in the moral sphere carry as clear and compelling a certitude as the attestations derived from sense.

Knowledge then is grounded on perceptions or impressions of outward existences, conveyed to the mind by the appropriate organs of sense or (in the case of certain abstract ideas and super-sensuous existences) of intellectual apprehension. But the perceptions are by no means equally valid ; and as soon as the perception has made itself felt and become a content of consciousness, it is for reason or understanding to test it, to pass judgment, and to accord approval or rejection.[1] The approving verdict, which affirms that the perception is a real representation corresponding to an actual object, is technically known as ' assent ' ; and this ' assent,' which, physically viewed, rests on right tension in the mental energy, may be strong or weak, mistaken or sound, true or false ; its action depends partly on the subjective condition of the perceiving and ratifying mind,

[1] vi. 52 ; vii. 16, 68 ; viii. 28, 47 ; xi. 16, 18 (7).

artly on the objective character of the representation
:self. It may yield a convinced assurance corresponding
ɔ a true and actual representation ; or again a convinced
ssurance which, however positive and dogmatic, is
ɔunded on a misleading or imperfect representation,
nd is consequently false or faulty in its assumptions ;
ɾ, finally a weaker sense of assurance passing through
arious grades of faltering conviction, until it ceases to
leserve even the name of 'opinion' (δόξα) at all.

The executive criteria then of knowledge, which must
ɪe applied to outer existences to test and measure their
eality, are twofold—sense and innate ideas. Reason
lirects their application, and in certain cases there ensues
according to Stoic belief) a specific and incontrovertible
ense of 'assent,' an answering affection and compulsion
ɪf the soul, that carries its own warrant of reality, and
.ssures to the Wise Man infallible apprehension of very
ruth.

Perception and sensation then consist of impressions
ɪpon the soul-organ, set in motion by objects of sense.
3ut those impressions—the dogma is essential, and the
ɪne guarantee of man's moral independence—are sub-
ect to the sovereignty of Reason. They play upon the
ɪrgans of sense, as strings upon the marionette ;[1] but
heir power and their authority stop there.[2] They try
ncessantly to force an entrance to the inner citadel, to
onfound reason and take it by storm, to anticipate or
way its verdicts ;[3] but it is the office of reason to keep

[1] ii. 2 ; iii. 16 ; vi. 16, 28 ; vii. 3, 29 ; xii. 19.
[2] vii. 16 ; viii. 41, etc.
For these various figures, iii. 6 ; v. 36 ; vi. 52 ; vii. 16 ; viii. 36, 48.

them at arm's length, standing without, stating their case, awaiting judgment.[1] Mind retains absolute power of self-determination, however imperiously impressions clamour and agitate. It is 'self-swayed, self-moved,' enabled by selective and circumscriptive power[2] to 'modify the objects upon which it plays into accord with the judgments which it approves.'[3] It is proof against the reactions of circumstance, for 'The view taken is everything,' as Marcus again and again reiterates.[4] 'Affect what will the parts of my being from without! the parts affected can if they please find fault. So long as I do not view the infliction as an evil, I remain uninjured.'[5] 'Efface impression; stay impulse; quench inclination; be master of your Inner Self'[6]—that is the business and prerogative of mind.

'This unconditional sovereignty of reason in the individual life secures to man that perfect independence of the will, which seemed the indispensable condition of virtue. Proof against affections of the flesh, disturbances of the emotions, and all 'slings and arrows' of outrageous fortune, he becomes 'a citadel impregnable to passion,'[7] a headland round which all billows of circumstance boil and break in vain.[8] But, as the event proved, his independence is gained at the expense of a yet more commanding subordination. If, as the life-power of the universe, the controlling faculty has rights

[1] iii. 16 ; iv. 3 ; v. 19 ; vii. 2, 68 ; viii. 28 ; ix. 15 ; xi. 16.
[2] v. 26 ; viii. 36 ; xii. 3.   [3] v. 19 ; vi. 8 ; vii. 16, 67 ; xi. 1.
[4] ii. 15 ; iii. 9 ; iv. 3, 39 ; vi. 52 ; xi. 18 (7) ; xii. 8, 22, 25, 26.
[5] vii. 14.   [6] ix. 7 ; cf. iv. 24 ; v. 2 ; vii. 29 ; viii. 29, 47.
[7] viii. 48.   [8] iv. 49.

indefeasible and unassailable within the little state of
man, it becomes on the same showing a part only, a\
single jot,[1] in the interminable sum and series of cosmic
being. And the inference was not evaded or denied;
the chain of causation [2] and of consequence was absolute
from the beginning; the history of the universe was but
the unfolding of the providence of God [3] in sequences
that followed one another with unalterable cyclic regu-
larity; [4] the recurrent processes of nature,[5] the rise and
fall of kingdoms,[6] the ceaseless round of human circumstance,[7] the destiny of individuals,[8] are all part of that
great ‘web of Klotho,’ which issues from the primal
cause, forewoven by the predestinations of eternity.[9]
The moral determinism, even more than the physical,
is absolute and irreversible: the one end of man lies in
conformity with ‘the inviolable necessity,’ [10] so that in
the last resort, as cosmic Monism necessarily implied,[11]
moral freedom resolves itself into a determination or
self-subjugation of the will into harmony with the working of destiny, into obedient *following* of reason and of
God.[12] Man’s attitude to circumstance, not the direction
of it, remains within his own control. Knowing or un-
knowing, willing or loth,[13] all work towards the inevitable
consummation—

ducunt volentem fata, nolentem trahunt.

---

[1] v. 24.   [2] v. 8.   [3] ii. 3.
[4] v. 13, 32; ix. 28; xi. 1   [5] viii. 6, 50; xii. 24.
[6] iv. 32; vii. 49; x. 27.   [7] iv. 32; vi. 37; vii. 1; ix. 14.
[8] v. 13.   [9] iv. 34; and cf. ii. 3; iii. 4, 11, 16; iv. 26;
v. 8; viii. 23; x. 5.   [10] xii. 14.   [11] See p. lxvi.
[12] iii. 9, 12; vii. 31; ix. 1; x. 11, 12, 28; xii. 27, 31.
[13] vi. 42; ʌ. 28.

The difficulties thus raised are fundamental, and on the monistic assumption, certainly as formulated by the Stoics, insuperable. The independence of the will as a true first principle or ἀρχή is incompatible with its identification with the world-soul. If, as Stoic masters taught, the highest consciousness of man represents the most complete and perfect embodiment of the world-spirit, the saving thought of self-determination towards some transcendent, and yet unapprehended, harmony is excluded. Not only is man part of the universal pre-destination, but the limits of that predestination are known and absolute. The subjection imposed becomes intolerable. It is impossible to identify the soul of man with the infinite creative spirit of the universe, and at the same time to circumscribe his outlook within the finite limitations of space and time and 'the material shell.'[1] Nature *as a whole* may be conceived as in some marvellous way at once self-circumscribed and self-sufficing:[2] but the individual limited isolated part cannot at once inherit and express the spiritual fulness of the whole, and at the same time acquiesce in the transient and incomplete appropriation of limitations that are final. Further, the facts of consciousness remain unsatisfied. The Stoics laboured the classification and nomenclature of various orders of emotion, but give no account of the inner antagonisms that exist between reason, desire, and impulse. They do not

[1] For enforcement of time limitations—see ii. 14, 17 ; iii. 10, 12 ; iv. 16, 19, 26, 49 ; vi. 32 ; vii. 29, 54 ; viii. 2, 7, 36, 44 ; ix. 25, 29 ; x. 11 ; xii. 1, 3, 26.
[2] viii. 50.

grapple with the central difficulty, the origin and existence of irregular and irrational impulses in the soul, or show how their presence is compatible with a nature that is 'altogether good.'[1] All alike are operations of the Pneuma, and the Pneuma is divided against itself. If lusts and affections, good desires and bad, all spring from the same fountain-head, every guarantee for the eventual prevalence of good is withdrawn. The destiny of creation reveals itself in never-ending cycles of unprogressive conflict, and no thought of moral evolution enters in to brace endeavour, or justify optimism. As part of this predestination, the basis of individual virtue itself becomes precarious. Such are some of the difficulties involved in the Stoic scheme.

To this extent then and by this route Greek thought approached the moral problems of 'free-will,' which it bequeathed in intensified form to Christianity. The Stoics did not push the issue to its ultimate contradictions; circumscribing and in effect sacrificing free personality, they were content to leave the conception of Order supreme and paramount; and their problem was not complicated by the idea of life as probation, by any doctrine of reward or punishment in a life to come, or by any need of provision for the remission of sins. The diseased or rebellious member might suffer loss; it might estrange or excommunicate itself as some malcontent from the social system;[2] it might entail upon itself forfeitures, pains, disabilities, or death; it might become a kind of tumour or excrescence on the body:[3]

---

[1] Compare p. lxv.

[2] ii. 16; viii. 34; ix. 23.   [3] iv. 29.

but even so 'the health of the world-order, the welfare and well-being of Zeus,'[1] was not impaired, nor its movement contravened; disaffection was powerless to interrupt or baulk the purposes of providence, and in opposing it does but become fuel for the flame,[2] feeding and strengthening what it essays to check and counteract.

By this narrowing of the field, Stoic belief escaped some of the difficulties which beset the Christian in accounting for the existence of pain and evil. Partly by allowing vicarious suffering of the part for the advantage of the whole, and partly by condoning evil as an incident and mode of the prevalence of good, it sought to break the direct impact of the argument, and to avoid the admission of any ultimate triumph of evil, or any final defeat of the power and wisdom and beneficence of God. But though the most urgent difficulties were thus evaded by Stoicism, and deeper difficulties—such, for instance, as those that hinge on environment, on heredity, or on erroneous belief—were not yet broached, yet it brought men face to face with the inscrutable problems of individual responsibility, and owned their exigence to an extent that may be measured by the distance which separates the stalwart bravado of Diogenes from the acceptant optimism of Epictetus, or the hard defiance of Cato from the devout resignation of Marcus Aurelius.

---

[1] v. 8.

[2] iv. 1; viii. 32, 35, 57; x. 31, 33.

IV.—STOICISM IN HISTORY

HISTORICALLY, Stoicism belongs to the age of the Diadochi; the career of Alexander was ended before Zeno repaired to Athens and enrolled himself among the disciples of Crates. The conquests of Alexander changed the moral as well as the political outlook of Hellenism; for ethically, as well as socially, it became impossible any longer to regard the πόλις as the supreme unit of morality. ‚The conception of the state enlarged to that of the nation, and nationality became cosmopolitan in its field of exercise. ‘Hellenism’ was no longer restricted to the cities and colonies of Greece, but was called upon to realise itself as a social and intellectual entity from the Ægean to the Indies. The reconstruction of Ethics was immediate and fundamental. In Plato it is a standing assumption that the city is ‘by nature’ the Greatest Common Measure of individual morality; in Aristotle the same idea still dominates the field of ethics, and moral prerogative is intimately bound up with civic status; ‘natural’ obligation is not identical for the slave and for the freeman, towards the citizen and towards the alien.

Greek ethics from the first expressed realised conditions of Greek life; and the changes of formula that are common to all the post-Aristotelian, or more truly to all post-Alexandrian, schools are another testimony to the freshness and sincerity of the Greek intelligence. In all alike—Stoic, Epicurean, or Cyrenaic—the civic basis is abandoned for the individualist and universal. The ethical ideal becomes internal and, as the city widens to the world, transcends limitations of status or franchise; and belongs to man as man, the common seal of his humanity. As a consequence of this it becomes, or appears to become, for a time, less vital in its effect upon the lives of individuals; it plays less obvious a part in history; the Athenian or the Spartan ideal, by virtue of its limitations, visibly dominates the lives and words and behaviour of representative Athenians or Spartans; it is tangible and unmistakable. A universal ideal is less determinate, and in so far frequently less efficacious; more remote and unattainable in practice, it is prone to compromise with tradition and environment; the Stoic Wise Man does not appear upon the stage of history, least of all in the days or place which first promulgated the idea. Stoic morality was indeed too novel, too many-sided, and too revolutionary for immediate realisation in the arena of public action. In repudiating the civic tie, it failed at first to supply effective substitutes and incentives to altruistic obligation: politically and socially, it was for a time sterile, and indeed rather a naturalised than native product of true Hellenism. Throughout the Hellenic stage, it is impossible to instance great personalities avowedly conforming aim and practice to Stoic principles. Though these gradually, no doubt, began to leaven moral

philosophy and to influence standards of action and
sentiment, Stoicism proper was an affair of the schools.
It was academic before it could become practical; it
was necessary for it to submit theory to the checks of
experience, before it could command allegiance from
the householder, the citizen, and the statesman, as well
as the scholar and recluse.   But in its Athenian home,
engaged in stimulating controversy with rival schools of
thought, strengthening defences, abandoning untenable
positions, and mellowing the individualist paradoxes
of Cynism by maturer conceptions of social aim and
obligation, it prepared itself for larger destinies.

In the historic embassy, which proceeded from
Athens to Rome in 155 B.C., to plead for toleration to
philosophers, the Stoic School was represented by
Diogenes; but its first effective apostle was Panætius of
Rhodes, who, a few years later, introduced it at Rome
under the most favourable auspices.   A man of means
and culture, belonging to one of the oldest and most
distinguished families of Rhodes, Panætius devoted himself by deliberate predilection, not by any accident or
secondary motive, to the lifelong pursuit of philosophy.
At Athens, after hearing the best masters of the day,
he attached himself to the Stoic School, of which he
was eventually to become the recognised head.   Like
Polybius, he became a member of that Scipionic circle,
which first naturalised Hellenic culture at Rome, and
by travel as well as domestic intercourse formed ties of
special intimacy with the younger Scipio.   Rome and
Athens were almost equally the centres of his activity,
and through him the Stoic philosophy, in a somewhat

eclectic and Platonic form, secured an early and abiding hold upon the intellectual leaders of Rome. The *De Officiis* of Cicero is a confessed adaptation from the cognate treatise of Panætius.

But apart from the personality of Panætius, Stoicism fell upon congenial soil; the time was ripe for its acceptance. The historical parallel is full of interest and meaning. Scipio, the friend and patron of Panætius, executed final doom on Carthage. As Stoicism sprang historically out of the supersession of Greek city-states and the expansion of Greece into the world-empire of Alexander, so too its second birth in Italy heralds the imperial stage in the destinies of the great Republic. Upon the fall of Carthage, Africa and Macedonia were constituted Provinces of Rome; a few years added Asia to the number; Rome was no more a city, but an Empire, and her mightiest task, the evolution of Imperial law and administration, lay before her. In the accomplishment of this, Stoicism was no unimportant factor. It was the one philosophy, which in its conceptions of social obligation, of world-citizenship, and of the solidarity and brotherhood of man, contained the germs of a great political order. True, the enactment of laws does not come within the province of schools of philosophy, and influence must filter through individuals, rather than proceed from accredited or formal organisations, but it must not for that reason be belittled or ignored, and in the case of Stoicism the proof rests on no mere inferential evidence. Its voice was continually heard among the official circles of Rome; the earliest of great Roman lawyers, M. Scævola the *Augur*, and the yet more

famous *Pontifex*, were among the first to give welcome
to Panætius ; Cato and Cicero, each in their own way,
are witnesses to its continued power ; among Augustan
lawyers it could claim S. Sulpicius Rufus, Sextus
Pompeius, and others as disciples ; throughout the
darkest days of Imperial oppression, it upheld the forms
of liberty ; carrying accepted weight in family and state,
and slowly mitigating the rigours and inequalities of the
old regime with the humaner influences that are the
glory of the Flavian and Antonine successions, it finally,
in the persons of the Antonines, father and son, took its
seat upon the throne.

In the field of letters, the position of Stoicism was
more assured and definite. At the middle of the
second century, when wealth, supply of slaves, and
empire had wrought an increase of luxury and leisure,
which made intellectual as well as other forms of recreation a necessity, Rome stood at the turning of the
ways. She must either create a literature at home, or
import it from abroad. Literature first finds form in
poetry, and the rough Saturnian, or uncouth pro-
vincialism of the Atellane farce, had no chance against
hexameter and iambic, and the finished perfection of
Greek drama. It was vain for Censor or Senate to
expel philosophers and lay a ban upon rhetoricians and
professors ; the last and stoutest champion of the Latin
school, Cato himself, in his old age accepted Greek
supremacy, and Rome imported literature as a part of
her plunder of the world. Terence vindicates his claim
to originality by the boast that his plays are drawn
direct and solely from the Greek.

In the earlier phases of this Græco-Roman literature, so far as it survives, the borrowing is too direct and crude, and the moral intention too unreflective, to give materials for judgment; but as soon as the national consciousness finds play in poets of Italian stock, and the yield of literature becomes full and representative, we see the whole national ethos reshaping itself upon the lines of Greek philosophy.   Rome showed the same docility in borrowing its moral, as its poetical formulas from Greece.   If Lucretius swings the blade of Epicurus in his fierce onset against the timid formalisms of the national religion, Vergil throughout conveys his national ideal in tones modulated from Stoicism.

> Principio caelum ac terras camposque liquentes
> lucentemque globum lunae Titaniaque astra
> spiritus intus alit, totamque infusa per artus
> mens agitat molem et magno se corpore miscet.
> inde hominum pecudumque genus vitaeque volantum
> et quae marmoreo fert monstra sub aequore pontus.
>
> .   .   .   .
>
> .hinc metuunt cupiuntque, dolent gaudentque.[1]

God is not banished . to fenced paradises of far *Intermundia*

> Where never creeps a cloud, or moves a wind,
> Nor ever falls the least white star of snow,
> Nor sound of human sorrow mounts to mar
> Their sacred, everlasting calm—

but reigns as that

> fortuna omnipotens et ineluctabile fatum

which irresistibly controls the destinies of nations.

[1] Aen. vi. 724-733.

Mythology is used for poetic machinery and embellishment, but the plot moves at the ordering and disposition of cosmic destiny. The Fortune or Majesty of Rome is not so much the work of man, as the visible march of God in history, the ordinance and monotone of Fate. Man is but the acceptant instrument of gods—

> desine fata deum flecti sperare precando.

In presence of an order too mighty for defiance, too impersonal for protest, and too august for sympathy, resolution and endurance, rather than confidence or exultation, become the poet's note.

> Tu ne cede malis, sed contra audentior ito

voices the same profound and tearless acceptance, as haunts the page of Marcus. Struggle will attain its unseen inevitable goal ; that is enough to give dignity and strength to resignation, but not to animate life with hope. The most characteristic and immortal of Vergilian notes—such for instance as

> sunt lacrimae rerum et mentem mortalia tangunt

or

> tendebantque manus ripae ulterioris amore

epitomise the mood which dominates the thoughts of Marcus.

Once genuinely naturalised, the earliest flowers of a transplanted and imitative literature are likely to prove the fairest ; they will not possess generative faculty or reproductive virtue. It was so with the Græco-Roman poetry of the Cæsarean and Augustan era. Its Golden Age is brief and isolated ; and as it subsides into the silver decadence, Seneca in his Tragedies,

Persius in his Satires, Lucan in his *Pharsalia*, remind us how much Stoicism did to fan the flickering after-glow of Latin poetry into life.   Satire and social epigram each bear testimony to its growing power and recognition as a factor in social development.

Prose tells a somewhat different tale.   There, at least in what may be called the political departments—History, Oratory, Memoirs, Epistolary correspondence, and Law—the Latin mind displayed unsurpassed constructive power.   These only reflect indirectly, or include as an incident of their main theme, the currents of philosophic thought.   But here too, it may be said that such moral inspirations as appear spring mainly, if not entirely, from Stoic impulses ; while in philosophic treatises Stoicism holds the field almost alone.   Cicero is indeed encyclopædic in his range of interest ; but it is hardly too much to say that he failed to commend to his own countrymen, or even to assimilate for his own purposes, anything that lay outside of Stoicism. His permanent contributions to moral philosophy were the *De Officiis* and the Tusculan Disputations.   The metaphysics of Plato and Aristotle, and the Sceptical dialectic of the later Academy, were meaningless and unintelligible to the Roman.   For him, Ethics were the sole content of philosophy ; and the only system that came into active competition with Stoicism was that of Epicurus.

Its earliest propaganda in Rome was vigorous and well sustained ; and Lucretius embraced it with an iconoclastic fervour that is without parallel in the history of the School.   But he found no following :

though the name and fashion of Epicureanism continued to prevail, it did not produce one spokesman or teacher of conviction and ability, and fast degenerated into the superficial and popular apologetics of self-indulgence : as such it found adherents among the *dilettanti* of the capital, but it touched no responsive chord in the national ethos of Rome, and was incapable of that accommodation to traditional beliefs which commended Stoicism to men of patriotic, conservative, and religious temperament.   Thus, though the School survived at Athens, and M. Aurelius himself included it among his professorial endowments, as an effective creed and theory of morals it was dead.

Stoicism was, in fact, the one philosophy congenial to the Roman type.   The emphasis it laid on morals, the firmness and austerity of its code, the harshness of its judgment on defaulters, the stern repudiation of emotional considerations or impulses, even the narrowness and inflexibility of its moral logic all commended it to Roman sympathies.   The strength of Rome, the secret of her empire, lay in *character*, in an operative code of honour, domestic, civic and (more at least than in other states) international.   And the Stoic conception of virtue corresponded closely to the range of qualities denoted by Roman *virtus*—manliness.   The traditional type of Roman patriot, the patrician stedfastness of a Camillus or Dentatus, the devotion of a Decius, the dogged self-sacrifice of a Regulus, the sternness of a Brutus ordering his disobedient son to execution, the immovable and often ruthless allegiance to the constituted order of the commonwealth were treasured historical

g

exemplifications of unformulated Stoicism. Its very
narrowness and obstinacy of view was in its favour.
Cato (of Utica) was typically Roman, and by his
faults and limitations as much as his backbone of virtue
became for a time the ideal of Roman Stoicism. 'The
Republican opposition,' as Mommsen in his scornful
manner puts it, 'borrowed from Cato its whole attitude
—stately, transcendental in its rhetoric, pretentiously
rigid, hopeless, and faithful to death ; and accordingly,
it began even immediately after his death to revere as a
saint the man who in his lifetime was not unfrequently
its laughing-stock and scandal.' The strength and the
persistence of these historical attachments finds testimony
in the *Thoughts* of Marcus,[1] and they enriched Stoicism
with that vein of sentiment, which in theory it plumed
itself upon repudiating. Roman Stoicism, as it were,
'believed in the communion of saints.'

Thus the more morality, political and personal,
became self-conscious, and the need of some reasoned
theory of conduct was pressed home by Greek influences
to men of character and culture, the more did everything that was serious at Rome gravitate towards
rational and tempered Stoicism as its creed. In the
long Reign of Terror, under which Rome cowered in
the first century, when virtue could only speak with
bated breath, and liberty and honour kept within
closed doors, Stoicism (like Christianity) was maturing
and effectualising its moral energies. It gains a breadth
and a reality unknown to it before, and takes shape as
'Roman Stoicism.' The Satires of Persius voice the

[1] See *infra*, p. cxxv.

almost inarticulate fury of indignation which it could
stir in the breasts of the young and chivalrous ; the life of
Epictetus proves how it laid hold of the conscience of
the slave and the freedman, as well as the high-born
and the cultured. The death of Arria the elder, with
its superb *finale*, the *salon* of the younger Arria, the
voluntary suicide of Paulina, the teaching of Musonius
Rufus, and the writings of Seneca, show how Stoicism
had won to itself that which was bravest and gentlest
in the womanhood of Rome. The women of this day
are the precursors of Lucilla, mother of Marcus
Antoninus. In the judgment of the people, to which
Tacitus is an impartial witness, the Stoics were, throughout this crisis, identified with all that was left of courage
and integrity in public life. When silence was the last
form of protest left, in the provinces and in the army,
the official journal was scanned to see ' *what Thrasea had
refused to do,*' and in his person Nero ' sought to murder
virtue herself.'

By Nero, by Vespasian, by Domitian, Stoics were
honourably singled out for exile, for proscription, and
for death. Musonius Rufus stedfastly bore exile in Gyara,
and penal servitude in Greece ; Rubellius Plautus,
Seneca, Thrasea Pætus, Helvidius Priscus, Rusticus, and
Senecio, all sealed their testimony with their blood.
When in the last years of Domitian a caitiff Senate
decreed the burning of the books of Arulenus Rusticus
and Herennius Senecio, ' they thought,' writes Tacitus,
himself ex-prætor to the tyrant, ' that in that flame
they were extinguishing the voice of Rome, the freedom
of the Senate, the conscience of the race, that in

expelling the philosophers and laying all goodness under ban, honour would nowhere any more rise and look them in the face.' It was no wonder that, when happier days dawned, a virtual monopoly of moral education fell to a school whose doctrines were certified thus.

· Upon the material side the age of the Antonines presents a picture of unsurpassed prosperity. Under Hadrian Rome touched its zenith of material pomp and affluence. The Forum was a blaze of temples, porticoes, basilicas; the Cæsars' palaces crowned the Palatine; the Golden House of Nero had been superseded by the yet more stupendous circles of the Colosseum; the Mausoleum of Hadrian rose in marble under the eyes of the boy Marcus; forums, baths, theatres, aqueducts, vied with each other in architectural magnificence. Among all the remains of Pagan opulence, there is none which so overpowers the imagination with sense of profusion of scale, as Hadrian's suburban villa, still in its ruins covering some eight square miles, with its maze of triclinia, audience chambers, baths, and colonnades, paved with mosaic, ceiled and enriched with scroll or tracery or arabesque, its fountains of porphyry, its fish-ponds and lakes, its mimic landscapes reproducing nature's choicest handiwork——vales of Tempe, ravines of Styx, harbours of Canopus——and everywhere the niches and pedestals provided for the unexhausted creations of the sculptor's skill. Though with the accession of the Antonines outlay on public buildings and extravagance in spectacles was much reduced, and imperial residences dismantled to meet necessities of state, yet the Antonine

Column and the sculptures of the Triumphal Arch show that traditions of good workmanship still lingered on.

Upon the intellectual side this huge material splendour leans wholly on the past. It is an age of culture and of decadence, not of production. The last Latin writers—Statius and Martial in verse, the Plinies, Tacitus, Quintilian, Columella in prose—belong to the preceding period, and after them Latin literature sinks to its lowest depths. Throughout the western world —for the first time it may be said for a thousand years —poetry ceased to exist. History sinks to the levels of Suetonius and then expires; rhetoric decays into the conceits of Fronto; while the new literature of Christianity is only in its cradle. The best work is done by Greeks, and is mainly exegetical or scientific; though Plutarch, Lucian, and others, redeem the age from total literary barrenness. But on the other hand it is, beyond precedent, an age of schools and universities, of recitations and prælections, of hospitals and orphanages; education, for the first time treated as a science by Quintilian, is on the moral side entrusted to the philosopher, on the intellectual to the grammarian and rhetorician.

The Stoic—in his extremer form a Cynic—everywhere predominates. He is the standing target for the spleen of the Satirist, or the mirth of the jester. He was to be found in all places of public resort, in the pulpit, in the drawing-room, and at Court. He is not limited to the *rôle* of schoolmaster or professor, but as private tutor, as secretary, and as ethical adviser, becomes a familiar figure in the households of the great.[1] Such households maintained large bodies of dependents, who as readers, scribes, stewards, doctors, and artists of all kinds, ministered to luxury and directed the labours of the slaves. Among them the position of the Stoic has been compared to that of the domestic chaplain of a bygone day. He was part of the decorum of a great house, with functions half moral and half social; he was expected to advise, to edify, to sympathise, to entertain, to ease the wheels of domestic life and intercourse. The position of such men, foreigners and pensioners, as professional moralists was full of difficulty, and there were no doubt professing Stoics, who (like other men) sacrificed dignity or paltered with morals, to keep in the good graces of an employer. The *Graeculus esuriens* at times found the Stoic garb the most convenient in which to ingratiate himself and get a livelihood. But the first book [2] of the *Thoughts* shows how much they contributed to set high standards of courtesy and conscientiousness and ethical refinement; and critics as well as eulogists admit that in the hour of trial the bereaved, the sick, and the dying turned for support to the presence and consolations of the philosopher.

Political history, except in its personal bearings upon Marcus, lies outside our compass. Throughout the vast area of the Empire peace, order, and good government prevailed; supervision, vigilant and effective, was exercised over military and civil governors, and the frontiers were kept with vigour and self-restraint; free developments of civic and provincial life were liberally

[1] Cf. i. 16. [2] i. 5-15.

encouraged ; and the blessings, which paternal government and enlightened bureaucracy are able to confer,
were extended in all directions.   But at the seat of rule
power and responsibility centred more and more in the
person of the Emperor.   Good jurists, upright officials
and industrious civil servants seem the best that Rome
could still produce ; as general, as writer, as statesman
Marcus seems the last of the Romans.

As prelude to the consideration of his *Thoughts*, it
may be useful to set forth his genealogy, and a brief
synopsis of events referred to in the following section.

SYNOPSIS OF EVENTS

<table>
<tr><td>

A.D.
121. April 6. Birth on Coelian Mt., his name being M. Annius Verus.

127. *Eques.*
129. Salic Priest.
133. Youthful addiction to Stoicism.
136. Assumes *Toga Virilis.*
137. *Præfectus feriarum Latinarum.*
138. Adopted by Antoninus, and becomes M. Aur. Antoninus—betrothed to Fabia, daughter of deceased L. Ælius Verus. *Quæstor.*

139. *Cæsar. Cos.Desig. Sevir Turmæ. Pont. Max., Augur, xvViv Sacr. Fac., viiVir Epul.*

140. *Cos.* I. This year, or later, marries Faustina.
145. Conversion to philosophy.
161. Commencement of sole rule. L. Verus at once made Augustus, and betrothed to Lucilla.

164. *Armeniacus.*

</td><td>

A.D.
121. July. Death of father, Annius Verus, then praetor.
     Grandfather, Annius Verus, Cos. II.
126. „   „   „   Cos. III.

137. Death of L. Ælius Verus, *Cæsar.*
138. Feb. 25. Antoninus adopted by Hadrian, and made *Imp. c. trib. pot.* He adopts M. Aur. Antoninus and Lucius Verus (son of late Cæsar).
     July 10. Death of Hadrian.
     Lucius Verus entitled *Augusti Filius.*

140. Death of Faustina, consort of Antoninus.

161. March 7. Death of Antoninus. Revolt in Britain. War with Chatti.
161-6. Parthian War, conducted by L. Verus.
164. Lucilla joins L. Verus at Ephesus.

</td></tr>
</table>

A.D.

166. Parthian Triumph. *Parthicus, Medicus, Pater Patriæ.*

-167. Marcus forms army. *Lectisternium* at Rome. Advance to Aquileia. Quadi sue for terms.

168. Summer campaign against Quadi.

169. Celebrates funeral of L. Verus at Rome. Marcomannic Wars (2nd Period).

169-75.

172. *Germanicus.*

173 (or 174). Visit to Rome.

174. *Sarmaticus.*

175. Tour in Asia and Egypt.

176. Travels in Asia and Greece. Dec. Triumph (with Commodus). *Pater Patriæ.*

177-8. Administration at Rome.

178-80. Marcomannic Wars (3rd period). Aug. M. leaves Rome.

180. March 17. Death of Marcus.

A.D.

166. Oct. 12. Commodus and Annius Verus made *Cæsars.* Plague in Italy.

167. Irruption of Northern Barbarians. Aquileia threatened. L. Verus marches north with Marcus.

168. L. Verus campaigns with Marcus.

169. Death of L. Verus at Altinum. Campaign against Iazyges.

173. Campaigns on Rhine by Pompeianus and Pertinax.

174. Quadi campaign. "The Thundering Legion,"

175. Commodus summoned to Pannonia.

176. Death of Faustina, wife of Marcus.

177. Commodus marries Crispina.

GENEALOGICAL TABLE

[The table is incomplete, and intended only for illustration of the *Thoughts*.]

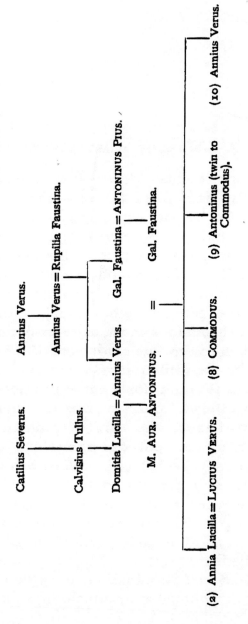

V.—Marcus Aurelius Antoninus

HISTORY represents Marcus as discoursing for three days to the assembled Senate—the days preceding his departure for his last campaign—upon the principles of philosophy and the way of virtue; and modern philosophic romance has drawn upon the Thoughts to dramatise the scene in full. While such a resetting is interesting and legitimate, and while it is possible to reproduce with certainty the general colour and contents which such Imperial exhortations must have exhibited, we must not be misled as to the true characters of the Thoughts themselves. These soliloquies were never meant, as some would seem to think, for a set exposition of philosophy; neither are they a homily or treatise intended for edification of readers or the ears of Roman Senators. For adaptation to that purpose something must be put in, and much must be left out. They belong to the privacy of the closet, addressed to no eye or ear but his own —reminiscences, reflections, interrogations, admonitions ' *To Himself.*' This is the one title that has any vestige of authority, and it were well if they had been always so described and known. They are a manual of personal duty and of self-examination, by which a solitary soul, charged with immense responsibilities, sought to understand, to discipline, and to confirm itself, and so in the conduct of life to attain a more susceptible appreciation, a more strenuous devotion, a perfected allegiance of will to the leadings of nature and God. Their counterpart has emanated more often from the cell or the hermitage than from the statesman's cabinet or the general's praetorium ; they are a *De Imitatione* such as might have been penned amid the isolations of Khartoum.

Among philosophers, Marcus is neither prophet, lawgiver, nor scribe ; he is not a teacher expounding a creed, confirming doubters or controverting opponents. He is a diarist conversing with himself, not claiming even for the doctrines of his school, much less for his own judgments, any absolute infallibility or certitude.[1] There is no pretence to completeness, little even to method, in the handling of ethical topics. Terminology is not always, from the scholastic point of view, exact or uniform. Words are used in the popular sense, as well as in the technical. Quotations are admitted from alien schools and teachers,[2]—for not even the straitest orthodoxy foregoes eclecticism in the privacy of meditation. Allowing this amount of latitude, it is true to say that the presentation of Stoicism found in the Thoughts is correct and careful beyond expectation. In early boyhood [3] he was attracted by its doctrines and its disciplines, in manhood he espoused them as his rule of life ; each day from its first waking hour,[4] each action

---

[1] v. 10.

[2] *E.g.* Epicurus vii. 64 ; Plato vii. 35, 44-48, 63 ; x. 23 ; Theophrastus ii. 10.   [3] i. 6.   [4] ii. 1 ; x. 13.

and each abstinence, each word and each silence,[1] each gesture and each look,[2] was a conscious and diligent observance of Stoic precept, till the tenets of the masters, so learned and practised and appropriated, became a second nature, prescribing not merely instinctive canons of behaviour, but even the inevitable moulds of thought and of expression.

Of most of the censures levelled at his inaccuracy it may be said, either that the language is to be judged by common sense and not intended to be technical, or that the term or tenet assailed is a genuine ingredient of Stoicism in its Græco-Roman form. His theory[3] of knowledge, impulse, and perception is in close accord with that of Epictetus; his attribution of non-reasoning 'Soul' to animals is express and deliberate[4]; his attitude to Atomism, or to the 'future state' of the Soul, is sound and coherent. The latter is a good typical instance for examination.

Depending as it necessarily did on distant and insecure hypotheses, and leaving ethical issues unaffected, the doctrine does not bulk largely in Stoic discussion. Death, a re-arrangement or dispersion of the bodily elements, could not imply annihilation of the Pneuma, a thing logically and physically inadmissible, but only cessation of the particular form of immanence. That after death the animating soul or pneuma was sooner or later re-assimilated into the stock of universal soul, all Stoics were agreed: but while some held that death connoted the end of separable existence, others thought

---

[1] i. 10; vi. 53; vii. 4, 30.   [2] vii. 24, 37, 60.
[3] Cf. Section III. § 4.   [4] So vi. 14; ix. 8, 9.

that, qualitatively at least, though not with any survival of personality, the soul-pneuma retained its independence until the general conflagration of the Universe, when a new cycle of being begins, and the Pneuma reproduces from itself the forms of immanence previously realised. Chrysippus limited even this qualitative retention of being to the souls of the wise, believing that in all other cases reabsorption took place before the final conflagration. From the nature of the case, and from Stoic distaste for gratuitous metaphysical hypotheses, there was room for difference of judgment, and Seneca illustrates the tendency of Roman Stoicism to make at least verbal concessions to the popular belief in some survival after death. In his own conviction Marcus nowhere seems to waver; death, wherever he has occasion to give clear and simple utterance to his own thoughts, is always a dissolution of being, that is, the end of action, impulse, will, or thought, that terminates every human activity, and bounds our brief span of life with an eternity that contains neither hint nor hope nor dread of further conscious being.[1] The bodily elements will pass to other uses, earth to earth and dust to dust, while the life-giving Pneuma will rejoin that ethereal or fiery being, of which it is a part. Death is the last word said of the greatest and the least, of Alexander or his stable-boy, and equally extinguishes the virtuous and vicious, the wise man and the fool :[2] 'had it been better otherwise, the gods would have had it so ; from its not being so, be assured it ought not so to be.'[3] So resolute and unequivocal falls his own utterance.

[1] ii. 11, 12; ix. 21; x. 29; xii. 35   [2] iii. 3; vi. 24, 47.   [3] xii. 5.

But there remain passages in which other possibilities are broached, and which some have interpreted as a wavering back on hope, inconsistent with his philosophic creed. This mistakes the writer's attitude. Just as the devout Christian will in his self-communings face the moral corollaries consequent on a denial of the Resurrection or of a future life ; so too Marcus will entertain and test the consequences of postulates to which he himself gives no assent. The inferences, set down as alternative hypotheses only, will be found to leave the moral issue, which is under consideration, strengthened or unaffected. In two passages [1] 'loss of sensation' at death is contrasted with 'sensation changed in kind and experiencing another life.' His own belief is that death ends sensation, but even on the other (the Platonic or the Pythagorean) assumption, the fear of death is groundless. Next in a series of parallel passages the alternative of 'dispersion' [2] is put forward as one account of death ; the term is regularly connected with the 'Atomic' theory of life, held by the Epicurean school, and in every instance Marcus is consciously quoting the view and terminology of adverse thinkers. Just as he contrasts the Cosmic interpretation of the world with the Atomic—not because conviction wavers, but because candour must not burke the alternative—so, too, side by side with that reabsorption, which follows from his own monistic system, he must set the corollary of 'dispersion' which follows from atomic materialism ; *in either case*, life is small and

---

[1] iii. 3 ; viii. 58.

[2] σκεδασμός and σκεδασθῆναι, vi. 4, 10, 24 ; vii. 32 ; viii. 25 ; x. 7.

transitory, but in the latter even life as it is loses all moral meaning and motive.[1] But besides the inadmissible alternatives, there remain hypotheses between which Marcus feels it unimportant to decide. Death may mean final extinction[2] of the Pneuma—a conclusion which Cicero imputes to another Roman Stoic, Cornutus, and to which Marcus feels at least no ethical objection. But in assuming the destruction instead of the reabsorption of the life-giving spirit, it does from the *physical* side sap the Stoic dogma, which regards the sum of Pneuma as constant and eternal; and in all serious discussion[3] of the subject Marcus adheres to the orthodox tenet of reabsorption. At the death of the body the soul undergoes change of place and phase,[4] and returns to something approaching its pre-incarnate condition. Some Stoics placed such disembodied souls 'in the upper regions,' or 'in the sub-lunar' or 'the stellar' sphere. And these speculations are in the writer's mind when he speaks of souls passing 'into the air,'[5] the upper or rarer air that is to say, akin to the 'fiery ether' of which soul is constituted. There, peradventure by progressive assimilation, analogous to the gradual decomposition of the mortal body, it is eventually reabsorbed or reassumed into the seminal principles of life,[6] out of which it originally sprang,

[1] vi. 10.

[2] σβέσις v. 33 ; vii. 32 ; viii. 25 ; x. 22, 31 ; xi. 3 ; cf. iii. 3 ; vi. 24 ; viii. 58.

[3] Esp. iv. 21.

[4] Denoted by τροπή x. 7 ; by μετάστασις in v. 33, vii. 32, and the verb iv. 21, viii. 25 ; by μεταβολή iv. 14, 21.

[5] iv. 21.   [6] iv. 14, 21 ; vi. 24 ; x. 7.

awaiting new activities or the complete reintegration which takes place at the final conflagration of the present order.   The denial of the 'hope of immortality' is settled and complete ; there is no place in the *Thoughts* for the rhetorical ambiguities of Seneca ; and for Marcus as indubitably as for Epictetus 'there is no work nor device nor wisdom nor knowledge in the grave whither , thou goest.'

This digression, if rather minute, will have served to illustrate the right method of studying the Thoughts, if we desire to get at the mind of Marcus and his exact relation to Stoic doctrine.   The quality of treatment is of a piece with the conditions and character of workmanship.   The ethical value of the work does not rest on exactness or originality of speculative thought. Receptiveness, not originality, was the note of his own genius, as well as of the age and society in which he lived.   For true self-realisation and that satisfaction of the energies which alone brings happiness, the problems of physics and metaphysics seemed almost as empty and unprofitable as the exercises in rhetoric from which he had turned impatiently when manhood was mature. The life of Reason was more than logic, and not the monopoly of schoolmen.,   'Do not,' he writes, 'because dialectic and physics lie beyond your ken, despair on that account of freedom, self-respect, unselfishness, and tractability toward God.'[2]   Stoic physics and logic are not to Marcus an arena for argument or speculation, but accepted presuppositions needed to make life coherent

---

[1] i. 7 and close of 17 ; viii. 1.

[2] vii. 67.

h

and intelligible. The interest lies in another plane, in the ethics of practical experience.

Epictetus is the teacher to whom Marcus Aurelius is most allied—in age, in doctrine, and in scope of thought. In the emphasis, as well as in the substance, of their teaching there is close resemblance; their psychology and their epistemology agree; they insist on the same main ethical dogmas; they take the same attitude towards abstract dialectic, and to rival schools of philosophy—Cynic, Epicurean, or Sceptic. In their concentration upon practical ethics, their recurrence to Socratic formulas, their abandonment of Stoic arrogations of certitude and indefectibility, their extension and enforcement of *social* obligation, their ethical realisation of the omnipresent immanence of God, they occupy the same position towards Stoicism. But the likeness goes deeper than mere general traits. Among his debts to his chief teacher Rusticus, Marcus recalls with crowning emphasis his gift of the *Memoirs of Epictetus*.[1] With the treatise of Ariston, they may be regarded as the instrument of his ‘conversion.’ The disciple names Epictetus[2] in the same category with Chrysippus and Socrates, quotes him[3] more often than any philosopher, and borrows from his stores his favourite excerpts, metaphors, and illustrations; thought and language are saturated with conscious and unconscious reminiscences, too numerous to recapitulate. The most noteworthy differences arise from Marcus' fuller recognition and

---

[1] i. 7.   [2] vii. 19.

[3] See iv. 41; v. 29; xi. 33, 34, 35, 36, 37. The citation from Plato in vii. 63 is in the form preserved only by Epictetus.

application of the idea of the cosmos. This makes itself felt in more than one direction; in duties to others the cosmic claim tends to absorb and supersede individual virtue and even social fellowship; in duties to self, the immanence of the indwelling God, while conceived more impersonally, becomes more vivid and imperious in operation; in physics, especially in the physiology of mind and spirit and in cosmic 'sympathy of parts,' surer foundations are provided for pantheistic reverence and belief.

The other and more obvious differences that separate them are the result of position and of temperament.

As a professed teacher, Epictetus was called upon to examine and weigh grounds of evidence and modes of proof, to accept or reject criteria, to formulate bases of belief, to confront and criticise the tenets of friendly or hostile schools; he addresses himself to all sorts and conditions of men,—the man of the study, the man of the market-place, and the man of the bureau; to philosophers and laymen, to prudes and profligates, misers and spendthrifts, to the privileged and the oppressed, to representatives of every class and age and station in life, from the patrician or proconsul to the freedman and the slave. For the moralist he classifies virtues and vices, tracks their affinities and exposes their disguises; for the crowd, he deals with the round of daily life, its faults, its foibles and its vicissitudes; he has shrewd counsels for the quarrelsome, the talkative or the affected; he holds up the mirror to indolence, hypocrisy, or stubbornness; he discourses upon manners no less than morals, discussing the ethics of dress, of theatre-going, of physical exercise, of personal cleanliness; he pokes fun at fashion or unmasks meanness; he spices his talk with homely and concrete illustration, racy and sometimes coarse; he appeals now to literature and history, now to anecdotes of philosophers or characters upon the stage; his humour is fresh, caustic and imperturbable, in personality and method reminding us of Socrates.

In manner, the contrast offered by Marcus is complete. No sense of mission, and no hankering after novelty or *éclat*, inspires his pen. He has neither objectors to gainsay, nor disciples to edify; he does not exhort or rebuke, spur the apathetic or shame the reprobate; he has no mixed audience to attract and hold, no diversity of circumstances to take into account. He need not season instruction with wit, or diversify his theme with illustration; such illustrations as occur are from the large analogies of nature or from the ordered round of day-by-day activities. The proofs and processes which Epictetus discusses and justifies, Marcus assumes as known and granted; it is beside his mark to complete or articulate his system as a whole, to formulate a moral casuistry for varieties of fortune, age, and circumstance. He has but a single auditor—serious, dispassionate, intent,—*himself.* And even so the range of introspection and of utterance is severely circumscribed. Temptations of the flesh, for instance, except in forms of weariness or pain, have passed out of sight. 'A few principles, brief and elemental'[1]—they are enough: he

[1] iv. 3, with which xi. 18 may be compared, as a summary of 'all the commandments.'

plays with no fancy, indulges no reverie, gives the rein
to no emotion; 'our fathers had no fuller vision, neither
will our children behold any new thing.'[1]   He meditates
and cross-examines self with the analytic voice of reason,
which restricts[2] each circumstance to its tiny sphere of
significance and power, which dissects each impression
into the sorry terms of its material counterpart,[3] which
disenchants sense of the illusions of movement and
colour, which 'views itself, determines itself,'[4] and
'maintains a motion of its own, towards its appointed
end.'[5]

On first perusal the *Thoughts* probably seem too
highly moralised to be entirely sincere or interesting
as a self-revelation.   They create an impression of
monotony, of formality, of reticence and schooled
decorum resulting from habitual self-restraint.   The cry
of pain, the outburst of indignation or impatience is
silenced almost as soon as said; it is an ejaculation only
or a sigh, that never becomes explicit in the name of an
offender or the description of an offence.   Feeling and
passion are hushed in principles and maxims, until the
record of spiritual experience becomes upon the surface
impersonal and colourless.   But as tone and manner
grow familiar, the individuality of the writer becomes
distinct, intense, and unmistakable.   Self-repression does
not obliterate the lines of personality, but unifies and in
a manner augments their effect; and the thoughts *To
Himself* become the one authentic testament and record
of philosophy upon the throne.   For once 'the

---

[1] xi. 1.   [2] viii. 36; ix. 25.
[3] For references, p. cxxxiv.   [4] xi. 1.   [5] viii. 60; v. 14.

philosopher was king,' and the experience is recorded
for all time. Behind the mask of monarchy the man's
lineaments are disclosed ; we overhear the wistful affections and the lone regrets, the sense of personal short-
coming[1] and wasted endeavour, the bitterness of
aspirations baffled and protests unheeded, the confes-
sions of despondency and sometimes of disgust,[2] we
realise the exhausting tedium of 'life at Court lived
well,'[3] the profound ennui of autocracy in its enforced
companionship with intrigue and meanness and malice
and self-seeking,[4] the stern demands of duty hampered
by power and realised in renunciation, the pride and the
patience, the weakness and the strength, the busy loneli-
ness,[5] the mournful serenity, the daily death in life, of
the Imperial sage.

Throughout, the Thoughts are homogeneous, one of
the simplest and sincerest self-presentments ever penned,
'the most human' Renan calls them 'of all books.'
This results at once from the characteristic limitations
of ethical appeal and the wide comprehensiveness of
application. Tradition has preserved for us the figure
of the apostle of love, aged with labours, and in his
last days summarising the lore of life and holiness in
the reiterated charge, 'Little children, love one another.'
And there is something of the same insistence, the
same arresting monotony of note in the very different
message of Marcus—the recurrent reference of each

[1] ii. 4, 6 ; v. 9 ; viii. 1 ; x. 8.
[2] iv. 28 ; vii. 21, 36 ; viii. 20, 24 ; ix. 17, 24.   [3] v. 16.
[4] *E.g.* ii. 1 ; v. 10 ; ix. 3, 27, 29, 30, 34, 42 ; x. 8, 9, 13, 36.
[5] ix. 29 ; x. 9, 13.

mood, each incident, each perplexity as it arises to the criterion of *cosmic* duty.   All is cosmos : of this cosmos thou art part : for thee and for it there is but 'one order, one god, one being, one law :'[1] not self-will, but the cosmos, the will of God, is the way of virtue and the rule of life.   And in applying this touchstone to the complicated vicissitudes, demands, and emergencies of life, he has not his eye upon a congregation, or a side-glance for posterity.   An *Eikon Basilike* such as this would have found wide vogue, had publication been designed or permitted, at a time when ' to be without an image of the author seemed a sacrilege.'   What accident of faithful piety concealed and preserved the document, cannot be guessed, but for nine centuries[2] no note or whisper betrays its existence.   Fourteen hundred years after they were written down, the Thoughts re-emerge,[3] a revelation of personality, without parallel in the literature of Greek or Roman philosophy.   Who can reconstruct for himself the personality of Plato or of Aristotle ?   We have full-length portraits of Socrates and Epictetus, which reproduce their lineaments and habits, their way of life, the shrewd and cheery optimism of their talk ; but even here we do not hold the key of individuality, or penetrate, as Marcus bids us, into the inner self.[4] While to the attentive reader of these self-communings Marcus Aurelius becomes so absolutely known, that

[1] vii. 9.

[2] Until Suidas, lexicographer of the eleventh century.

[3] *Editio princeps* by Xylander, Zürich 1558, from a manuscript subsequently lost.

[4] iv. 38 ; vi. 3 ; vii. 59 ; viii. 61.

mere records of fact and observations of historians
become almost superfluous. His nature contained no
surprises; he is always his own man; so that each
record seems, as it were, inevitable, a something of which
we had heard before, something familiar or divined,
though memory had dropped the detail.

The chroniclers tell us that 'from childhood he was
of a serious cast'; that his demeanour was that of 'a
courteous gentleman, modest yet strenuous, grave but
affable;'[1] that 'he never changed his countenance for
grief or gladness.'[2] His bodily health was weakly from
the first, and strained by overwork; notwithstanding
scrupulous care it was a constant source of suffering
and disablement, and in later life power of digestion
and sleep wholly gave way.[3] His private bearing and
menage were of extreme simplicity : as Cæsar, he would
receive at his small private house, in ordinary citizen
attire; abroad, he wore plain woollen stuffs, and when
not in attendance on the Emperor would dispense
entirely with suite or outrunners. In family relations
he loved his mother and his children dearly,[4] and
grieved deeply at their loss; he condoned the faults of
Lucius Verus,[5] and in mourning remembered none of
the mortal frailties of Faustina.[6] Faithful and diligent

[1] Cf. i. 10; v. 31; vi. 53; vii. 4, 30. These and the following references note chance coincidences or correspondences occurring
in the Thoughts. On dress and equipage, cf. i. 7, 16, 17.

[2] vii. 24, 37, 60.

[3] Cf. i. 8, 15, 16, 17; iv. 3; v. 1, 5; vi. 2; vii. 64; viii. 12.

[4] i. 3, 11, 13, 17; vi. 12. [5] i. 14, 17.

[6] i. 17, his one notice of Faustina, breathes enduring affection
and respect. After her death their statues, wrought in silver,

in his attachments, he found time even as Emperor to keep up personal correspondence [1] with the circle of his friends. The fidelity of Antoninus to Hadrian earned him the sobriquet of Pius; but the official assiduity of Marcus was yet more unrelaxed in its devotion; [2] during three-and-twenty years, we read, he absented himself for two nights only from the side of Antoninus; he never missed a meeting of the Senate, or left before its close; he would give days to the hearing of a single case, and extended the days of assize to 230 in the year. His intellectual traits were love of reading, [3] taste for antiquities and history, [4] addiction to philosophy, and extreme docility of temperament; in manhood as in youth 'he never dropped attendance upon lectures;' as Emperor he sat at the feet of Sextus and of Apollonius; [5] he visited the schools of Smyrna and of Alexandria; he endowed chairs of all the philosophies [6] at Athens. At Eleusis he underwent solitary initiation. Citizens and soldiers believed in the efficacy of his prayers, [7] as the sculptures of the Antonine column to this day bear witness. His self-distrust declared itself in the misgivings with which he entered on the Cæsarship, and in the

became the shrine to which all the brides and bridegrooms of Rome repaired to make their nuptial vows (*Dio Cass.* 71, 31)— a more significant testimony than coins, or votive memorials, or ceremonial apotheosis.

[1] i. 12.   [2] Cf. i. 16.   [3] ii. 2, 3; xi. 7.

[4] Cf. i. 14; iii. 14; iv. 32, 33; vii. 1; viii. 3, 25, 31, 37; x. 27, 37; xii. 27.   [5] i. 8, 9, 17.

[6] i. 12; ii. 10, 15; vii. 64; ix. 41 : and various quotations recognise non-Stoic schools. Cf. ὁμοθαμνεῖν, μὴ ὁμοδογματεῖν, xi. 8.

[7] vi. 23, 44; ix. 40; x. 36.

offer of abdication with which he met the rebellion of Avidius Cassius.

His laws and rescripts aim chiefly at protecting orphans, wards, and minors, at relieving debtors and the destitute, at enlarging the rights of women, at curbing the arbitrary privileges of 'fathers' and 'masters,' at emancipating and giving civil rights to slaves, in a word at imbuing Roman jurisprudence with the principles of Stoic justice, and so realising a world-citizenship in 'an equal commonwealth based on equality of right and equality of speech, and an imperial rule respecting first and foremost the liberty of the subject.'[1] He mitigated, so far as a Cæsar could, the ferocity of gladiatorial shows;[2] he introduced buttons on the foils of the fencers, and nets under the high-rope dancers. At Rome he erected a temple, of new and unique dedication, to *Beneficence.* He upheld law and civic obligation, and approved the sentence of Justin, and the execution of the Christian confessors of Lyons.[3] Rigorous in public economics and strict in the distribution of largess,[4] he craved permission of the Senate to sell Imperial treasures to defray the needs of war, with the words, 'Nothing we have is our own; even the house we live in is yours.' Each word and trait finds some echo or counterpart in the Thoughts, and the reader makes answer to himself, Of course he thus acted, or said, or looked; how could he otherwise? Dio Cassius and Capitolinus become, as it were, commentaries upon his own soliloquies.

[1] i. 14; cf. i. 16, 17; vi. 30.   [2] x. 8.   [3] xi. 3.
[4] i. 16, 17.

With the Thoughts in our hands he is far more intelligible and unmistakable to us to-day, than to his own contemporaries. Silence makes men enigmas to their fellows. Though by tenacity of moral will he was the strongest man of his generation, Avidius Cassius took him for 'a philosophic mule,' interpreting his sufferance of evil-doers and his leniency to traitors as an index of stupidity, hypocrisy, and weakness. When, in days of gloom and terror, death for the fourth time put forth his hand and took from him his little son, his last but Commodus, Rome saw only the unmoved face; but the reader of the Thoughts knows how the loss of a dear child[1] recurs as the type instance of a poignant grief, and how twice—brooding over Commodus—he combines the desolate citations

> Lives are reaped like ears of corn,
> One is spared, another shorn.

> Though I and both my sons be spurned of God,
> There is, be sure, a reason.[2]

There are men, often of highly sensitive nature, who pass for unemotional, because they will not give the rein to individual passion, but find satisfaction for their emotions in general rather than in personal affections; their very sensitiveness and restraint takes refuge in reserve. This is the temper which has animated reformers, patriots, philanthropists of the Mazzini, Howard, or Wilberforce type,—the men who have espoused causes and principles and large enthusiasms of humanity, and

[1] i. 8; viii. 49; ix. 40; x. 34, 35; xi. 34.
[2] vii. 40; xi. 6.

this it is which in varied notes of aspiration, disappointment, and resolve gives depth and pathos to the Thoughts of Marcus Aurelius. 'To be misunderstood even by those whom one loves,' writes Amiel, 'is the cross and bitterness of life. It is the secret of that sad and melancholy smile on the lips of great men which so few understand.' This, and the obstinate contradiction between attainment and desire. To stand well-nigh single-handed for reason and for right; to work with worthless instruments; to withhold vain interference and correction; to let second-bests alone; to silence scruples and endure compromise; to crave for peace and spend his years in hunting down Sarmatians;[1] to preside at the tedious butchery of gladiatorial games with the heart that cried, 'How long, how long?'[2] to turn forgiving eyes and unreproachful lips upon the perilous debaucheries of Lucius and the frailties of Faustina; to live friendless and exiled for his people's sake; to cling to the belief in reason and just dealing against the day-by-day experience of unreason, violence, and greed; patiently, resolutely ἀνέχεσθαι καὶ ἀπέχεσθαι, 'to endure and to refrain'; to exhaust body and soul in the long effort to save Rome, and in return for all this to partake always 'the king's portion—Well-doing, Ill report';[3] to be isolated, thwarted, maligned, and misinterpreted—this was no light bearing of the cross. Through the cadences of patience and renunciation and resolve there seems to float continually the refrain of Epicurus—'Pain past bearing brings an end; pain that lasts, may be borne'[4]—and accent and

---

[1] x. 10.   [2] vi. 46.

[3] vii. 36.   [4] vii. 33, 64, 66; viii. 36, 46; x. 3.

tone adjust themselves completely to the grave lineaments the sculptor has transcribed for us in stone,[1] the countenance of reflective and enduring fortitude, not so wholly sad but that it is tinged with the far-off vision of fruitions not yet revealed, but possibly in store for humankind; acquainted sadly with the worth and worthlessness of Cæsarean estate; not unaware of low motives or mean men, yet bent on dispensation of an even justice to the conquered, the captive, or the coward; 'a priest and minister of gods,'[2] passing in an imperial calm the proffered homage of barbarians and the noisy plaudits of the crowd,[3] unelated, unillusioned, and 'till god sounds the withdrawal, still ready for the march.'[4]

Throughout the Thoughts the moral standpoint is *imperial*. It is not only or chiefly that the Ideal Prince is set forth in the pattern of Antoninus,[5] that there are references to Court life and its conditions,[6] or to the duty of 'the ram to the flock and the bull to the herd'.[7]; it is the moral climate of the whole, that which makes the work unique in interest and use. Here is no Stoic declamation about chains and racks, tyrants and libertines, but a Cæsar of Rome—to whom the emptiness of riches, the vanity of power, and the hollowness of praise or fame[8] are not a topic but an experience—

---

[1] The reliefs from the Triumphal Arch of Marcus Aurelius, particularly the scenes of Sacrifice and of Pardon.

[2] iii. 4.   [3] x. 34.   [4] iii. 5.   [5] i. 16, 17 ; vi. 30.

[6] iv. 3 ; v. 16 ; vi. 12 ; viii. 9, 31 ; x. 27, etc.

[7] xi. 18 (1); cf. iii. 5.

[8] ii. 12, 17 ; iii. 6, 10 ; iv. 3, 19, 20, 33 ; v. 33 ; vi. 16 ; vii. 6 ; viii. 21, 44, 52, 53 ; ix. 30, 34 ; x. 34 ; xii. 8.

taking counsel with himself how to 'choose the highest and hold it fast.'[1]

The cardinal virtues of Stoicism—Justice, Truth, Wisdom, and Courage [2]—are applied to the estate of monarchy. Justice does not wield the sword, but comes pressing the plea of the weak and the obligation of the strong — 'forbearance is one part of justice,'[3] and recognising the tie of kind will not overlook the allowance due to ignorance; and a still more imperial note animates a reflection such as this : 'We are not true to justice if we strive for things secondary, or if we allow ourselves to be imposed upon, or draw hasty and fallible conclusions.'[4] So again, Truth [5] is never figured as protest or contradiction, but as that simplicity of bearing, that openness of mind, that singleness of word and act, that quiet undeviating 'pursuit of the straight course,' which power and place make doubly difficult. Courage and Wisdom are viewed from the same outlook, as of one 'strong and patient and provoked every day.'

Herein lies the salient contrast between Epictetus the freedman and Marcus Aurelius the Emperor. How could Epictetus, reviewing life, have numbered among its blessings, 'that he had never been called upon to borrow from another,'[6] or have regarded it as the worst ignominy 'to receive favours he could not return.'?[7]

---

[1] iii. 6 ; v. 21.   [2] Enumerated iii. 6.

[3] iv. 3 ; cf. iii. 11 ; ix. 22.   [4] xi. 10.

[5] Among many passages, cf. esp. i. 11 ; iii. 4, 16 ; iv. 18, 51 ; v. 3 ; vi. 30 ; ix. 1 ; x. 13 ; xii. 29.

[6] i. 17.   [7] xi. 25.

The virtues sought, the vices eschewed, in range, in treatment, and in distribution of emphasis, presuppose the position of authority. Throughout, men are regarded as recipients, rather than dispensers of kindnesses; duties to *equals*, and duties to *inferiors* monopolise the field; all coarser and more flagrant forms of vice, or actions that could be called criminal, are merely named as objects of repulsion. The moral distractions and perturbations which he dreads are those which beset power and place and privilege, to disturb serenity of soul. The regards are fixed on 'sins of respectability,' on indolence, impatience, discourtesy, officiousness,[1] and on such more delicate forms of moral delinquency as self-absorption in the press of current duties,[2] as want of moral nerve and allowance of morbid self-distrusts,[3] as uncertainty of purpose, frivolity, and aimlessness [4] of life, or as the intellectual indolence which rushes to hasty conclusions and leaves us at the mercy of unwarranted impressions or desires. The treatment of virtues is no less characteristic and discriminating. Beside the solid virtues and charities incumbent on the ruler, are set the social graces which adorn the gentleman—consideration, candour, modesty, attentive and intelligent perception, tact and address in conversation;[5] and the compass of morality is extended to such refinements as cheerfulness in leadership,[6] belief in friends' affection,[7] wise husbandry and just apportionment [8] of powers, careful selection

---

[1] ii. 1 ; iii. 5.   [2] i. 12.

[3] v. 5.   [4] i. 15 ; ii. 7, 16, 17 ; vii. 4 ; xi. 21.

[5] i. 10 ; vi. 53 ; vii. 4, 30 ; viii. 22, 30 ; xi. 13, 18 (9).

[6] iii. 5.   [7] i. 14.   [8] iii. 11 ; iv. 32 ; vii. 3 ; viii. 29, 43.

among competing claims,[1] reserve of leisure[2] for purposes
of self-examination and recreation of the inner life.
Leisure as well as labour, thought as well as action,[3] de-
portment [4] as well as motive, are scrupulously moralised.

Although these finer sensibilities attest the humanising
influences of Hellenic culture and good taste, Greek
draperies and accent do not obscure the Roman heredity
and type. In some sense indeed he is 'the last of the
Romans,' the final specimen and representative of the
political traditions of Rome. The Western Empire will
indeed, largely by acquired momentum and inertia, still
last out two centuries, but its few good Emperors will
be soldiers of fortune or versatile Orientals. The blood
of Marcus was of Spanish and Italian stock, trained
in the best traditions of Roman administration. His
grandfather, Annius Verus, was Prefect of the City, and
three times held the Consulship; the earliest of Marcus'
remembrances was the impression of his dignified official
suavity.[5] His father's career [6] was cut short during his
tenure of the prætorship. Upon the mother's side,
grandfather and great-grandfather [7] were both twice
Consul, and from a child he was at home among the
best Patrician circles. The Emperor Hadrian, with
playful pleasantry, would call him as a little boy *Veris-
simus* [8] instead of Verus. He learned his principles of

[1] iv. 24.
[2] Cf. *e.g.* i. 12 ; ii. 5, 7 ; iv. 3, 24 ; vi. 11 ; viii. 51.
[3] i. 3 ; iii. 4.   [4] vii. 24, 37, 60 ; xi. 15.
[5] i. 1.   [6] i. 2.
[7] Calvisius Tullus, and Catilius Severus, referred to i. 4.
[8] Dio Cass. 69, 21 ; but so too on medal, and in dedication of
Justin's First Apology.

government from Antoninus, who was *par excellence* the State official.   The Flavian dynasty and Trajan had been Imperial Commanders-in-Chief: Hadrian, by a new conception of the Imperial function, had become the universal ' *Visitor* ' of his immense domain, mould-ing, comprehending, and unifying the whole on broad Imperial lines.   In Antoninus there emerges the new type, the Imperial 'official,' becoming more and more the autocratic chief of a highly-organised bureaucracy, which—through its various departments of Civil Law, Exchequer, Public Works, Police, War, Posts, and the like—directed the world of provinces from Rome.   In this assiduous, watchful, and highly conservative [1] school of statesmanship Marcus was nursed.

In boyhood, antiquities and history fascinated his attention, and constant touches reveal the hold these subjects had upon him.   The old names,[2] Camillus Caeso Volesus, have a pleasant savour of the past; among the Quadi he deplores that he may not re-read his 'deeds of ancient Rome and Greece, garnered for old age';[3] he founds his political ideals upon the patriots of Rome, Cato and Brutus, Thrasea and Helvidius.[4]   He had a reverence for old forms and offices and usages ; he treated the Senate with punc-tilious respect,[5] exhibiting a ceremonious and almost sentimental deference to prerogatives that were hardly more than titular.

Moribus antiquis res stat Romana virisque

was his reminder to generals in the field ; and if any-

[1] i. 16, πάντα κατὰ τὰ πάτρια πράσσων.   [2] iv. 33.
[3] iii. 14.   [4] i. 14 ; cf. vi. 44.   [5] Cf. viii. 30.

i

where in the Thoughts there sounds a ring of martial exhilaration it is associated with the word 'Roman.'[1] He not only gave its Golden Age to Rome, but pushed the empire to its furthest geographical extension. He 'triumphed'[2] over Parthians in the East, over Germans and Sarmatians in the North; through fourteen stubborn years of war he held and secured the marches of the Danube; the Antonine Column is no vain or boastful trophy, it is the monument of victories that secured to the Empire the two last centuries out of which the new order of the world, East and West, was born. Softened and chastened though it is by his age and the circumstances of life and upbringing, his character is Roman to the core,—Roman in resolution and repression, Roman in civic nobility and pride, Roman in tenacity of imperial aim, Roman in respect for law, Roman in self-effacement for service of the State.

Tu regere imperio populos, Romane, memento—
hae tibi erunt artes—pacisque imponere morem,
parcere subiectis et debellare superbos.

One other trait of temperament is Roman—religiousness of mind. For poetry and literature, Rome borrowed her mythology from Greece; but for life and conduct, belief centred upon embodiments of the divine as *numina*, —powers and influences rather than persons, regulating all actions and phenomena. In their impersonal ubiquity

[1] iii. 5 ; cf. ii. 5.
[2] The Parthian triumph—the first for sixty years—was in 166, with titles *Parthicus, Medicus, Pater Patriae;* the Marcomannic, following titles *Germanicus* and *Sarmaticus*, in 176.

they seem almost prepared for a creed of pantheistic immanence. In infancy, Vaticanus urged the baby's new-born cry; Fabulinus prompted his first word; Cuba rocked his cot. In outgoing and incoming, Iterduca set him on his road and Domiduca gave safe return. On the farm Terminus kept his boundary, Robigo mildewed his crop, Cloacina ordered his drains, Sterquilinus gave virtue to his manure. For Rome, the Fortune or the Safety or the Majesty of the City extended and preserved the empire; in house and town, the ancestral Penates of the hearth and the Lares of the streets guarded the intercourse of life; in the individual breast, a ministering Genius shaped his destinies and responded to each mood of melancholy or of mirth. Thus all life lay under the regimen of spiritual powers, to be propitiated or appeased by appointed observances and ritual and forms of prayer. To this punctilious and devout form of Paganism Marcus was inured from childhood; at the vintage festival he took his part in chant and sacrifice; at eight years old he was admitted to the Salian priesthood; 'he was observed to perform all his sacerdotal functions with a constancy and exactness unusual at that age; was soon a master of the sacred music; and had all the forms and liturgies by heart.'[1] Our earliest statue depicts him as a youth offering incense; and in his triumphal bas-reliefs he stands before the altar, a robed and sacrificing priest. To him ' prayer and sacrifice, and all observances by which we own the presence and nearness of the gods' are 'covenants and sacred ministries' admitting to

---

[1] Cf. Capit. 4. In 139, he became *Pontifex Maximus, Augur, Quindecemvir Sacris Faciundis, Septemvir Epulonum.*

'intimate communion with the divine.'[1]   This habit of
mind accommodated itself perfectly to Stoic teaching, to
an interpretation of the universe which (in the words of
Epictetus) averred that 'all earth is crammed with gods
and spiritual powers.'[2]   Stoicism in fact provided an intelligible theology and theocratic basis for the intricate
mechanism of sign and formula and rite, which natural
magic had gradually riveted upon a simple, scrupulous,
and superstitious folk.   Dream and oracle and even
ordered coincidences of phrase become channels of
spiritual grace and revelation.[3]   Philosophy and religion
clasp hands as means of reconciliation with God, and
deliverance from invisible powers of evil.   With the
exception, in a sense, of Julian, whose religious revival
bordered on caricature, Marcus is the most 'god-fearing'[4]
figure in Roman history, and perhaps the only one
which can be called devout.   He not only inaugurated
his campaigns with antique rites and solemn *lectisternia*,
but as Emperor fulfilled his desire of receiving the mystic
initiations of Eleusis.   And this sense of religion pervades
his writing like an atmosphere.   The tone is changed
from that of earlier Stoicism ; the pantheism is less
physical, and the language more theistic.   Life is the
presence of God ; the course of the world is the evolution

[1] vi. 44 ; xii. 5 ; cf. v. 7 ; vi. 23 ; ix. 40 ; *. 36 ; xii. 1.
[2] Epict. 3, 13, 15.
[3] i. 17 ; ix. 27.
[4] vi. 30 ; cf. i. 16.   Amm. Marc. notes the likeness, and re-
applies to Julian the epigram directed against M. Aurelius :—

> We the white bulls bid Marcus Cæsar hail !
> Win but one victory more, our kind will fail.

of Providence; the hand of God, or gods[1]—for the theistic or polytheistic forms of belief are alike covered and interpreted by Pantheism—is operative everywhere; above all his voice is articulate within man's self, as his indwelling life and soul.

In this way man enters into partnership with God, and shares his franchise in the universe;[2] God in man, man with God are spiritual confederates; life is continuous ministration to the divine;[3] man's moral sense, 'an efflux of God'[4] 'a particle of Zeus'[5] 'an effluence of the disposing reason of the world'[6] is one with the moral movement of the universe—

> The soul that rises with us, our life's star,
> Hath had elsewhere its setting
> And cometh from afar.

The word of Heraclitus ἦθος ἀνθρώπῳ δαίμων—*Character is man's destiny*—is filled with new reality of meaning; the indwelling Genius, which Romans reverenced, is an embodied conscience responsible for every act and word not to the individual merely, but to the august tribunal from which it draws its sanction. Seneca handles the theme with more rhetorical artifice, Epictetus with warmer touches of personal relationship, but in neither is the assurance of the 'god within' more intense

---

1 'God' and 'gods' will be found almost equally common. In the Translation I have written both with the small 'g,' as alone consonant with Stoic mood and way of thought. *Zeus* is used iv. 23; v. 8, 27; xi. 8.

2 See ii. 1; viii. 2; x. 1.

3 λειτουργεῖν v. 31; vi. 28; x. 22, and cf. iii. 4.

4 xii. 26.   5 v. 27.   6 ii. 4.

in conviction, or more elevated in expression than in Marcus.[1] His 'ruler and guide,' his 'pilot' and his 'lawgiver,' his 'monarch and lord,' man must 'keep the deity enshrined within his heart unsoiled and unperturbed, serenely concerting the divine Order by truth of utterance and justice of act.' By this, 'the most precious organ we possess, we attain faith, honour, truth, law, and a good god within.'[2]

In this way Marcus grafts public and personal religion into the central tenet of Cosmic order and inherence which dominates his universe of thought. This determines for him the life 'in conformity with nature,'[3] and from it may be deduced all the main affirmations which make up his moral system.

The *individual* is *part of a whole*, knit together in essential unity of being, operation, and design. The action of the part has meaning only as a function of the whole. To recognise the function is reason, to discharge it life 'in smooth flow.' All obligation is cosmic in its source and sanction. Justice, the base of all the virtues,[4] expresses itself towards man, but is in essence a part of holiness,[5] a consonance of will with God; so likewise injustice is no mere infringement or misappropriation of another's right, but a transgression of the primal will, a sin of irreverence committed not against man but God.[6]

[1] Cf. ii. 13, 17; iii. 3, 4, 5, 6, 7, 12, 16; iv. 1, 12; v. 10, 26, 27; vii. 64; viii. 45; x. 13; xii. 1, 19, 26.
[2] x. 13.
[3] iv. 23, 29, 49; v. 1, 25; vi. 16; vii. 11, 18; viii. 1, 5, 54; x. 2, 25, 28; xi. 16, 20, etc.
[4] xi. 10.   [5] xi. 20; xii. 1.   [6] xi. 1.

Truth similarly is spoken of as 'a name for nature,' and to
fall from truth is not merely to mislead or wrong another,
but 'to fight against the order of the universe, and to be
at civil war with one's own being.'[1]   Belief in its cosmic
import enlarges and elates the thought of duty.   It is
a covenant that, in so far as we identify ourselves with
the power outside ourselves, by which we live and move
and have our being, effort will not be wasted or misspent.[2]
It consecrates patience, enabling us to acquiesce in
apparent failure or impotence; 'even in sleep we are
fellow-workers with god.'[3]   It heightens contentment
in well-doing,[4] while it chastens self-complacency; duty
is life kept natural, and 'moving in smooth flow.'[5]   'The
horse runs, the hound hunts, the bee makes honey; so
the man that does his duty does not raise a shout, but
passes on to the next act, as a vine to the bearing of
clusters for next season.'[6]   It only can keep 'the straight
way'[7] through life's distracting maze, speak peace among
the bawling of tongues,[8] and conduct the storm-tossed
mariner to 'still waters and a waveless bay.'[9]

The doctrine of tranquillity is ultimately pushed to
lengths that threaten moral energy.   Founded on the
thought of cosmic determinism,[10] and divorced from the
compensations and suggestions of redress that the hope
of immortality supplies, this view of life entails the sad,

---

[1] ix. 1.   [2] Cf. iii. 12.   [3] vi. 42; cf. vi. 14, 43; vii. 13.
[4] On the *joy* of virtue, iii. 6; iv. 24; v. 9; vi. 7; vii. 13; viii.
26, 43; x. 33; xi. 1, 16; xii. 29.
[5] ii. 5: v. 9, 34; x. 6.   [6] v. 6.
[7] iv. 18, 51; v. 3; vi. 17; vii. 55; x. 11.   [8] vii. 68.
[9] xii. 22.   [10] See pp. lxvi. and lxxxi.

and even sombre, resignation which enwraps the *Thoughts.*
The part 'loses its life' in a continuous act of cosmic
participation and surrender, enforcing no claim and cher-
ishing no hope upon its own individual behalf. Things
without will not 'dazzle or daunt';[1] it will 'neither seek
nor shun'[2] the appointments of destiny; 'for me nothing
is early and nothing late that is in season for thee, great
Universe.'[3] Unmurmuring it accepts pain, sickness,
failure, or bereavement; 'pain, if past bearing, ceases
to be borne.' It foregoes its right not only to realise
itself, but even to exist: it accepts the decree that the
holiest and noblest should be utterly extinguished and
cease to be: the part is but for the perfection of the
whole; accepting its apportionment, it refuses under
any provocation 'to find fault with god.'[4] Such self-
submission—contrasting strangely with the proud self-
sufficiencies of infant Stoicism—sounding the last depths
of self-effacement, silencing but not satisfying the
authentic instincts of finite personality, can only be
maintained by suppressing factors in consciousness,
whose claims are indefeasible.

The Stoic doctrine of Apathy, instead of perceiving
in Reason and Will a directive self-adjustment of the
emotions into true harmony with their surroundings,
summons them to refuse and expunge and override
the motions and affections which are conscious of the
outer stimulus. The kingdom of the Ego is divided

---

[1] xii. 1, 13; cf. i. 15.

[2] iii. 7, 12; vii. 34; viii. 52; ix. 1; x. 13, 34; xi. 11.

[3] iv. 23.

[4] vi. 16, 41; viii. 17; ix. 1, 39; x. 1; xii. 12, 24.

against itself, and the parts warring against each other are brought to moral impotence. Suppression of the emotions is destruction, not conservation or adjustment of energy, and so far as it takes effect involves waste, or even self-expenditure, of the one source of motive power. Good order and contentment in the soul are based on long-suffering, inexorable coercion of all un-satisfied affections, with sure sapping of the moral energies. 'Apathy,' on this showing, becomes a passion-less heroism in which moral responsibility declines into fatalistic acquiescence, and the independence and being of the self are finally annulled. Not only ignoble and selfish emotions are to be suppressed, but also the most ennobling and energetic, all that aspire beyond the present, all that do well to be angry in resisting antagonism to wrong, all that kindle duty into desire and suffuse it with emotional warmth. 'Teach men or bear with them,' 'Blame none' become aphorisms of the virtue, which moves only within the prescriptions of the individual reason. Disabled for inspiration or for reproach, it becomes an anxious exercise of self-con--straint, patient, restricted, and ineffectual. Hence the deep individual pessimism which appears side by side with the pantheistic optimism, and which so broadly distinguishes the Stoic and the Christian doctrines of resignation. The universal optimism of the Stoic allows and even rests on pessimism in the particulars ; the part is of necessity the whole in a form of incomplete and like wise imperfect realisation ; its interest and its existence is subordinate to the well-being of the whole, and its transi-ence and insignificance become topics of consolation.

The *individual is part of the whole*—but how in-
finitesimally small a part! and how ephemeral! A
morsel of soul, upon a grain of earth, man occupies a
moment between the two infinities.[1] No compensating
assurance of spiritual permanence or of larger contingent
issues is permitted to relieve the littleness of life.
'Grains of frankincense on the same altar, one drops
sooner, another later—it makes no difference.'[2] The
quantitative insignificance of man—and on a basis of
strictly monistic materialism the inference is logical—
has its counterpart in the qualitative. Material things
—and all things are material—may be analysed into
their constituents of cause and substance,[3] and their
content is nothing more than the material analysis dis-
closes. 'Just as we analyse the food we eat into the
dead carcase of bird or beast, the purple robe we wear
into sheep's wool dipped in secretions of the shell-fish,
so should we do through the whole range of life:' 'push
analysis to the component parts, and you are disenchanted; apply the process to life too as a whole.'[4]
So in reiterated diminutives, half-pitying and half-con-
temptuous, things are one by one reduced to the beggarly
elements of which they are made up. Man is but 'the
puff of breath' that for a day 'carries its corpse.'[5] But
the same argument which forecloses aspiration, also annuls
the power of vain desires. Life finds its sole complete-

---

[1] iv. 3, 50; v. 13, 23; ix. 32; xii. 7, 32.
[2] iv. 15, and cf. ii. 17; iv. 32, 35, 44; vi. 36, 37, 46; vii.
1; ix. 14; xi. 1; xii. 24.
[3] ii. 12; iii. 11: v. 13; vii. 29; viii. 11; ix. 25; xii. 10, 29.
[4] vi. 13; viii. 21; ix. 36; xi. 2, 17.   [5] ix. 24.

ness in itself, in the realisation and fulfilment of its
cosmic part, undistracted by baits of worthless pleasure,
or lures of wealth or state, or the evanescent bubble of
fame.   Stripped of their husks and veils,[1] none of
these things can either tempt, or satisfy, or last.

But man's cosmic relationship carries other and far
more inspiring implications.   If inherence in the unitary
whole circumscribes individuality, it implies at the same
time a fellowship of interest among the parts, that to
' nature's sincere familiar '[2] becomes a conscious and en-
gaging bond.   And this sympathetic tie of parts touches
chords in the imagination and the heart of Marcus that
had not before been sounded.   There is not only a
vague and wistful sense of unity, but an almost personal
tenderness towards nature, both in organic and inorganic
phases of action, that is new to literature.   The
harmonious courses of the stars,[3] the free bounties of
air and rain and sunlight,[4] the ordered industries and
happy societies of bird and beast and insect,[5] the co-
operations of feet and hands and eyelids and teeth,[6] the
ripening and the passing of vine and fig and olive,[7] the
distinctive beauties of youth and prime and age,[8] and
even the more baleful aspects of the immanent world-
life—'the lion's scowl, and the foam that flecks the wild
boar's mouth '[9]—proclaim one origin, one life, one end,
and stir 'an accent of emotion' that opens up new

[1] xii. 2, 8.   [2] iii. 2.   [3] vii. 47 ; ix. 9 ; xi. 27.
[4] viii. 57 ; ix. 8 ; xii. 30.
[5] v. 1, 6 ; vi. 14 ; ix. 9 ; xi. 18 (9).   [6] ii. 1 ; ix. 42.
[7] iv. 6 ; v. 6 ; viii. 19.   [8] iii. 2, cf. iv. 20 ; vii. 24.
[9] iii. 2 ; vi. 36.

vistas of poetic utterance. *"Earth is in love with rain, and holy aether loves.* Yes, the world-order is in love with fashioning whatever is to be. To the world-order I profess ' Thy love is mine.' "[1] The very modernness of touch may cause the rarity and novelty of such a section as iii. 2 to escape the reader's notice. The directness and the delicacy of the realism go far beyond the generalities of the Hymn of Cleanthes, and anticipate notes such as those of the *Prometheus Unbound* :—

> The wandering voices and the shadows these
> Of all that man becomes, the mediators
> Of that best worship, love, by him and us
> Given and returned ; swift shapes and sounds, which grow
> More fair and soft, as man grows wise and kind,
> And, veil by veil, evil and error fall.
>
> .   .   .   .
>
> And men and beasts in happy dreams shall gather
> Strength for the coming day and all its joy.
> And death shall be the last embrace of her
> Who takes the life she gave, even as a mother,
> Folding her child, says, ' Leave me not again.'

Thus man has conscious communion with all parts of the great whole : but a special tie of kind unites him with one member of the order,—his fellow-men. In the economy of nature all things exist for sake of something else, the lower ever subserving the needs of the higher.[2] Man, the crown of nature, differentiated from all other creatures by the gift of Reason,[3] is called to minister to

[1] x. 21 ; cf. v. 4.
[2] v. 16, 30 ; vii. 55 ; xi. 10, 18.
[3] iii. 4, 6, 9 ; iv. 3, 4, 29 ; v. 16, 34 ; vi. 14, 23 ; ix. 8, 9 ; xi. 1, 20, etc.

man. We are made for one another: 'the bond of kind makes all things human dear.'[1]   The rational and social element is as inherent in the constitution of man, as gravity in the various elements of matter.[2]   He cannot escape or annul this property of nature; he is (as Aristotle too had said) 'a social being,' made for social action; its authentications are paramount and binding, its performance his refreshment and delight.[3]   It is in the pages of Marcus that the conception of the social tie gains fullest recognition and enforcement.   Rational soul only attains its height, in realising 'catholic and social aims.'[4]   The seed of this is found historically in the bond of *citizenship*, which supplied the Athenian Greek with his basis of morality and human obligation. The Stoic philosopher, proclaiming the moral autonomy of the individual, disclaimed the strictly political bond and sanction, to found morality upon bases that were universal.   The civic obligation (in its narrower application) was annulled and superseded by the cosmic, but the name and the associations of 'citizenship' were too deeply grafted into moral consciousness to be killed out. They survived into the idea of a 'world-citizenship.' 'The world is as it were a city,'[5] and if to the Athenian Athens was *Dear City of Cecrops*, to the Stoic the universe is *Dear City of God*.[6]   At the outset the phrase

[1] ii. 1, 13; iii. 4; iv. 3, 4; v. 1, 16, 30; vi. 39; vii. 13, 22, 31, 55; viii. 8, 26, 56, 59; ix. 1, 27; xi. 1, 10, 18; xii. 30.
[2] ix. 9; xi. 20.
[3] iii. 6, 11; v. 1, 6, 16; vi. 7, 14, 30; vii. 5, 55, 74; viii. 12, 23; ix. 31, 42; x. 6; xi. 21; xii. 20.   [4] vi. 14, etc.
[5] ii. 16; iii. 11; iv. 3, 4, 23; vi. 44; vii. 8; x. 6, 15; xii. 36.   [6] iv. 23.

'world-citizenship' had perhaps more sound than meaning, and so far as it possessed positive content, connoted
status and franchise, rather than claims of sacrifice or
service.   But noble phrases are pregnant: as the ob-,
ligations involved in status gradually compelled the
moral assent, as the 'part' (*meros*) learned to recognise
and own its contributory offices as 'member' (*melos*),[1] the
idea of 'world-citizenship' came to include the whole
range of social duty and endeavour.   Implicit in all
human relationship, the social tie affects every contact of
man with man, establishing a bond of brotherhood, which
forbids all selfish isolation of interest.   'What is not
good for the swarm is not good for the bee.'[2]   It ensures
community of sentiment with every man.   'Enter into
every man's Inner Self, and let every other man enter
into thine.'[3]   It inspires, impels the life of active service.
'We are made for cooperation, as feet, as hands, as
eyelids, as the upper and the lower teeth.'   And this
law of service is as binding on the Cæsar as on the
churl.   Moreover, do what we will or resist as we may,
the great bond is inalienable; no temporary disclaimer
or repudiation can annul it.   The individual may for a
moment violate, but he cannot impair or destroy the
solidarity of man.   'Consider the goodness of god,
with which he has honoured man: he has put it in his
power never to be sundered at all from the whole; and
if sundered, then to rejoin it once more, and coalesce,
and resume his contributory place.'[4]   Men, in spite of
themselves, remain 'members of the body.'   And, as

[1] vii. 13.   [2] ii. 3; v. 8, 22; vi. 45, 54; x. 6, 33.
[3] viii. 61.   [4] viii. 34; xi. 8.

it contemplates the comprehending unity, the thought clothes itself in noble phraseology, and summons man, as man, to become 'the peer and fellow-citizen of god' and the sharer of his law and franchise.[1]

Clearly this thought of 'world-citizenship' transcends _political_ relationships of any narrower kind ; but yet the political circumstances of his age and the personal position from which the Emperor applied philosophy to life, contributed to invest the formula with new conviction and reality.   The realisation of a confederate 'world-city,' of a _Civitas Dei_ upon earth coextensive with the sway and genius of Rome, floats before the vision of the Emperor as a consummation of world-history.   Rome, in the 'Golden Age' of the Antonines, stood for Law and Order from the Euphrates to the Atlantic, from the Northumbrian wall of Antoninus to Mount Atlas and the tropic of Cancer.   Already in the hands of the great jurists, whose labours began to shape the Perpetual Edict, the _lex naturae_, which stands above human caprice or national vicissitude, was becoming formulated as _ius naturale_—natural right, which Stoic influences helped to secure as the moral basis of Imperial code law.   'Cosmopolitanism, the dream of philosophers in the downfall of Greek independence, becomes at last upon the throne of Roman Cæsars a proud self-consciousness of Rome's historic mission.'

This large recognition of the social tie makes Stoicism humane and catholic, redeeming it from the dryness, which resulted from the too exclusive emphasis on reason, and from the intolerance consequent on a purely

[1] viii. 2 ; x. 1.

individualistic morality. Stoicism insisted from the first on the inwardness of virtue, and placed morality in disposition and motive, not in obedience to prescribed canons of action. As long as the gaze turned inward, and mere self-consistency satisfied the demand of conformity to nature, pride and self-centred egoism were the natural and almost inevitable outcome. But the acceptance of a cosmic standard of reference, while leaving the stress on motive and disposition unimpaired, safeguards against selfish and self-satisfied contraction of view. Excess of individualism, *eccentricity* of thought or behaviour, is checked instead of encouraged; and the moral pedantry of a Brutus or even a Helvidius, or the aggressive spleen of a Juvenal or Persius, become as alien to the temper of Marcus, as the tasteless vagaries of a Diogenes. Alongside of modesty, forbearance, and all that makes up 'temperance,' a liberal enlargement is given to the active emotions, which right reason can approve and authorise. Patience may extend to pity[1]; pride and indifference give way to meekness and unselfish concern for others; virtue may find delights in offices of good; and all the more temperate forms of love—kindness, charity, goodwill, and such like—come into free play.[2] But one restriction remains. The quality of love is various, and Greek discriminates where English is ambiguous. The forms in which this sympathy for man is set forth, are devoid of emotion; if the term of passion ever escapes the sage's lips, it is

[1] ii. 13 ; vii. 26.
[2] The stress laid on the virtues here mentioned is reiterated. For virtue as delight, see refs. p. cxxxi. *note.*

the thought of Nature, not of man that stirs it. The⁻
love of neighbour is not an outgoing of personal affection, but at most a befriending care for kind; it falls
short of 'brotherhood' (the term adopted in translation[1])—for it is not indeed direct from man to man,
but transmitted through the cosmos. It remains impersonal and generic, belonging to the same moral
category as patriotism, or political fraternity, or devotion
to a cause : but, spread over a larger and less tangible
object, it falls short of these in ardour of desire, and
much more lacks the effusion, the joy, the impulsive
energy and the quick indignations of altruistic love.
Therefore to the last it condemns the Stoic to some
lukewarmness of faith and ineffectiveness of personal
appeal ; and leaves him content 'to better men or bear
with them,'[2] 'to keep in charity with liars and with
rogues,'[3] 'to blame none,'[4] and to accept misunderstanding and dislike as normal items of experience.[5] Life
will have little glow and death no sting.

Death is the seal of man's position in the cosmos.
He is but a part, insignificant in space and time ; the part
passes, only the whole abides. Death is an incident[6]
in the brief incident of its existence ; it is for nature's
good, acceptable not terrible.[7] The Thoughts are

[1] ii. 1, 13 ; iii. 4 ; vii. 22 ; ix. 22 ; xi. 9 ; xii. 26.
[2] v. 28 ; vi. 27, 50 ; viii. 59 ; ix. 11 ; x. 4 ; xi. 18. [3] vi. 47.
[4] Cf. ii. 1 ; iv. 3 ; v. 22, 25 ; vi. 27, 55 ; vii. 22, 29 ;
viii. 14, 17 ; ix. 4, 11, 20, 38, 42 ; x. 4 ; xi. 16, 18 ; xii.
12, 16.
[5] ii. 1 ; x. 36. [6] iv. 5 ; vi. 2 ; ix. 3 ; x. 36 ; xii. 23.
[7] ii. 12 ; iii. 5, 7, 16 ; iv. 48 ; v. 29, 33 ; ix. 3, 21 ; x. 8,
29, 36 ; xii. 35.

k

steeped in the near consciousness of its approach.[1]   For
just appreciation of their purport, and sympathetic
rapport with their mood, they must be regarded as
farewell reflections upon life and a greeting given in
advance to death.   The first book is a retrospect on
life, moving among its treasured memories of help and
friendship; 'thou art an old man'[2] is the prelude to the
second; 'thy life is all but finished,' 'its tale fully told
and its service accomplished;'[3] it remained, while the
powers of mind and body still held out,[4] to adjust
himself as in the presence of death for reunion with the
whole.   Life's day had been laborious, and its setting
was grey and solitary.   At seventeen he had entered
the responsibilities of Cæsarship, and from that day the
wear and tear of office had been continuous.   At forty
the whole weight of Empire fell upon his shoulders,
and the colleagueship of L. Verus proved an addition
rather than a relief to care.   At forty-six came the
imperious call which summoned him to the long exile
of the Camp : and the imminent fate of Rome hung on
the staunchness of his resolution.   'As man, as Roman,
as Imperator, he held the van—keeping a brave face.'[5]
But the strain of self-sustainment, — 'upright, not
uprighted,'[6]—was exhausting.   The attachments of his
youth had been to older men, and death or circumstance
had withdrawn them from his side; the philosophers
and councillors shunned the privations of the camp;

[1] ii. 5, 11, 17 ; iii. 16 ; iv. 37 ; v. 33 ; vi. 30 ; vii. 29, 69 ;
xi. 18 ; xii. 1.

[2] ii. 2 ; cf. iii. 5.   [3] ii. 6 ; v. 31.   [4] iii. 1.

[5] iii. 5.   [6] iii. 5 ; vii. 12.

Galen loved Rome too well to attend him on the Danube, and no poet or man of letters has told the story of his Marcomannic wars. Even the solace and companionship of books was missing.[1] The surroundings and associates of war were harsh and uncongenial,[2] yet his presence was necessary with the legions. In the home affections, on which he had most leaned, the hand of bereavement had pressed heavily; of five sons, death had spared only Commodus, and in 176 his spirit was broken by the death of Faustina. It must have taxed all his fortitude to stand out 'life's remainder,'[3] waiting for the 'retreat to sound,' with powers at the last stage of exhaustion. The Thoughts are the cry of isolation that escaped him, as 'Among the Quadi,' and 'At Carnuntum,'[4] he bore the load of empire and the solitude of power. Nerves and digestion under long strain had quite worn out, so that he scarcely ate or slept. Theriac—a sedative drug—had, Galen tells us, become almost his food; and Julian introduces him among the Cæsars, as 'very grave, his eyes and features drawn somewhat with hard toils, and his body luminous and transparent with abstemiousness from food.' 'Death is rest:' 'depart then with serenity—serene as he who gives thee thy discharge.'[5]

The impressive pathos, which attaches to this convinced presentiment of death, is more than personal. The funeral notes, which culminate in the *Nunc Dimittis*

[1] ii. 2, 3 ; iii. 14 ; iv. 30 ; and perhaps viii. 8.
[2] ii. 1 ; v. 10 ; viii. 44 ; ix. 3, 27, 29, 30, 34 ; x. 1, 8, 9, 13, 36.
[3] iii. 4 ; iv. 31 ; x. 15 ; xi. 16 ; xii. 3.
[4] Subscription to Books I. and II.   [5] vi. 28 ; xii. 36.

of the closing book, are the knell of a dying age. Over the tomb of Marcus, too, the historian might fitly inscribe the mournful epitaph LAST OF HIS LINE.[1] Last of Roman Stoics, he is also the last of Emperors in whom the ancient stock of Roman virtue survived. He stood, but half unconsciously, at the outgoings of an age, filled with a sense of transitoriness in all things human, of epochs, empires, dynasties as well as individuals passing to dust and oblivion. The gloom of decadence haunted and oppressed him. Rome was in truth already bankrupt—bankrupt in purse, bankrupt in intellect, bankrupt in moral and even in animal vigour. Power centred more and more in the hands of the Chief of state, not because the Emperor strained after prerogative,—to which the whole bent of Marcus was opposed,—but because Senate and Patricians had lost the capacity and almost the ambition for rule. When the barbarian invaders knocked at the gates of Aquileia the Emperor had to sell the imperial personalties to raise funds for war; ravaged by plague, Italy could not recruit her legions except from slaves and gladiators; the procreation of children seemed to fail; and from this time forth the face of the Campagna began to assume the desolation of a place of tombs. Though outwardly 'the Eternal City' stood in plenitude of world-wide power, signs of the times declared the beginning of the end. The golden pause of the Antonine age is the moment of equilibrium before the quickening acceleration of 'The Decline and Fall:' its

[1] viii. 31.

era dates from 17th March 180 A.D., the death-day of Marcus Antoninus.

His end was as his life, deliberate, unflinching, resolute. Six days of inability to eat or drink, through which the habit of duty still struggled with the failing body; the summons to his friends; words tinged with a sad irony upon the vanity of life; the passionless farewell 'Why weep for me? think of the army and its safety : I do but go on before. Farewell!' Then the brief wanderings of delirium — *haec luctuosi belli opera sunt*, then the covered head, and the everlasting rest. Rome forgot the Emperor in the man — 'Marcus my father! Marcus my brother! Marcus my son!' cried the bereaved citizens. At his funeral the ordinary lamentations were omitted; and men said to one another, 'He whom the gods lent us, has rejoined the gods.'

Stoicism, by its treatment of the emotions, set itself at a disadvantage; it tended to make all life joyless, and the best life impossible. Notwithstanding, Marcus Aurelius Antoninus survives as perhaps the loftiest exemplar of unassisted duty, whom history records — unalterably loyal to the noblest hypothesis of life he knew. For him, life was indeed 'more like wrestling than dancing,'[1] yet 'in his patience he won his soul.' He lived when national virtue was dead, and almost buried; yet by integrity, by industry, and by mere fairness of mind, he helped not a little to make Roman Law the mother of codes and the saviour of society. War was to him a hateful 'hunting of Sarmatians,' yet 'duty made him a great Captain,' and he stayed the

[1] vii. 61.

barbarian till Western civilisation was Christian, and safe. Intellectually, he had neither genius nor learning, and wrote only for relief of sleeplessness and solitude: yet the centuries still turn to him for wisdom; and the Thoughts remain imperishable, dignifying duty, shaming weakness, and rebuking discontent.

MARCUS AURELIUS ANTONINUS

TO HIMSELF

BOOK I

ΜΈΜΝΗΟΟ ΤῶΝ ΔΟΓΜΆΤωΝ

FROM my grandfather Verus, integrity and 1
command of temper.

From the reputation and the memory of my 2
father, self-respect and manliness.

From my mother, to be god-fearing and liberal; 3
to check not malicious action only, but each
malicious thought; simplicity in daily living and
avoidance of the ways of opulence.

Thanks to my great-grandfather, I did not 4
attend public lectures, but was supplied with good
masters at home, and learned that in such matters
free outlay is no extravagance.

From my tutor, not to take sides with the 5
Greens or the Blues, the Big Shields or Little
Shields : to be industrious, of few wants, and to

B

wait upon myself; to mind my own business and
to scout slander.

From Diognetus, nobility of aim : disbelief in
sorcerers and wizards and their spells, in tales of
exorcism and such like : distaste for quail-fighting
and other such excitements : tolerance in argument : familiarisation with philosophy, and attendance first on Bacchius, then on Tandasis and
Marcianus ; my boyish essays, and my aspirations
after the plank bed and skin, with the other
requirements of Greek training.

From Rusticus, I first conceived the need
of moral correction and amendment: renounced
sophistic ambitions and essays on philosophy, discourses provocative to virtue, or fancy portraitures
of the Sage or the philanthropist : learned to
eschew rhetoric and poetry and fine language :
not to wear full dress about the house, or other
affectations of the kind : in my letters to keep to
the simplicity of his own, from Sinuessa, to my
mother : to be encouraging and conciliatory towards any one who was offended or out of temper,
at the first offer of advances upon their side.   He
taught me to read accurately, and not to be
satisfied with vague general apprehension ; and

not to give hasty assent to chatterers. He introduced me to the memoirs of Epictetus, presenting
me with a copy from his own stores.

From Apollonius, to keep free and to stake 8
nothing on the hazards of chance ; never, for one
instant, to lose sight of reason ; to keep equable
in temper, under assaults of pain, or the loss of
a child, or in tedious illnesses. His example was
a living demonstration, that the utmost intensity
admits of occasional relaxation. He was a model
of patience in explanation ; and visibly one who
made the least of his own experience and proficiency in philosophic exposition ; he taught me how
to receive factitious favours, without either sacrifice
of self-respect or churlish disregard.

From Sextus, kindliness ; and the model of a 9
well-ordered household ; the idea of life in conformity with nature ; dignity without affectation ;
sympathetic concern for friends ; tolerance for the
simple and unlettered ; the universal cordiality,
which made his society more agreeable than any
flattery, while never for a moment failing to command respect ; his steady intuition for discerning
and methodising the principles essential to right
living, avoiding all display of anger or emotion, and

showing a perfect combination of unimpassioned yet
affectionate concern.   In his commendation there
was no loudness, and about his learning no parade.

10   From Alexander the grammarian, to be un-
censorious; not to be carping and severe upon
lapses of grammar or idiom or phrase, but dexter-
ously to supply the proper expression, by way of
rejoinder or corroboration, or discussion of the
matter rather than the language, or some other
graceful reminder or hint.

11   From Fronto, to understand that malice and
doubleness and insincerity are characteristic of
the tyrant, and that Patricians, as we call them,
only too often fail in natural affection.

12   From Alexander the Platonist, seldom and
only when driven to it, to say or write, ' I have no
time ' ; and not to indulge the tendency to cry off
from duties arising out of our natural relations with
those about us, on the pretext of press of business.

13   From Catulus, never to slight a friend's
remonstrances, even though they happen to be
unreasonable, but to try and restore him to good
humour ; to be hearty in praise of my teachers,
as in the memoirs of Domitius and Athenodotus ;
and genuinely fond of my children.

From my brother Verus, love of belongings, 14
love of truth, and love of justice ; my knowledge
of Thrasea, Helvidius, Cato, Dion, and Brutus,
and the conception of an equal commonwealth
based on equality of right and equality of speech, ⨯
and of imperial rule respecting first and foremost
the liberty of the subject. From him too I
learned harmonious well-attuned devotion to philosophy : freehanded zeal for the good of others ;
hopefulness, and belief in friends' affection ; not
to withhold the expression of disapproval, and
not to leave friends to conjecture what one wanted
or did not want, but to be plain with them.

 From Maximus, self-mastery and concentra- 15
tion of aim ; cheerfulness under sickness or other
visitations ; a pleasant blending of affability and
dignity ; with unruffled alacrity in the performance
of appointed tasks. He inspired every one with
the belief that whatever he said he thought, and
that whatever he did was done from pure motives.
Nothing could dazzle, and nothing daunt him ;
there was no pressing forward, no hanging back,
no hesitation ; no ogling and fawning on one
hand, or frets and frowns on the other. Kind,
generous, and genuine, he gave one the impression

of goodness undeviating and even incorruptible. No one could ever have felt him patronising, yet no one could have borne to account himself his better ; so gracious was his manner.

16   From my father I learned gentleness, and unshaken adherence to judgments deliberately formed ; indifference to outward show and compliment ; industry and assiduity ; an ear open to all suggestions for the public weal ; recognition inflexibly proportioned to desert ; the tact that knew where severity was called for, or the reverse ; renunciation of all boy favourites ; disinterestedness of purpose. His friends had free leave to be absent from the imperial table, or to dispense themselves from attendance in his suite, and his sentiments were unchanged towards those who were detained on various calls. At the council - board his investigations were searching and persistent, where others would have been content with ready-made impressions and neglected strict inquiry. Stedfast in friendships, he avoided either caprice or extravagance. He seemed always up to the mark and bright. His forethought was remarkable, and his unostentatious prevision for the smallest trifles. Personal applause or flattery

of any kind he kept in check. Vigilant in
providing for imperial necessities, he carefully
husbanded his resources, without flinching from
the consequent complaints. Towards the gods
he was not superstitious ; towards men, he neither
courted popularity nor pandered to the mob, but
was in all points sober and safe, distrustful of
flash or novelty. The luxuries which tend to
refine life, and of which fortune is so lavish, he
enjoyed at once modestly and unfeignedly ; if
there, he partook unaffectedly, if absent, he did
not feel the lack. No one could charge him with
crotchets or vulgarity or pedantry, or fail to
recognise the manly ripeness and maturity of one
superior to flattery, and well able to govern both
himself and others. Added to this, he esteemed
all true philosophers ; to the rest he was
never acrimonious, yet contrived to keep his
distance. His manner was friendly, gracious
but not carried to excess. In attention to the
body he hit the happy mean : there was no
excessive hugging of life, no foppishness, and on
the other hand no undue neglect ; his wise self-
management made him almost independent of
doctoring, or of medicines or embrocations. He

was ready and generous in recognising any
real proficiency, in rhetoric for instance, or jurisprudence, or national customs, or any other
subject ; and eager to assist any to shine in their
particular sphere of excellence.   In everything
a loyal son of Rome, he did not in such matters
study appearances.   He was free from caprice
or humours, constant in attachment to the same
places and the same things.   After paroxysms
of headache, he would return fresh and vigorous
to his usual avocations.   His official secrets were
few, the rare and occasional exceptions being
solely matters of public importance.   He was
discerning and moderate in organising public
spectacles, in executing public works, in distribution of largess and the like ; always with
an eye to the actual need, rather than to the
popularity they brought.   He never bathed at
odd hours, or took a passion for building ; never
set up for a connoisseur of eatables, of the texture
and tints of clothes, or of personal charms.   His
dress came from Lorium where his country house
was, and was generally of Lanuvian wool.   The
story of his conduct to the apologetic tax-collector
at Tusculum is a sample of his general demeanour.

There was no perversity about him, no black looks or fits : he never forced things, as one says, 'past sweating point'; but was invariably rational and discriminating—giving judgments leisurely, calm, systematic, vigorous, and consistent. One might fairly apply to him what was claimed for Socrates, that he could either enjoy or leave things which most people find themselves too weak to abstain from, and too self-indulgent to enjoy. Strength, and with strength endurance, and sobriety in both, attest the perfected inviolable soul, as the illness of Maximus showed.

From the gods—good grandsires, good parents, 17 a good sister, good teachers ; good associates, kinsmen, friends, good almost every one : and that I did not hastily take offence with any one of them, though my natural disposition might easily enough have betrayed me into it ; but by the goodness of the gods circumstances never conspired to put me to the test. Thanks to the gods that I was removed when I was, from the side of my grandfather's mistress ; that I kept the flower of my youth ; that I did not force my virility, but patiently bided my time. That in my imperial father I found a chief, who eradicated

conceit, and brought me up to the idea, that court
life need not entail men-at-arms or brocaded
robes or flambeaux or statues or such like pomp ;
but that a prince may contract his state to the
style of a private citizen, without therefore demeaning himself or relaxing imperial and representative
position.   The gods granted me a brother, whose
influence stimulated me to cultivate my natural
powers, while his respect and affection gave me
new heart ; children of good parts, and free from
bodily deformities.   They saved me from making
too much way with rhetoric and poetry and the
rest, in which I might have become absorbed,
had I found it all smooth going.   Thanks to
them, I early advanced my tutors to the position
and dignity to which I saw they aspired, and did
not put them off with hopes of my eventually
doing so, as for the present they were still young :
I became acquainted with Apollonius, Rusticus,
and Maximus ; and I got clear and rooted impressions of what is meant by living in accordance
with nature.   The gods have done their part ;
their gifts, their aid, their inspirations have not
been wanting to help me to realise the life conformed to nature ; that I still fall short of it is

'my own fault, and comes of not heeding stedfastly the reminders, I may almost say the dictates of the gods. Thanks to the gods, my physical strength has stood as it has, the strain imposed : thanks to them, I kept clear both of Benedicta and Theodotus, and came safe out of later loves. Though often vexed with Rusticus, I never went to extremes that I might have repented. Though my mother was destined to die young, at least her latest years were spent with me. Whenever I wanted to help a case of poverty or other need, I was never told that I had no funds for the purpose; while I have never found myself similarly obliged to accept charity from another. Thanks too for such a wife, so submissive, so affectionate, so simple : for abundance of good tutors for my children : for help vouchsafed in dreams, more particularly for relief from bloodspitting and dizziness : and for the Caietan's response 'That depends on you.' Thanks too that, in spite of my ardour for philosophy, I did not fall into the hands of any sophist, or sit poring over essays or syllogisms, or become engrossed in scientific speculation. All this is by the help of the gods and destiny.

Among the Quadi, by the Gran.

BOOK II

ὀ ἀνεξέταστος βίος ἀβίωτος.—PLATO

1 WHEN you wake, say to yourself—To-day I
shall encounter meddling, ingratitude, violence,
cunning, malice, self-seeking; all of them the
results of men not knowing what is good and
what is evil. But seeing that I have beheld the
nature and nobility of good, and the nature and
meanness of evil, and the nature of the sinner,
who is my brother, participating not indeed in
the same flesh and blood, but in the same mind
and partnership with the divine, I cannot be
injured by any of them; for no man can involve
me in what demeans. Neither can I be angry
with my brother, or quarrel with him; for we are
made for co-operation, like the feet, the hands, the
eyelids, the upper and the lower rows of teeth.
To thwart one another is contrary to nature; and

one form of thwarting is resentment and estrangement.

Flesh, breath, and the Inner Self—that is all. 2
Good-bye, my books! strain after them no more;
they are not your portion.   As in the near
presence of death, despise poor flesh—this refuse
of blood and bones, this web and tissue of nerves
and veins and arteries.   Breath too! what is it?
a puff of wind, never the same, but every moment
exhaling, and again inhaled.   Last comes the
Inner Self—on that stake all: you are an old
man; do not let it be a slave any longer, pulled
puppet-like by self-seeking impulse; nor resist
destiny, either chafing at the present, or bemoaning the future.

In the gods' work there is providence every- 3
where.   For the action of chance is the course of
nature, or the web and woof of the dispositions
of providence.   From providence flows all; and
side by side with it is necessity and the advantage
of the Universe, of which you are a part.   To
every part of nature that which Nature brings,
and which helps towards its conservation, is good.
The conservation of the world-order depends not
only on the changes of the elements, but also on

those of the compounded wholes. Be content with what you have, find there your principles of life. No more of thirsting after books, that you may die not murmuring but in serenity, truly and heartily grateful to the gods.

4   Think how long you have gone on postponing, how often the gods have granted days of grace, which you have failed to use. It is high time to give heed to the order of which you are a part, and to the great disposer, of whom your being is an effluence; and to perceive that the limit of your time is circumscribed; use it to gain the unclouded calm, or 'twill be gone, and nevermore within your power.

Every hour staunchly, as a Roman and a man, resolve to do the work in hand, with scrupulous and unaffected dignity, affectionately, freely, justly; securing respite for yourself from all other intruding regards. And this you will secure, if you perform each task as though it were your last, free from all waywardness, from passions that estrange from reason's dictates, from insincerity, self-love, and discontent with destiny. See how few things a man need hold fast, to secure the smooth flow of a godly life—for the gods will require nothing more of him who keeps true to these.

✳ Is violence done you? Then do not violence 6
to thyself, my soul. Not for long will thy day
for self-reverence be. Each lives but once ; thy ⊃
life is all but finished, and still instead of respecting thyself alone, thou dost stake thy fortunes
upon the souls of others.

Pressure of outer claims distracts you. Then 7
give yourself some respite from the taskwork of
new good, and have done with the restless whirl.
But there is want of concentration in its other form
to guard against ; there are the triflers in action,
tired of life, with no fixed aim towards which to
direct each endeavour, yes, and each regard.

It were hard to find a man distempered by 8
not understanding what is passing in another's
soul ; but those who do not intelligently follow
the motions of their own, cannot but be in a
distemper.

Ever bear in mind what Nature is at large, 9
what my own nature is, how this stands to that,
how small a portion of how great a whole, and ⊅
further, that no man can prevent you from
keeping act and word always accordant with that
nature of which you are a part.

In comparing sins——so far as they admit of 10

general comparison — Theophrastus sagely observes that sins of desire are more heinous than sins of passion. For passion is an estrangement from reason, accompanied by sense of pain and inward constriction ; but sins of desire, in which pleasure gets the better of us, imply more of feminine incontinence. And surely it is right and philosophical to say that sinning with pleasure is more culpable than sinning with pain. The latter is like acting under provocation, and being driven into passion by pain : the former is a spontaneous impulse towards wrong, driving one to satisfaction of desire.

11   Whatever you do or say or think, it is in your power, remember, to take leave of life. In departing from this world, if indeed there are gods, there is nothing to be afraid of ; for gods will not let you fall into evil. But if there are no gods, or if they do not concern themselves with men, why live on in a world devoid of gods, or devoid of providence ? But there do exist gods, who do concern themselves with men. And they have put it wholly in the power of man not to fall into any true evil. Were there real evil in what remains against that too they would have pro-

vided, putting within man's power an absolute
immunity. But how can that, which does not
make a man worse, make his life worse? Nature
could never have made the oversight, either un-
knowingly, or yet knowingly, through inability to
guard against it or set it right. Nature could not,
either through lack of power or lack of skill, have
made such a blunder as to let good and evil indifferently befall the good and bad indiscriminately.
Yet death and life, good report and evil report,
pain and pleasure, riches and poverty, and all such
things fall to the good and bad indifferently, and
neither ennoble nor demean. The inference is that
they are neither good nor evil.

By mind-power we apprehend how quickly all
things vanish, bodies in the material world, their
memories in the lapse of time ; we understand
the nature of all things of sense, particularly
those which decoy us with the bait of pleasure, or
terrify us with the threat of pain, or are dinned
into our ears by self-conceit ; how cheap they are
and despicable, filthy, perishable, dead. Intelligence appraises those, whose views and voices
bestow repute ; it teaches the nature of death,
and shows that any one who looks it fairly in the

face, and mentally analyses the idea into the impressions which it contains, will come to regard it
simply as an act of nature ; and none but a child
is terrified at that.   Nay, and not merely an
act of nature, but for nature's good.   Finally, by
intellect we learn how man has touch with god,
and with what part of his being, and how, when
this takes place, the said part is affected.

13   Nothing is more disheartening than the weary
round of spying out everything, probing (as
Pindar says) 'the depths of earth,' guessing and
prying at the secrets of our neighbours' souls,
instead of realising that it is enough to keep
solely to the god within, and to serve him with
all honesty ; and our service to god is to keep
him pure from passion, and waywardness, and discontent with that which comes from gods or men.
The gods' works command respect, by virtue of
their excellence ; men's love, by virtue of the
bond of brotherhood ; and sometimes withal pity,
by reason of their ignorance of good and evil, a
blindness as disabling as that which obliterates
distinction between black and white.

14   Though you live three thousand years, ay or
three million, no man, remember, can lose another

life than that which he now lives, or live another than that which he now loses. The longest and the shortest come to the same thing. The present is the same for all (even though the loss be not the same); what you lose, or win, is just the flying moment. A man cannot be losing either past or future—how can he be deprived of that which is not his? Remember then two things— first, that all things from all eternity are of one and the same recurrent form, and that it makes no difference whether a man watches the same show for a hundred years, or for two hundred, or for an infinity; secondly, that the loss of the longest-lived and the shortest is one and the same. It is the present only of which a man can be deprived, that and that only being his, and what is not his he cannot lose.

The view taken is everything. The objections 15 urged against Monimus the Cynic are obvious; but so too is the value of the *dictum*, if one accepts the gist of it, so far as it is true.

Man's soul does violence to itself, first and 16 foremost when it makes itself, so far as it can, a kind of tumour and excrescence on the universe; any chafing against the order of things is a rebellion against nature, whose unity includes the various natures of the several parts. And again, secondly, when it estranges itself, or actively opposes another to his hurt, as happens in fits of anger. Thirdly, there is self-violence, when it succumbs to pleasure or to pain. Fourthly, when it plays false, by feigned and untrue act or word. Fifthly, when in action or endeavour it becomes aimless and works at random and unintelligently, when even trifles demand reference to an end ; and the end of rational beings is, to walk as followers of the reason and the ordinance of the city and commonwealth most high.

17   In man's life, time is but a moment ; being, a flux ; sense is dim ; the material frame corruptible ; soul, an eddy of breath ; destiny hard to divine, and fame ill at appraise. In brief, things of the body are but a stream that flows, things of the soul a dream and vapour ; life, a warfare and a sojourning ; and after-fame, oblivion. What then can direct our goings ? One thing and one alone, philosophy ; which is, to keep the deity within inviolate and free from scathe, superior to pleasures and to pains, doing nothing at random, nothing falsely or disingenuously, and

lacking for naught, whatever others do or leave undone ; accepting the apportioned lot, as coming from the same source as man himself; and finally, in all serenity awaiting death, the natural dissolution of the elements of which each creature is compounded. And if the component elements have nought to fear in the continuous change from form to form, why should one look askance at the change and dissolution of the whole ? It is of nature ; and nature knows no evil.

At Carnuntum.

BOOK III

1 WE must take into account, not only that each day consumes so much of life, and leaves so much less behind, but also that, even if life is prolonged, there remains the uncertainty whether the understanding will still retain ,discernment and the perceptive intuitions which bring insight into things divine and human. Dotage may set in, involving no failure of respiration, nutrition, impression, impulse, or the like ; but premature decay of full self-mastery, of nice exactitude in calculating duties, of just correlation of them as a whole, of clear perception whether the time has come to quit the scene, and such like criteria of active and well-ordered intelligence. We must press forward then, not only because each day is one step nearer death, but also because apprehension and intelligence may prematurely fail.

Watch well the grace and charm, that belong 2
even to the consequents of nature's work.   The
cracks for instance and crevices in bread-crust,
though in a sense flaws in the baking, yet have a
fitness of their own and a special stimulus to tickle
the appetite.   Figs again, just at perfection, gape.
In ripe olives the very nearness of decay adds its
own beauty to the fruit.   The bending ears of
corn, the lion's scowl, the foam that drips from
the wild boar's mouth, and many other things,
though in themselves far from beautiful, yet looked
at as consequents on nature's handiwork, add new
beauty and appeal to the soul, so that if only
one attains deeper feeling and insight for the
workings of the universe, almost everything, even
in its consequents and accidents, seems to yield
some pleasing combination of its own.   Thus
the actual jaws of living beasts will be not less
picturesque than the imitations produced by artists
and sculptors.   The old woman and the old man
will have an ideal loveliness, as youth its ravishing
charm, made visible to eyes that have the skill.
Such things will not appeal to all, but will strike
him only who is in harmony with nature and her
sincere familiar.

3   Hippocrates cured many sick, but himself fell
sick and died.   The Chaldeans foretold many
deaths, but fate overtook them too.   Alexander,
Pompey, Julius Cæsar, razed city after city to
the ground, and cut thousands and thousands to
pieces, horse and foot, upon the field of battle,
but for them too came the hour of departure.
Heraclitus after all his speculations on the conflagration of the universe, was water-logged with
dropsy, and died in a plaster of cow dung.
Democritus was killed by vermin ; and Socrates
by vermin of another kind.   What does it all
come to ?   This.   You embark, you make life's
voyage, you come to port : step out.   If for
another life, there are gods everywhere, there
as here.   If out of all sensation, then pains and
pleasures will solicit you no more, and you will
drudge no more for the carnal shell, which is so
unworthy of its ministering servant.   For the
spirit is mind and god, the body refuse clay.

4   Do not waste what is left of life in regarding
other men, except when bent upon some unselfish
gain.   Why miss opportunities for action by thus
persistently regarding what so-and-so is doing
and why, what he is saying or thinking or

planning, or anything else that dazes and distracts
you from allegiance to your Inner Self? In the
sequence of your regards, shun wayward random
thoughts, and, above all, meddling and ill-nature ;
limit yourself habitually to such regards, that if
suddenly asked ' What is in your thoughts now ?,'
you could tell at once the candid and unhesitating
truth—a direct plain proof, that all your thoughts
were simple and in charity, such as befit a social
being, who eschews voluptuous or even self-indulgent fancies, or jealousy of any kind, or malice
and suspicion, or any other mood which you would
blush to own. A man so minded, and committed
finally to the pursuit of virtue, is indeed a priest
and minister of gods, true to that inward and
implanted power, which keeps a man unsoiled by
pleasure, invulnerable by pain, free from all touch
of arrogance, innocent of all baseness, a combatant
in the greatest of all combats, which is the mastery
of passion, steeped in justice to the core, and with
his whole heart welcoming all that befalls him as
his portion : seldom, and only in view of some
large unselfish gain, does he regard what other
men say or do or think. In action his own
conduct is his sole concern, and he realises

without fail the web of his own destiny ; action he
makes high, convinced that destiny is good ; for
his apportioned destiny sweeps man on with the
vaster sweep of things.   He forgets not his bond
of brotherhood with every rational creature ; nor
that the law of man's nature implies concern for
all men ; and that he must not hold by the
opinion of the world, but of those only who live
conformably to nature.   He bears steadily in
mind what manner of men they are who do not
so live, and at home and abroad, by night and
by day, what kind of company they keep ; nor
can he take account of such men's praise, when
they do not even please or satisfy themselves.

5   Let action be willing, disinterested, well-
advised, ungrudging ; thought modest and un-
pretentious.   No overtalking and no overdoing.
Give the god within the control of what you are
—a living man, full-aged, a citizen, a Roman, an
Imperator ; you have held the van ; you are as
one who waits for the retreat from life to sound,
ready for the march, needing not oath nor witness.
Herein is the secret of brightness, of self-complete-
ness without others' aid, and without the peace
which is in others' gift.   Upright, not uprighted.

Does man's life offer anything higher than justice, truth, wisdom, and courage, in a word, than the understanding at peace with itself, in conforming action to the law of reason, and with destiny in all apportionments that lie beyond its own control? If you sight anything higher still, turn to it, say I, with your whole heart, and have fruition of your goodly find. But if there appear nothing higher than the implanted deity within, which gives the impulses their mandate, which scrutinises the impressions, which (in the words of Socrates) is weaned from the affections of sense, which takes its mandate from the gods, and concerns itself for men; and if all else proves mean and cheap in comparison with this, allow no scope to any rival attraction or seduction, which will preclude you from the undistracted cultivation of your own peculiar good. No outer claimant—not popular applause, nor power, nor wealth, nor self-indulgence—may compete with the authorisations of the social reason. For a moment they may seem to harmonise, but suddenly they take the mastery, and sweep you from your moorings. I say then, simply and freely, choose the highest and hold it fast. The highest is that in which lies true advantage. If your advantage as a reasoning being, make sure of it ; if only as a living thing, so state the case, not bolstering your judgment by any self-conceit, only be sure there lurks no error in your scrutiny.

7   Never prize anything as self-advantage, which will compel you to break faith, to forfeit self-respect, to suspect or hate or execrate another, to play false, to desire anything which requires screens or veils. He who is loyal to his own indwelling mind and god, and a willing votary of that inward grace, makes no scene, heaves no sighs, needs not a wilderness nor yet a crowd. The best is his, the life that neither seeks nor shuns. Whether his soul in its material shell remains at his disposal for a longer or a shorter space, he cares not a whit. So soon as it is time for him to take his leave, he is as ready to go his way as to engage in any other seemly or self-respecting act ; careful of one thing only, that while life shall last, his understanding shall never disown the relation of a being possessed of mind and social aim.

8   In the understanding throughly purged and chastened, there is no place for ulcerous sore or fester. Destiny cannot cut short the man's career

still incomplete, like an actor quitting the stage
before the piece is finished and played out.   He
does not cringe nor brag, he does not lean nor
yet stand off, he is accountable to none and yet
has no concealments.

Treat reverently your assumptive faculty : by 9
it and it alone is your Inner Self secured against
assumptions not in harmony with nature and with
the constitution of a rational creature.   It is our
warranty for mental circumspection, for community
with men, and for the walk with gods.

Casting all else away, hold fast these few 10
verities.   And bear in mind withal that every man
lives only in the present, this passing moment ;
all else is life outlived, or yet undisclosed.   Man's
life has but a tiny span, tiny as the corner of earth
on which he lives, short as fame's longest tenure,
handed along the line of short-lived mortals, who
do not even know themselves, far less the dead
of long ago.   ·

To these add yet one injunction more.   Always 11
define and outline carefully the object of perception, so as to realise its naked substance, to discriminate its own totality by aid of its surroundings,
to master its specific attributes, and those of the

component elements into which it can be analysed.
Nothing so emancipates the mind, as the power of
systematically and truthfully testing everything
that affects our life, and looking into them in such
a way as to infer the kind of order to which each
belongs, the special use which it subserves, its
relation and value to the universe, and in particular
to man as a citizen and member of that supreme
world-city, of which all other cities form as it
were households.   What is the object, ask, which
now produces the given impression upon me? of
what is it compounded? how long has it to last?
on what virtue does it make demand? gentleness,
courage, truth, good faith, simplicity, self-help, or
what?   In each case say, This comes from god;
or, This is part of the coordination, the concaten-
ating web, the concurrence of destiny: or, This is
from one who is of the same stock and kind and
fellowship as I, but who is ignorant of his true
relation to nature; I am not ignorant, and therefore in accordance with nature's law of fellowship
I treat him kindly and justly; though at the same
time in things relative I strive to hit their proper
worth.

12   If you put to use the present, earnestly, vigor-

ously, and considerately, following the law of reason ; if, careless of by-gains you keep your god within pure and erect, as though at any moment liable to be re-claimed ; if, waiting for nothing and shunning nothing, you keep your being whole, conforming present action to nature's law, and content with even truth of word and utterance, then you will be in the way of perfection. And none has power to hinder.

As surgeons keep their instruments and knives 13 at hand for sudden calls upon their skill, keep you your principles ever ready to test things divine and human, in every act however trifling remembering the mutual bond between the two. No human act can be right without co-reference to the divine, nor conversely.

Be not misguided any more : you will not now 14 re-read your *Memorabilia*, nor your deeds of ancient Rome and Greece, nor the essays and extracts which you garnered for old age. No, push forward to the end, fling empty hopes away, and as you care for self, to your own rescue, while you yet may.

They little know the full meaning of to steal, to 15 sow, to buy, to be at peace, to see the right course : such seeing needs another organ than the eye.

16 Body, soul, mind, these three : to the body belong sensations, to the soul impulses, to the mind principles. The impressions of sense we share with cattle of the field : the pulls of impulse with brute beasts, with catamites, with Phalaris, or Nero ; and mind is still the guide to obvious duties, even for the atheist, the traitor, and for those who lock the door for sin. Well then, if all else is shared, the good man's one distinction is to welcome gladly all that in the web of destiny befalls ; to keep the god implanted in his breast unsoiled, not perturbed by any tumult of impressions, keeping his watch serene, a seemly follower of god, not false to truth in utterance, or to justice in act. Though the whole world misdoubt him because his life is simple, self-respecting, and cheerful, he is angered with no man, and does not turn aside from the path that leads to his life's goal, unto which he must come pure and peaceful and ready to depart, in unrebellious harmony with his appointed portion.

BOOK IV

ἐκ coŷ ΓὰΡ Γένοc ἐcΜέΝ.—Cleanthes
πάΝΤΑ θεῶΝ ΜεcΤὰ Καὶ ΔΑΙΜόΝωΝ.—Epictetus

WHEN the sovereign power within is true to 1
nature, its attitude towards outer circumstance is.
that of ready adjustment to whatever is possible
and offered for acceptance. It does not set its
affections on any determinate material, but keeps
each impulse and preference conditional and subject
to reservation. Obstacles encountered it converts
into material for itself, just as fire lays hold of
accumulations, which would have choked a feeble
light ; for a blaze of fire at once assimilates all
that is heaped on, consumes it, and derives new
vigour from the process.

Let no act be performed at random, or without 2
full philosophic consideration.

Men seek retirement in country house, on shore 3

D

or hill ; and you too know full well what that yearn-
ing means.   Surely a very simple wish; for at what
hour you will, you can retire into yourself.   Nowhere can man find retirement more peaceful and
untroubled than in his own soul ; specially he who
hath stores within, a glance at which straightway
sets him at perfect ease ; meaning by ease good
order in the soul, this and nothing else.   Ever
and anon grant yourself this retirement, and so
renew yourself.   Have a few principles brief and
elemental, recurrence to which will suffice to shut
out the court and all its ways, and anon send you
back unchafing to the tasks to which you must
return.   What is it chafes you ?   Men's evil-doing ?
Do but fall back upon your tenet, that rational
beings exist for one another, that forbearance is a
part of justice, that wrong-doing is involuntary,
and think of all the feuds, suspicions, hates and
brawls, that ere now lie stretched in ashes ; think,
and be at rest. · Or is it the portion assigned
you in the universe, at which you chafe ?   Recall
to mind the alternative—either a foreseeing providence, or blind atoms—and all the abounding
proofs that the world is as it were a city.   Or is
it bodily troubles that assail ?   Realise again that

when the understanding has once possessed itself
and recognised its own prerogative, it is not bound
up any more with the pneuma-current, smooth or
rough, and recur to all that you have learned and
accepted regarding pain and pleasure. Or does
some bubble of fame torment you? Then fix
your gaze on swift oblivion, on the gulf of infinity
this way and that, on the empty rattle of plaudits
and the undiscriminating fickleness of professed
applause, on the narrow range within which you
are circumscribed. The whole earth is but a
point, your habitation but a tiny nook thereon :
and on the earth how many are there who will
praise you, and what are they worth? Well then,
remember to retire within that little field[1] of self.
Above all do not strain or strive, but be free, and
look at things as a man, as a human being, as a
citizen, as a mortal. Foremost among the maxims
to which you can bend your glance, be these two—
first, things cannot touch the soul, but stand without it stationary ; tumult can arise only from views
within ourselves : secondly, all things you see,
in a moment change and will be no more ; ay;
think of all the changes in which you have

[1] See x. 23, note.

yourself borne part.   The world is a process of variation ; life a process of views.

4   If the mind-element is common to us all, so likewise is that reason which makes us rational ; and therefore too that reason, which bids us do or leave undone ; and therefore the world-law ; therefore we are fellow-citizens, and share a common citizenship ; and the world is as it were a city. What other citizenship is common to the whole of humankind ?   From thence, even from this common citizenship, comes our franchise——mind, reason, and law.   If not, whence indeed ?   For just as the earthy element in me is derived from earth, the watery from another element, breath from a given source, and again the hot and igneous from its own proper source——for nothing comes from nothing, or can pass into nothing——so assuredly the mind-element has likewise its own origin.

5   Death, like birth, is a revelation of nature ; a composition of elements and answering dissolution. There is nothing in it to cause us shame.   It is in consonance with the nature of a being possessed of mind, and does not contradict the reason of its constitution.

6   That from such and such causes given effects

result is inevitable ; he who would not have it so,
would have the fig-tree yield no juice.   Fret not.
Remember too that in a little you and he will both
be dead ; soon not even your names will survive.

Get rid of the assumption, and therewith you   7
get rid of the sense ' I am an injured man ' ; get
rid of the sense of injury, you get rid of the injury
itself.

What does not make the man himself worse,   8
does not make his life worse either, nor injure him,
without or within.

It is a necessity demanded by the general good.   9

' All that happens, happens aright.'   Watch 10
narrowly, and you will find it so.   Not merely in
the order of events, but in just order of right, as
though some power apportions all according to
worth.   Watch on then, as you have begun ; in
all that you do, let goodness go with the doing—
goodness in the strict meaning of the word.   In
every action make sure of this.

Do not take the views adopted by him who 11
does the wrong, nor those he would have you
adopt ; just look at facts, as they truly are.

Two rules of readiness ; be ready, first, to do 12
just that which reason, your king and lawgiver,

suggests for the help of men ; and, secondly, be
ready to change your course, should some one after
all correct and convert you out of your conceit.
Only the conversion must be due to some convincing consideration, such as justice or public
gain, and the appeal must be of that order only,
not apparent pleasure or popularity.

13   Have you reason?—I have.—Then why not use
it ?   Let reason do its work, and what more would
you have ?

14 >   You exist but as a part inherent in a greater
whole.   You will vanish into that which gave you
being ; or rather, you will be retransmuted into
the seminal and universal reason.

15   Many grains of frankincense on the same altar ;
one drops sooner, another later—it makes no
difference.

16   In ten days, instead of a monkey or a beast,
you can become in the gods' eyes as a god, if you
do but revert to the principles of your creed and
to reverence for reason.

17   Do not live as though you had a thousand
years before you.   The common due impends ;
while you live, and while you may, be good.

18   How much valuable time may be gained by

not looking at what some neighbour says or does
or thinks, but only taking care that our own acts
are just and holy ; the good man must not heed
black hearts, but head straight for the goal, casting
not a glance behind.

He who is aflutter for fame perceives not, that 19
of those who remember him every man will soon
be dead ; so too in due course will each of their
successors, till the last flicker of memory, through
flutterings and failings, dies altogether out. Nay
assume that those who remember you are immortal,
and memory immortal, what is that to you ? To
you dead, absolutely nothing. Well but to you
living, what good is praise except indeed for some
secondary end ? Why then neglect unseasonably
nature's present gift, and cling to what one or
another says hereafter ?

Anything in any wise beautiful or noble, owes 20
the beauty to itself, and with itself its beauty ends ;
praise forms no part of it ; for praise does not
make its object worse or better. This is true of
the commoner forms of beauty—material objects
for instance and works of art—no less than of the
ideal ; true beauty needs no addition, any more
than law, or truth, or kindness, or self-respect.

For which of these can praise beautify, or censure,
mar? Is the emerald less perfect, for lacking
praise? or is gold, or ivory, or purple? a lyre or
a poniard, a floweret or a shrub?

21   If souls survive death, how can the air hold
them from all eternity? How, we reply, does
earth hold the bodies of generation after generation
committed to the grave? Just as on earth, after
a certain term of survival, change and dissolution
of substance makes room for other dead bodies,
so too the souls transmuted into air, after a period
of survival, change by processes of diffusion and
of ignition, and are resumed into the seminal principle of the universe, and in this way make room
for others to take up their habitation in their stead.
Such is the natural answer, assuming the survival
of souls. And we must consider not only the sum
total of bodies duly buried, but also of creatures
daily devoured by ourselves and the other animals.
What numbers are thus consumed, and as it were
buried in the bodies of those who feed on them!
Yet the requisite room is provided by the assimilation into blood, and forms of variation into air or fire.
How can the truth be searched out in this case?
By distinguishing between matter and cause.

Do not be dazed by the whirl. Whatever the 22
impulse, satisfy justice ; whatever the impression,
make sure of certitude.

I am in harmony with all, that is a part of thy 23
harmony, great Universe. For me nothing is early
and nothing late, that is in season for thee. All
is fruit for me, which thy seasons bear, O Nature !
from thee, in thee, and unto thee are all things.
" *Dear City of Cecrops!* " saith the poet : and wilt
not thou say, ' Dear City of God.'

" *Do few things, if you would have cheer.*" A 24
better rule methinks is to do only things necessary,
things which in a social being reason dictates, and
as it dictates. For this brings the cheer that
comes of doing a few things, and doing them well.
Most of the things we say or do are not necessary ;
get rid of them, and you will gain time and tranquillity. Thus in every case a man should ask
himself, Is this one of the things not necessary ?
and we ought to get rid not only of actions, that
are not necessary, but likewise of impressions ;
then superfluous actions will not follow in their
train.

Make trial of the good man's life and see how 25
in your case it succeeds——of the man satisfied with

his allotted portion in the universe, and content to keep his action just, his disposition charitable.

26   You have seen the other side of the picture? Now look on this. Be tranquil: be simple. Does another do wrong? The wrong is his own. Does aught befall you? It is well—a part of the destiny of the universe ordained for you from the beginning; all that befalls was part of the great web. In fine, *Life is short;* let us redeem the present by help of reasonableness and right. In relaxation, be sober.

27   Either an ordered universe, or else a welter of confusion. Assuredly then a world-order. Or think you that order subsisting within yourself is compatible with disorder in the All? And that too when all things, however distributed and diffused, are affected sympathetically.

28   "*A black heart*"—ay, a womanish, a perverse heart, a heart of brute beast or babe or cattle, stupid and false and hypocritical, a huckster's or a tyrant's.

29   If he who does not recognise what is in the universe is a stranger to the universe, none the less is he who does not recognise what is passing there. He is an exile, expatriated from the com-

munity of reason ; a blind man, with cataract of the
mental eye ; a pauper, who needs another's help, .
and cannot provide his own living ; an excrescence,
who as it were excretes and separates himself from
the order of nature, by discontent with his surroundings ; for the same nature which produced
you, produced them too ; a social outcast, who
dissevers his individual soul from the one common
soul of reasoning things.

One philosopher goes without coat; another 80
without book.   Quoth our half-clad friend, 'Bread
I have none, yet I hold fast to reason.'   And so
say I, 'Provender of learning I have none, and
yet hold fast.'

'Love your trade, however humble,' and find in 81
it refreshment.   Spend life's remainder, as one who
with his whole heart has committed his all to the
gods, and is neither tyrant nor slave to any man.

Picture, for instance, the times of Vespasian— 82
there you see folk marrying, rearing children,
falling sick, dying, warring, feasting, trading, farm-
ing, flattering, pushing, suspecting, plotting, praying
for deaths, grumbling at fate, loving, amassing,
coveting consulships or crowns.   Yet, where now
is all that restless life ?   Or pass a step on to the

times of Trajan!   Again it is the same.   That life too is dead.   So likewise scan the many registers of ages and of nations ; see how hard they strove, how fast they fell, and were resolved into the elements.   Above all dwell in retrospect on those whom you yourself have seen straining after vanities, instead of following out the law of their own being, and, clinging tight to that, resting content.   This acts as a sure reminder that interest in an object must be in proportion to the real worth of the particular object.   It will save you from disheartenment not to become unduly engrossed in things of lesser moment.

33   The accustomed phrases of old days are the archaisms of to-day.   So too the names that were once on all men's lips, are now as it were archaisms ——Camillus, Caeso, Volesus, Dentatus ; and a little later, Scipio and Cato ; yes even Augustus, and so with Hadrian and Antoninus.   All things fade, as a tale that is told, and soon are buried in complete oblivion.   This is true even of the shining lights of fame.   As for the rest, no sooner is the breath out of them, than they are ' to fortune and to fame unknown.'[1]   And what, after all, is eternity of

[1] Marcus quotes two familiar epithets from Homer, *Od.* i. 242.

fame? Just <u>emptiness</u>. What then remains, worthy of devotion? One thing only; the understanding just, action unselfish, speech that abhors a lie, and the disposition that welcomes all that befalls, as inevitable, as familiar, and as flowing from a like origin and source.

Freely resign yourself to Clotho, helping her 34 to spin her thread of what stuff she will.

Everything is but for a day, remembrancer alike 85 and the remembered.

Watch how all things continually change, and 86 accustom yourself to realise that Nature's prime delight is in changing things that are, and making new things in their likeness. All that is, is as it were the seed of that which shall issue from it. You must not limit your idea of seed to seeds planted in the earth or in the womb—which is most unphilosophical.

Death is at hand—but not yet are you simple, 87 or unperturbed, or incredulous of possible injury from without, or serene towards all, or convinced that in just dealing alone is wisdom.

Descry men's Inner Selves, and see what the 88 wise shun or seek.

Evil for you lies not in any self external to 89

your own ; nor yet in any phase or alteration of your material shell. Where is it then ? In that part of you which forms your views of what is evil. Refuse the view, and all is well. Though the poor flesh, to which it is so near allied, be cut or burned, fester or rot, still let this judging faculty remain at peace, adjudging nothing either bad or good, that can equally befall the bad man and the good. For that which equally befalls a man, whether he conforms to nature or no, is neither for nor against nature.

40   Constantly picture the universe as a living organism, controlling a single substance and a single soul, and note how all things are assimilated to a single world-sense, all act by a single impulse, and all co-operate towards all that comes to pass ; and mark the contexture and concatenation of the web.

41   What am I ? "*A poor soul, laden with a corpse*" —said Epictetus.

42   Things in change take no harm, nor the products of change good.

43   Time is a river, the mighty current of created things. No sooner is a thing in sight, than it is swept past, and another comes sweeping on, and will anon be by.

All that befalls is as accustomed and familiar 44
as spring rose, or summer fruit; so it is with
disease, death, slander, intrigue, and all else that
joys or vexes fools.

Subsequents follow antecedents by bond of 45
inner consequence; it is no merely numerical
sequence of arbitrary and isolated units, but a
rational interconnexion. And just as things existent exhibit harmonious coordination, so too
things coming into being display not bare succession but a marvellous internal relationship.

Remember the word of Heraclitus.——"The 46
death of earth the birth of water, the death of
water the birth of air, the death of air fire," and
so conversely. Remember too his "reveller, unconscious which way his road leads"; and again,
"men quarrel with their ever-present friend," even
with the reason that disposes the universe; and
his "To what they meet each day, men still keep
strange." And again, "We must not act and speak
like men asleep," albeit even then we seem to act
and speak;[1] nor yet "as children from their father's
lips," that is to say, blindly take all for granted.

Suppose some god informed you that to-morrow, 47

[1] The same *mot* is cited again vi. 42.

or at most the day after, you would be dead, you would not be greatly exercised whether it were the day after rather than to-morrow, not if you have a spark of spirit——for what difference is there worth considering? So, too, never mind whether it is ever so many years hence, or to-morrow.

48 Constantly realise how many physicians are dead, who have often enough knit their brows over their patients; how many astrologers, who have pompously predicted others' deaths; philosophers, who have held disquisitions without end on death or immortality; mighty men, who have slain their thousands; tyrants, who in exercise of their prerogative of death have blustered as though they were Immortals; whole cities buried bodily, Helice, Pompeii, Herculaneum, and others without end. Then count up those whom you have known, one by one; how one buried another, was in his turn laid low, and another buried him; and all this in a little span! In a word, look at all human things, behold how fleeting and how sorry——but yesterday a mucus-clot, to-morrow dust or ashes! Spend your brief moment then according to nature's law, and serenely greet the journey's end, as an olive

falls when it is ripe, blessing the branch that bare it and giving thanks to the tree which gave it life.

Be like the headland, on which the billows dash 49 themselves continually ; but it stands fast, till about its base the boiling breakers are lulled to rest. Say you, ' How unfortunate for me that this should have happened ? '   Nay rather, ' How fortunate, that in spite of this, I own no pang, uncrushed by the present, unterrified at the future ! '   The thing might have happened to any one, but not every one could have endured without a pang.   Why think that a misfortune, rather than this a good fortune ?   Can you apply the term misfortune at all to that which is not a frustration of men's nature? or can you regard anything as a frustration of his nature, which is not contrary to the will of that nature ?   Think rather—You have learned the will of nature.   Can that which has befallen you possibly prevent you from being just, lofty, temperate, discerning, circumspect, truthful, self-respecting, free, and all else in which man's nature finds its full reward.   Remember then henceforth in every case where you are tempted to repine, to apply this principle—not, ' The thing is a misfortune,' but ' To bear it bravely is good fortune.'

E

50   A simple, yet effectual, help towards disregard of death, is to dwell on those who have clung tenaciously to life. What have they got by it, more than those taken in their prime? Somewhere, somewhen; in any case they lie low, Cadicianus, Fabius, Julianus, Lepidus, and the rest who, however many they first carried to the grave, came thither themselves at last. How slight the difference after all, and that too how beset, how ill-companioned, how bodily mis-housed! It is as nothing, compared with the unfathomable past and the infinite beyond. In the presence of that, is not 'Trigerenian Nestor'[1] as the three days' babe?

51   Ever run the short way: and the short way is the way of nature, aiming at perfect soundness in every word and every act. Such is the rule that gives deliverance from worry and irresolution and all secondary aims and artifice.

---

[1] M. plays upon the familiar epithet 'Gerenian' of Nestor, the typical ancient of Greek literature, and Trigeron (τριγέρων) 'thrice-aged,' an epithet applied to Nestor by the Greek epigrammatists.

BOOK V

わ hi, oh why, this person
life is so short!
you don't understand.
'private occupa'

ἀνέχου καὶ ἀπέχου

IN the morning, when you feel loth to rise, fall 1
back upon the thought 'I am rising for man's
work. Why make a grievance of setting about
that for which I was born, and for sake of which
I have been brought into the world? Is the end
of my existence to lie snug in the blankets and
keep warm?'—'It is more pleasant so.'—'Is it
for pleasure you were made? not for doing,
and for action? Look at the plants, the sparrows,
the ants, spiders, bees, all doing their business
helping to weld the order of the world. And
will you refuse man's part? and not run the
way of nature's ordering?'—'Well, but I must
have rest.'—'True, yet to rest too nature sets
bounds, no less than to eating and to drinking: in
spite of which you pass the bounds, you transgress

nature's allowance : while in action, far from that, you stop short of what is within your power. You do not truly love yourself ; if you did, you would love your nature, and that nature's will. True lovers of their art grow heart and soul absorbed in working at it, going unwashed, unfed ; you honour your nature less than the carver does his carving, or the dancer his dancing, or the hoarder his heap, or the vainglorious man his glory. They, for their darling pursuit, readily forego food and sleep, to advance that upon which they are bent. To you, does social action seem cheaper than such things, and worth less devotion ? '

What a solace to banish and efface every tumultuous, unauthorised impression, and straight-way to be lapped in calm !

Claim your right to every word or action that accords with nature. Do not be distracted by the consequent criticism or talk, but if a thing is good to be done or said, do not disclaim your proper right. Other men's self is their own affair, they follow their own impulse : do not you heed them, but keep the straight course, following your own nature and the nature of the universe ; and the way of both is one.

I walk the ways of nature, until I fall and 4 shall find rest, exhaling my last breath into that element from which day by day I draw it, and falling upon that wherefrom my father stored my seed of life, my mother the blood, my nurse the milk ; which for these many years provides my daily meat and drink, supports my tread, bears each indignity of daily use.

You have no special keenness of wit. So be 5 it—yet there are many other qualities of which you cannot say, ' I have no gift that way.' Do but practise them : they are wholly in your power ; be sincere, dignified, industrious, serious, not too critical or too exacting, but considerate and frank, with due reserves in action, speech, and accent of authority. See how many good qualities you might exhibit, for which you cannot plead natural incapacity or unfitness, and how you fail to rise to your opportunities. When you murmur, when you are mean, when you flatter, when you complain of ill-health, when you are self-satisfied and give yourself airs and indulge one humour after another, is it forced on you by lack of natural gifts ? Heavens ! You might long since have been delivered from all that. It is only after all a question of some slowness, some lack of quickness in perception ; and this you can train and discipline, if, you do not shut your eyes to it or indulge your own stupidity.

6   There is a kind of man, who, whenever he does a good turn, makes a point of claiming credit for it; and though he does not perhaps press the claim, yet all the same at heart he takes up the position of creditor, and does not forget what he has done. But there is another, who so to say forgets what he has done: he is like the vine that bears a cluster, and having once borne its proper fruit seeks no further recompense.   As the horse that runs, the hound that hunts, the bee that hives its honey, so the man who does the kindness does not raise a shout, but passes on to the next act, as a vine to the bearing of clusters for next season.— ' What ! ' you object, ' are we to class ourselves with things that act unconsciously, without intelligence ? '—' Yes indeed ; but to do so is to assert intelligence ; for it is a characteristic of the social being to perceive consciously that his action is social.'—' Yes i' faith, and to wish the recipient too to perceive the same.'—' What you say is true : but if you thus pervert the maxim's mean-

ing, it will make you one of those described above ; who indeed are misled by plausible appeals to reason. Once master the true meaning, and never fear that it will lead you into neglect of any social act.'

An Athenian prayer—*Rain, rain, dear Zeus,* 7 *upon Athenian tilth and plains.* We should either not pray at all, or else in this simple, noble sort.

We talk of doctors' orders, and say : Æscula- 8 pius has prescribed him horse exercise, or cold baths, or walking barefoot. It is the same with Nature's orders, when she prescribes disease, mutilation, amputation, or some other form of disablement. Just as doctors' orders mean such and such treatment, ordered as specific for such and such state of health, so every individual has circumstances ordered for him specifically in the way of destiny. Circumstances may be said to *fit* our case, just as masons talk of *fitting* squared stones in bastions or pyramids, when they adjust them so as to complete a given whole. The adjustment is a perfect fit. Just as the universe is the full sum of all the constituent parts, so is destiny the cause and sum of all existent causes. The most unphilosophical recog-

nise it, in such phrases as 'So it came to pass for
him.'   So and so then was brought to pass, was
'ordered' for the man.   Let us accept such
orders, as we do the orders of our Æsculapius.
They are rough oftentimes, yet we welcome them
in hope of health.   Try to think of the execution
and consummation of Nature's good pleasure as
you do of bodily good health.   Welcome all that
comes, perverse though it may seem, for it leads
you to the goal, the health of the world-order,
the welfare and well-being of Zeus.   He would not
bring this on the individual, were it not for the
good of the whole.   Each change and chance
that nature brings, is in correspondence with that
which exists by her disposal.   On two grounds
then you should accept with acquiescence whatever befalls—first, because it happened to you,
was ordered for you, affected you, as part
of the web issuing from the primal causation ;
secondly, because that which comes upon the
individual contributes to the welfare, the consummation, yea and the survival, of the power
which disposes all things.   As with the parts, so
is it with the causes ; you cannot sever any
fragment of the connected unity, without mutilat-

ing the perfection of the whole. In every act of
discontent, you inflict, so far as in you lies, such
severance and so to say undoing.

Do not give way to disgust, do not lose heart, 9
do not be discouraged at flaws in strict consistency
of conduct : after each check, return to the charge,
thankful, if in most things you acquit yourself like
a man ; and returning, love that to which you
return ; turn once and again to philosophy, not
as the urchin to his master, but as the sore-eyed
to the sponge and egg, or others to salves or
fomentation. Obedience to reason will thus
become not a question of outward show, but of
inward refreshment. Philosophy, remember, wills
only that, which nature within you wills ; while
you willed something not in accord with nature.
'Why what is more agreeable?' says pleasure,
with beguiling voice. Nay but consider, is it
more truly agreeable than loftiness of soul, free,
simple, gracious and holy? What can be more
agreeable than wisdom itself, when you consider
the smooth unhalting flow of its intelligence and
apprehension ?

Things are so wrapped in veils, that to gifted 10
philosophers not a few all certitude seems un-

attainable. Nay to the Stoics themselves such
attainment seems precarious ; and every act of
intellectual assent is fallible ; for where is the
infallible man ?   Pass to the material world ; how
transitory, how worthless it all is, lying at the
disposal of the rake, the harlot or the robber !
Or take the characters of those with whom you
consort ; to bear with even the most gentle-minded
is hard work, nay hard enough to put up even
with oneself. In all this darkness and filth, in
this incessant flux of being and of time, of motion
and things moved, I can imagine nothing that
deserves high prizing or intent pursuit. On
the contrary one must take comfort to oneself,
while awaiting natural dissolution and not chafing
at the delay, and find refreshment solely in
these thoughts——first, nothing will happen to me,
that is not in accord with Nature : secondly, I
need do nothing contrary to the god and deity
within me ; for that no man can compel me to
transgress.

11   What use am I now making of my soul ? that
is the question. Put it to yourself at every turn
and ask——How goes it with that part of me,
known as the governing Inner Self ? Whose soul

have I now? the child's? the lad's? the woman's?
the tyrant's? the cattle's? or the beast's?

This may serve you as a test of what the world 12
calls 'goods.' When once a man pictures the
reality of true and veritable 'goods,'—goods such
as wisdom self-restraint justice and courage—he
cannot with that picture in his mind add the
proverbial jest upon excess of goods; it will not
fit. So long as the goods he pictures are goods
in the popular sense, he will have an open ear
for the poet's epigram, and accept it as perfectly
in point. It is true enough of excellence, as
regarded by the world : otherwise the witticism
would not fail to shock and offend; and applied
to wealth, and the appurtenances of luxury or
show, we accept it as a smart and pointed
epigram. To it then, and ask yourself—Can
I accord the dignity or the idea of 'goods' to
things which do not by their conception preclude
the opprobrious taunt, that the abundance of them
leaves the owner not a corner 'to ease himself in'?[1]

---

[1] The reference is to a fragment of Menander, restored by Cobet
with the help of this paragraph, and running thus :—

There's an old proverb, sir, against profusion,
If you'll excuse the somewhat coarse allusion—
With such a glut of goods, amid the pelf
You've not a corner left in which to ease yourself.

13   I consist of two elements, the causal and the material ; neither of which can perish or cease to exist, any more than they came into being from previous non-existence. It follows then that every part of me will be coordinated by change into some other part of the world-order, and that again into some new part, and so on *ad infinitum.* My existence is but a stage in the succession, and so too that of my parents, and so backwards once more *ad infinitum.* There is no objection to this view, even supposing the world is ordered in finite cosmic cycles.

14   Reason and the reasoning process are in themselves and their action self-sufficing faculties. They derive their impulse from their own beginning ; they march to their appointed end. Hence the term rectitude[1] applied to conduct, signifying that it never swerves from the right path.

15   Nothing strictly appertains to man, which is not appointed for man, as man. Such things are not among man's requirements, they have no warranty in man's nature, and they do not perfect or complete that nature. Neither therefore does

[1] The etymological correspondence between κατόρθωσις *rectitude* or *rightness of action,* and ὀρθότης *directness* of movement, baffles literal translation.

man's true end lie in them, nor that which con-
summates the end, to wit the good. Were any
of these things appointed for man, contempt and
mutiny against them could not be appointed likewise ; nor could self-detachment from them be
laudable ; nor, if they were truly goods, could
going short of them minister to goodness.
Whereas, the more a man deprives himself of
such things, or acquiesces in such deprivation, the
better he becomes.

Repeat impressions, and your understanding 16
will assimilate itself to them ; for the soul takes
the dye of its impressions. Steep it then constantly in such sequences as these :——where life is
possible, so too is right life ; you live at court,
then at court too live aright. Or again——for
whatsoever purpose each thing is constituted,
thereto it tends ; and whereto it tends, there lies
its end ; and where its end is, there too is each
thing's gain and good. It follows that the good
of the reasoning creature lies in social action ; for
it has been long since shown, that we are made
for social action. Is it not palpable, that the
lower forms exist for the higher, and the higher
for one another ? And things with breath of life

are higher than things without ; and things with reason than with breath alone.

17   Pursuit of the impossible is idiotcy ; yet for the worthless to abstain from such pursuit is impossible.

18   Whatever comes upon a man, nature has formed him to bear. The same trials befall another ; from ignorance of what has happened, or for show of superiority, he stands stedfast and undemoralised. What ! ignorance and self-complacency more strong than wisdom ! For shame !

19   Things material cannot touch the soul in any way whatever, nor find entrance there, nor have power to sway or move it. Soul is self-swayed, self-moved ; and soul modifies the objects upon which it plays into accord with the judgments which it approves.

20   In one respect man stands to us in the closest of all relations—we must do good to them and bear with them. But in so far as individuals obstruct my proper action, man falls into the category of things indifferent, just as much as sun or wind or wild beast. They may indeed contravene some particular action, but inner impulse and disposition they cannot contravene, for these are subject to reservation and also have inner modifying power. For the understanding modifies and converts every

hindrance to action into furtherance of its prime
aim ; so that checks to action actually advance it,
and obstacles in the way promote progress.

In the universe honour that which is highest ; 21
and the highest is that which all else subserves,
and which overrules all. So too within yourself
honour the highest ;. there too it is the same in
kind : it is that within you which all other powers
subserve, and by which your life is disposed.

What is not injurious to the city, cannot injure 22
the citizen. Whenever you feel the sense of
injury, apply this criterion——If the city is not
injured, neither am I myself. If the city is
injured, do not fly into a rage with the author of
the injury ; ask, what misconception prompted it ?

Bethink thee often of the swiftness with which 23
things that are or come to be sweep past and
disappear. Being is a river in continual flow ; its
action for ever changing, its causes infinite in
variation. Hardly a thing stands fast, even within
your own purview. Infinity past and to come is
a fathomless gulf, into which vanish all things.
How foolish then in such a world to pant, to
strain, to fume, as though time and troubling
were for long !

24 Think of the sum of being, and in what a morsel of it you partake ; the sum of time, compared with the brief atom assigned to you ; of destiny, and the jot you are of it !

25 Does another wrong me ? See he to that——his disposition, his actions are his own. For me, I have at this present just that which universal nature wills me to have, and am doing just that which my own nature wills me to do.

26 Whether the physical currents run smooth or rough, let them not sway the governing and sovereign self within. It must not confound itself with them, but remain self-determinant, and circumscribe all such affections to the parts affected. When these assimilate themselves to the understanding by that sympathy of parts which exists in an organic unity, we must not attempt to resist the physical sensation ; but on the other hand the Inner Self must not go on to assume on its own authority, that the affection is either good or bad.

27 Live with the gods. And he lives with the gods, who ever presents to them his soul acceptant of their dispensations, and busy about the will of god, even that particle of Zeus, which Zeus gives

to every man for his controller and governor—to wit, his mind and reason.

Do you get angry at rank armpits? or 28 at foul breath? What would be the good? Mouth, armpits are what they are, and being so, the given effluvia must result.—'Yes, but nature has given man reason, man can comprehend and understand what offends!'—'Very good! *Ergo* you too have reason; use your moral reason to move his; show him his error, admonish him. If he attends, you will amend him; no need for anger—you are not a ranter, or a whore.'

You can live here on earth, as you think to 29 live after your departure hence. If others disallow, then indeed it is time to quit; yet even so, not as one aggrieved. The cabin smokes—so I take leave of it. Why make ado? But so long as there is no such notice to quit, I remain free, and none will hinder me from doing what I will; that is, to conform to the nature of a reasonable social being.

The mind of the universe is social. For see, 30 it has made the lower for sake of the higher; and combines the higher in a mutual harmony. See how it gives its mandate, secures coordination,

F

apportions everywhere according to worth, and combines the dominants in mutual accord.

31   What of your past behaviour to the gods, to your parents, brothers, wife, children, teachers, tutors, friends, intimates, household? Can you, in respect of all, say——

> I wrought no froward deed, said no rude word.[1]

Yet recollect all that you have gone through, and all you have found strength to bear: remember that the story of your life is fully told and its service accomplished; recollect how many sights of beauty you have seen; how many pleasures and pains foregone; how many ambitions disregarded; and how often you have shown grace to the graceless.

32   How is it that souls untrained and ignorant confound the trained and wise? The answer is, What soul is trained and wise? That only which knows the beginning and the end, and the reason diffused through all being, which through all eternity administers the universe in periodic cycles.

33   A little while and you will be ashes or a skeleton, a name or not so much as a name; and

---

[1] Homer, *Od.* iv. 690.

what is a name but so much rattle and sound?
Life and all its prizes are empty, rotten, insignificant, snapping puppies or quarrelsome children,
that laugh and anon fall to crying. Faith and
honour, justice and truth have taken wing—

From widewayed earth to heaven.[1]

What then still detains you here? The objects
of sense are changeful and unstable; the organs
of sense dim, and easily imposed upon ; poor soul
itself mere exhalation of the blood. And good
repute in such a world is emptiness. What then?
serenely you await the end, be it extinction or
transmutation. While the hour yet tarries, what
help is there? what, but to reverence and bless
the gods, to do good to men, "to endure and
to refrain"? and of all that lies outside the
bounds of flesh and breath, to remember that it is
not yours, nor in your power.

Life in smooth flow is yours, if only you hold 34
straight on, keeping the track in views and acts.
Two things are common to the soul of god, the
soul of man, and the soul of every rational creature.
First, another cannot contravene their purpose;
secondly, in disposition and action attuned to

[1] Hesiod, *Works and Days*, v. 197.

justice lies their good, and therewith cessation of desire.

35   If the fault is not in me, nor the act by fault of mine, nor the common weal injured, why trouble more about it ?   What injury is it to the common weal ?

36   Do not let impression overbear judgment; cope with it according to your power, and by scale of worth.   Should you come short at all in things of secondary worth, do not regard it as an injury —that were an evil habitude.   Like the old man in the play, who at parting begged for his foster-child's top, but did not forget that after all it was a top and nothing more—so be it too with life.

Declaiming from the rostra you cry, ' My good man, have you forgotten what these good things come to after all ? '—' True,' comes the answer, ' but for all that eagerly pursued.'—' Is that a good reason for your joining in the folly ? '—Whereso-ever stranded, I can at any time become a man ' of fortune.'   For ' fortune ' means self-appropriation of endowments truly good, and good endowments are—good moods, good impulses, good acts.[1]

---

[1] The references that might clear up this section have perished, and both in language and arrangement much is obscure and unintelligible.

BOOK VI

ΝΟῦϹ ΔΙΕΚΌϹΜΗϹΕ ΠΆΝΤΑ.—ANAXAGORAS

THE substance of the universe is tractable and 1
plastic : and in the disposing reason there inheres
no cause that makes for evil, for it contains no evil,
does no evil, and inflicts no injury on anything.   By
it all things come into being and run their course.

Do your duty—whether shivering or warm, 2
never mind ; heavy-eyed, or with your fill of sleep ;
in evil report or in good report ; dying or with
other work in hand.   Dying after all is but one
among life's acts ; there too our business is 'to
make the best of it.'

Look within ; do not let the specific quality or 3
worth of anything escape you.

All material things soon change—by evapora- 4
tion, where there is unity of being ; otherwise, by
dispersion.

5   The disposing reason knows its condition, its action, and the material on which it works.

6   Not to do likewise is the best revenge.

7   Be it your one delight and refreshment, to pass from social act to social act, remembering god.

8   Our Inner governing Self is that which is self-excited and self-swayed, which makes itself just what it wills to be, and which makes all that befalls seem to itself what it wills.

9   All things run their course in accordance with the nature of the universe ; there is no other competing nature, that either comprehends this from without, or is itself comprehended within, or that exists externally and unattached.

10   The world is either a welter of alternate combination and dispersion, or a unity of order and providence. If the former, why crave to linger on in such a random medley and confusion? why take thought for anything except the eventual ‘dust to dust’? why vex myself? do what I will, dispersion will overtake me. But on the other alternative, I reverence, I stand stedfast, I find heart in the power that disposes all.

11   When torn in pieces as it were by press of work, straightway fall back upon yourself, and do

not break tune or rhythm more than you must ; by thus habitually falling back on self, you will be more master of the harmony.

Had you a stepmother and a mother too, you 12 would be courteous to the former, but for companionship would turn continually to your mother. For you the court is one, philosophy the other. To her then turn and turn again, and find your refreshment ; for she makes even court life seem bearable to you, and you in it.

In regarding meats or eatables, you say, So 13 and so is the carcase of a fish, or fowl, or pig ; or again, Falernian is so much extract of grape juice ; the purple robe sheep's wool dyed with juices of the shell-fish ; copulation, a mere physical process. Regards of this kind explore and search the actual facts, opening your eyes to what things really are. So should you deal with life as a whole, and where regards are over-credulous, strip the facts bare, see through their worthlessness, and so get rid of their vaunted embellishments. Pride is the arch sophist ; and when you flatter yourself you are most engrossed in virtuous ends, then are you most befooled. Remember what Crates says of Xenocrates himself.

14   Ordinary admiration fastens as a rule on natural objects, whose unity is due to 'inward hold'[1] or to organic growth, such for instance as stones, timber, fig-trees, vines or olives : as intelligence advances, it takes note of soul-unities as seen in flocks and herds: the yet more gentle-minded are appealed to by the indwelling of rational soul, not as yet universal in range, but manifesting itself in art, or some form of proficiency, or in the bare possession of troops of slaves.[2] But he who honours rational soul, of universal and social aims, no longer heeds aught else, but strives before everything to keep his own soul alive and quick to rational and social impulses, and joins with all of like kind in working to this end.

15   Things hasten into being, things hasten out of it ; even as a thing comes into being, this or that part is extinct : phases of flux and variation continuously renew the world, just as the unfailing

[1] The terminology is technical : for explanation, see Introduction, p. lvi.

[2] The reference to slaves may seem abrupt and irrelevant. But at Rome the connoisseur gratified his tastes, or established his reputation, by the employment of slaves : the men of light and leading kept their 'slave' establishment of painters, gem-cutters, grammarians, scribes, philosophers, and the like, just as the wealthy of to-day collect libraries or pictures or blue china.

current of time perennially renews eternity.   In
this river of existence how can one prize much any
of the things that race by, on none of which one
can take firm stand ? it were like setting one's love
on some sparrow that flits past and in an instant
is out of sight.   Life itself may be regarded as so
much exhalation of blood and respiration of air.
A single breath, an inhalation and emission, such
as we perform every moment, fitly compares with
that final emission of the quickening *pneuma*, which
you received but yesterday at birth, and now render
back to the element from which you first drew it.

What is worth prizing ?   Not the power of 16
transpiration, which we share with plants ; nor
respiration, shared with cattle and brute beasts ; nor
the impressions of sense ; nor the pulls of impulse ;
nor herding with each other ; nor nutrition, which
after all is no better than excretion.   What then ?
the clapping of men's hands ?   No, nor clapping
of their tongues ; for the applause of the multitude
is but a clatter of tongues.   Discarding reputation
then, what is there that remains prizeworthy ?
To my mind, this—command of one's appointed
being, alike for action and inaction, in the direction
of its guiding pursuits and arts.   For the aim of

every art is right adaptation of the product to the end for which it is produced ; the gardener who tends the vine, the horse-breaker, the dog-trainer, all seek this end ; all forms of training and teaching make for some object ; there lies the true end of worth : secure that, and you need lay claim to nothing else.   Give up prizing a multitude of other things, or you will never be free, self-sufficing, passionless.   Inevitably you will envy, grudge, and look askance at those who can rob you of your prize, and plot against those who have what you yourself covet : the sense of something lacking makes discord within, and leads on to constant complaining against the gods.   To respect and honour your own understanding alone will put you at satisfaction with yourself, in harmony with all things social, and in accord with the gods, well pleased that is to say with their dispensation and world-ordering.

17   Upwards, downwards, round and round, course the elements.   But the motion of virtue is none of these ; of some diviner mould, it pursues the even tenor of courses unimagined.

18   What a thing is man !   To contemporaries living at their side they will not give a good word,

yet themselves set store on the good word of
posterity, whom they have never seen nor will see.
It comes near to being vexed at not having the
good word of your ancestors !

Because your own strength is unequal to the 19
task, do not assume that it is beyond the powers
of man ; but if anything is within the powers and
province of man, believe that it is within your
own compass also.

In the gymnasium, when some one scratches 20
us with his nails or in lunging hits our head, we
do not protest, or take offence, or harbour rooted
suspicions of design ; no, we just keep our eye
upon him, not with hostility or suspicion, but with
good-tempered avoidance. So too with the rest
of life ; let us shut our eyes to much in those who
are as it were tussling at our side. It is open
to us to avoid ; we need not suspect or quarrel.

If any one can convince and show me that 21
some view or action of mine is wrong, I will cheerfully change : I seek the truth, which never yet
hurt any man. What hurts is persisting in self-
deceit and ignorance.

I do my own duty ; all things else distract me 22
not ; for they are either things without breath, or

things without reason, or things misguided, that know not the way.

23   You have reason ; unreasoning creatures and the world of material things have none : therefore in your dealings with them rise superior and free. Men have reason ; therefore in your dealings with them, own the social tie. In all things call upon the gods. And trouble not over the time it occupies ; three hours so spent avail.

24   Death put Alexander of Macedon and his stable boy on a par. Either they were received into the seminal principles of the universe, or were alike dispersed into atoms.

25   Consider how many things, physical and psychical, go on at one and the same moment within each one of us ; no wonder then that many more, yea all things created, co-inhere together in the one great whole, which we call the universe.

26   If some one asks you, ' How is Antoninus spelt ? ', will you excite yourself over the utterance of each letter ? Well then, if some one flies into a rage, are you going to rage back ? Will you not rather quietly enumerate the characters in order one by one ? Here too remember that every duty is the sum of given units. Keep

steadily to these, without perturbation and with
out retaliation of ill-will, pursuing methodically
the appointed end.

Cruel, is it not, to prevent men from pushing 27
for what looks like their own advantage? Yet in
a sense you forbid them that, when you resent
their going wrong. They are doubtless bent
upon their own objects and advantage.—'Not
so,' you say, 'in reality.'—Teach them so then
and prove it, instead of resenting it.

Death is rest from impressions of sense, from 28
pulls of impulse, from searchings of thought, and
from service of the flesh.

Shame on it! in this mortal life, the soul to 29
lose heart before the body!

See that you be not be-Cæsared, steeped in 30
that dye, as too often happens. Keep yourself
simple, good, sincere, grave, unaffected, a friend to
justice, god-fearing, considerate, affectionate, and
strenuous in duty. Struggle to remain such as
philosophy would have you. Respect the gods,
save men. *Life is short;* and the earthly life
has but one fruit, inward holiness and social acts.
In all things the disciple of Antoninus. Remember his resolute championship of reason, his

unvarying equability, his holiness, his serenity of
look, his affability, his dislike of ostentation, his
keenness for certitude about the facts ; how he
would never drop a subject, till he saw into it
thoroughly and understood clearly ; how he bore
unjust reproaches without a word ; how he was
never in a hurry ; how he gave no ear to slander ;
how accurately he scrutinised character and
action ; never carping, or craven, or suspicious, or
pedantic ; how frugal were his requirements, in
house and bed and dress and food and service ;
how industrious he was and how long-suffering ;
how, thanks to his abstemious living, he could
restrain himself till evening, without even relieving his physical needs at the usual hour.
Remember his constancy and evenness in friendship, his forbearance to outspoken opposition,
his cheerful acceptance of correction ; and how
god-fearing he was, though without superstition.
Remember all this, that so your last hour may
find you with a conscience clear as his.

31   Recall your true, your sober self : shake off
the slumber and realise that they were dreams
that troubled you.   Now wide awake once more,
look on it all as a dream.

I am of body and soul. To the body all 32
things are indifferent ; it has no power to make
differences.   To the understanding all things are
indifferent, excepting its own activities.   But its
own activities are all within its own control :—
Moreover, even of these, it is concerned only with
the present ; future or past activities are at the
moment themselves indifferent.

No pain of hand or of foot is contrary to 33
nature, so long as the foot is doing foot's work,
and the hand hand's.   So too to man, as man,
no pain is contrary to nature, so long as he is
doing man's work.   If it violates nature, for him
it ceases to exist and is no evil for him.

What rare pleasures please robbers, rakes, 34
parricides, tyrants !

See how common craftsmen accommodate 35
themselves to some extent to ignorant employers,
but all the same hold fast to the principles of their
craft and decline to depart from them.   Shame
on us, that the architect and the doctor should
have more respect to the principles of their craft,
than man to his, which he shares with the gods.

In the universe Asia and Europe are but 36
corners ; ocean a drop ; Athos a grain ; the span

of time, a moment in eternity. All things are small, unstable, vanishing. All issue from one source, starting directly from the universal Soul, or derivatively consequent. Even the lion's jaw, venom, and all things baleful, thorns mud or what not, are consequents of things grand and beautiful. Do not regard them as alien to that which you worship, but reflect upon the common source of all.

37   He who sees what now is, hath seen all, all that was from eternity, all that shall be without end ; for all things are of one kind and of one form.

38   Consider oftentimes the bond that knits all things in the world-order, and their mutual relationship. All things as it were intertwine, all are in so far mutually dear ; for thing follows thing in order, as the result of the continuous vibration that thrills through all, and the unity of all being.

39   Put yourself in harmony with the things among which your lot is cast ; love those with whom you have your portion, with a true love.

40   If any tool, or implement, or utensil is doing the work for which it was produced, it is well

with it ; though there the producer is no longer by. But in nature's unities the power which produced is still within them and abides : so much the more then must you have respect to it, and believe that, if you handle and employ all according to its will, you have all to your mind. So is it with the universe, whose all is to its mind.

If you assume anything that lies outside your 41 own control to be a good for you or an evil, then the incidence of such evil or the depriva-tion of such good drives you into finding fault with the gods, and hating the men who bring about, or as you suspect will bring about, such deprivation or incidence : and oftentimes we sin, from being bent upon such things. But if we account only that which is in our own control as good or bad, there remains no reason either for arraigning god, or setting ourselves at feud with man.

One and all we work towards one consumma- 42 tion, some knowingly and intelligently, others unconsciously. Just as Heraclitus, was it not, said of those who sleep, that they too are at work, fellow-workers in the conduct of the universe. One works in one way, another in another ; and

G

not least, he who finds fault and who tries to resist and undo what is done. Even of such the world has need. It remains then to make sure, in which ranks you range yourself; he who disposes all things will in any case make good use of you, and will receive you into the number of his fellow-workers and auxiliaries. Only do not you play foil to the rest like the coarse jest in the Comedy, to use the figure of Chrysippus.[1]

43   Does the sun claim the rain's work? or Æsculapius that of Ceres? or again, each single star—are not all different, yet all co-operating to the same end?

44   If the gods took counsel about me and what ought to befall me, doubtless they counselled well: a god of ill counsel one can scarce imagine. And what should impel them to seek my hurt? What advantage were it either to them or to the universe, which is the first object of their providence? If they took no counsel about me in particular, for the universe at all events

---

[1] Plutarch, *De Comm. Not.* xiv., elucidates the reference. 'Just as comedies introduce jests which are vulgar enough in themselves, yet improve the piece as a whole; so too you may criticise evil regarded by itself, yet allow that taken with all else it has its use.'

they did, and the consequent results I am bound
to welcome acquiescently. If indeed they take
no thought for anything at all——an impious
creed,——then let us have done with sacrifice and
prayer and oaths, and all other observances by
which we own the presence and the nearness of
the gods. But if after all they take no thought
for anything to do with us, then it is in my own
power to take thought for myself ; and what I
have to consider is my own interest ; and the
true interest of everything is to conform to its
own constitution and nature ; and my nature
owns reason and social obligation ; socially, as
Antoninus, my city and country is Rome, as a
man, the world. These are the societies, whose ˋ
advantage can alone be good to me.

All that befalls the individual is for the good 45
of the whole. That might suffice. But looking
closer you will perceive the general rule, that
what is good for one man is good for others too.
But 'good' or 'interest' must be regarded as
wider in range than things indifferent.

As in the amphitheatre or other places of 46
amusement the monotony of tedious repetitions
makes the spectacle pall, so is it with the experi-

ence of life; up and down, everything is one
monotonous round.   How long?   How long?

47   Constantly realise the dead—men of all kinds,
of every vocation, of every nationality, all dead.
Come down if you will to Philistion, Phœbus,
Origanion.   Pass now to other 'tribes of the
great dead': we too must pass whither so many
have gone before—skilled orators, august philosophers, Heraclitus, Pythagoras, and Socrates;
the heroes of old time; generals and monarchs
that came after; and in their train Eudoxus,
Hipparchus, Archimedes, minds keen and lofty,
wits busy supple and precocious; yes and the
Menippuses too, who have made man's fateful
fleeting life their jest.   Realise all these, all long
since in the dust.   What matters it to them?
what, still more, to those who have not even left
a name?   Here one thing is of real worth, to
live out life in truth and justice, with charity even
to the false and the unjust.

48   When you want to cheer your spirits, consider the excellences of those about you—one so
effective, another so unassuming, another so open-
handed, and so on and so on.   Nothing is more
cheering than exemplifications of virtue in the

characters of those about us, suggesting themselves as copiously as possible. We should keep
them always ready to hand.

Does it annoy you to weigh so many pounds 49
only, instead of three hundred? It is the same
with living so many years only, and not more.
You are content with the quantum of matter
allowed you; be so too with the time.

Try to persuade men: but act, whether it is 50
liked or not, when principles of justice so demand.
If some one obstructs you by force, welcome the
rebuff and own no pang, utilising the hindrance for
exercise of virtue in another form. Endeavour,
remember, was subject to reservation, and you
did not aspire to impossibilities. To what then
did you aspire? To the endeavour just such as
it was. Gain that, and the object, for which we
were sent into the world, is realised.

The ambitious man rests personal good upon 51
action that depends on others; the man of pleasure
upon personal affections of the body; the man of
mind upon personal action.

You can refuse to entertain the view, and with 52
it all tumult of soul; things in themselves have
no power to force our judgments.

53 Practise attention to what others say, and do your best to get into the speaker's mind.

54 What is not good for the swarm is not good for the bee.

55 If the sailors abused the pilot, or the sick the physician, would they have any other object, than to make him save the crew or heal the patients?

56 How many with whom I came into the world have already quitted it!

57 To the jaundiced honey seems bitter; to the hydrophobe water is horrible; to children a ball is a thing of beauty. Then why lose my temper? Think you false opinion takes less effect, than bile in the jaundiced or the virus in hydrophobia?

58 No one can stop you from living according to the principle of your own nature: nothing will happen to you contrary to the principle of the universal nature.

59 Think what men are! whom they care to satisfy! for what results! and by what actions! How soon time will bury all! how much it has buried already!

BOOK VII

Ἦθος ἀνθρώπου Δαίμων.—HERACLITUS
Ἦθος πηγὴ Βίου.—ZENO

WHAT is evil? It is what you have seen again 1
and again ; and in every case that occurs, remind
yourself that it is what you have seen again and
again. Up and down, everywhere you will find
the same things, repeating themselves at every
page of history, ancient mediæval or quite recent ;
repeating themselves every day in our own cities
and homes. Nothing is new ; all is stale and all
is fleeting.

Look to first principles ; and how can they be 2
deadened, but by the extinction of the impressions
to which they correspond? and these you may
continually kindle into glow. On any given thing,
I have the power to take the right view ; if so,
why vex myself? Things outside my own under-

standing are nothing to my understanding. Grasp that, and you stand upright : you can ever renew your life.   See things once more as you saw them before ; and therein you have new life.

A mimic pageant, a stage spectacle, flocking sheep and herding cows, an armed brawl, a bone flung to curs, a crumb dropped in the fish-tanks, toiling of burdened ants, the scamper of scurrying mice, puppets pulled with strings——such is life.   In such surroundings you must take your stand, considerate and undisdainful ; yet under-stand the while, that the measure of the man's worth is the worth of his aims.

In talk we must intelligently understand what is said, and in endeavour what is done.   In the latter, look straight at the aim to which it tends ; in the former, watch carefully the meaning conveyed.

Have I understanding equal to the task, yes or no?   If yes, I use it for the work, as a tool supplied by Nature : if no, either I step aside in favour of some one better able to accomplish the work, or, if duty for some reason forbids that, I act as best I can, securing the help of some one, who availing himself of my direction can carry out

what is opportune and serviceable for the common
fellowship. For all I do, whether alone or with
another's help, should aim solely at what promotes
the service and harmony of all.

How many, after choruses of praise, have 6
dropped into oblivion ; how many, who swelled the
chorus, have long since disappeared !

Do not be ashamed of being helped. It is 7
incumbent upon you to do your appointed work,
like a soldier in the breach. What if you are lame
and cannot scale the battlement alone, but can
with another's help ?

Let not the future perturb you. You will face 8
it, if so be, with the same reason which is yours to
meet the present.

All things intertwine one with another, in a 9
holy bond : scarce one thing is disconnected from
another. In due co-ordination they combine for
one and the same order. For the world-order
is one made out of all things, and god is one
pervading all, and being is one, and law is one,
even the common reason of all beings possessed of
mind, and truth is one : seeing that truth is the
one perfecting of beings one in kind and endowed
with the same reason.

10   Every material thing fast vanishes into the sum of being ; and every cause is quickly re-assumed into the universal reason ; and the memory of everything is quickly buried beneath eternity.

11   To the reasoning being the act which is according to nature is likewise according to reason.   •

12   Upright or uprighted.

13   As in physical organisms the unity is made up of separate limbs, so among reasoning things the reason is distributed among individuals, constituted for unity of co-operation.   This thought will strike more home, if you constantly repeat to yourself ' I am a member of the sum of reasoning things.' If you substitute *meros* for *melos*—part for member—you do not yet love men from your heart ; you have yet no certitude of joy in doing kindnesses ; they are still bare duty, not yet a good deed to yourself.

14   Affect what will the parts of my being liable to affection from without ! the parts affected can if they please find fault.   So long as I do not view the infliction as an evil, I remain uninjured. And I need not so view it.

15   Whatever any one else does or says, my duty

is to be good; just as gold or emerald or purple for ever says, Whatever any one else does or says, my duty is to be emerald and keep my proper hue.

The Inner Self does not agitate itself—does 16 not, for instance, terrify itself or excite its own desires. If some one else can terrify or vex it, let him. It will never itself induce such moods by self-assumption. The body must take thought for its own hurts, as best it can, and if hurt say so; the soul, to which belong terror, vexation or any assumption of the kind, refuses hurt; you cannot wrest it to any such judgment. The Inner Self is self-complete, subject to none but self-created needs, and free accordingly from every perturbation or contravention, except such as arise from its own action.

Happiness — literally, god within, or good.[1] 17 What are you about here, Impression, you deceiver? Be off, sir—as you came: I will none of you.—'You have come as an old friend,' you say?—Well, peace be with you: only, begone!

Does change terrify you? Yet what can come 18

[1] A play on the derivation of the Greek word *Eudaimonia*, and untranslatable.

into being without change? What after all is dearer, or more proper to Nature? Can you have your bath, without change passing upon the firewood? or nourishment, without change passing upon the viands? Can any serviceable thing be accomplished without change? Do you not see that change within yourself is of a piece with this, and equally indispensable to Nature?

19   Being is as it were a torrent, in and out of which all bodies pass, coalescing and co-operating with the whole, as the various parts in us do with one another. How many a Chrysippus, how many a Socrates, how many an Epictetus has time past swallowed up! Extend the thought to every man and every thing whatsoever.

20   One thing alone torments me, the fear of doing something which is not meant for the constitution of man, or in the way not meant, or not meant as yet.

21   Soon you will have forgotten all; soon all will have forgotten you.

22   It is man's special gift to love even those who fall into blunders: it operates as soon as it suggests, that men are your brothers, that sin is of ignorance and unintentional, that in a little you will both be dead, that, above all, no injury is done

you ; your Inner Self is not made worse than it was before.

From the sum of being, as from wax, Nature 23 now moulds a nag ; then breaks it up, and utilises the material to make a tree ; next, a man ; next, some other thing ; and each has but a brief exist- ence. But it is no hardship for the chest to be broken up, any more than to be knocked together.

A scowl upon the face is a violation of nature. 24 Repeated often, beauty dies with it, and finally becomes quenched, past all rekindling. From this fact try to understand, that it is contrary to reason ; if once sensibility to sin is lost, what object in still living on ?

A little while, and nature which disposeth all 25 things will change all that you see, and of their substance make new things, and others again of theirs, that the world may be ever fresh.

When any one does you a wrong, set yourself 26 at once to consider, what was the point of view, good or bad, that led him wrong. As soon as you perceive it, you will be sorry for him, not surprised or angry. For your own view of good is either the same as his, or something like in kind : and you will make allowance. Or supposing your own view of good and bad has altered, you will find charity for his mistake come easier.

27   Do not imagine yourself to have what you have not ; but take full account of the excellences which you do possess, and in gratitude remember how you would hanker after them, if you had them not.   At the same time take care that in thus hugging them, you do not get into the habit of prizing them so much, that without them you would be perturbed.

28   Withdraw into yourself.   By nature our reasoning Inner Self finds self-contentment in just dealing and the calm which follows in its train.

29   Efface impression.   Check the pulls of impulse. Circumscribe time to the present.   Recognise all that befalls, either yourself, or another.   Divide and analyse each material thing into cause and matter.   Realise your last hour.   Let the wrong remain with him, with whom it first originated.

30   Keep thought intent on what is said ; enter with your mind into what is done and what is doing it.

31   Be your brightness that of simplicity and self-respect, and of indifference to all that is not virtue or vice.   Love mankind.   Walk with God. " *All things by law* " saith the sage.   Yes !

Gods or atoms, it suffices to remember that *All things are by law.* Two words sum all.

Of Death. Death, in a universe of atoms, is 32 dispersion ; but if all is a unity, death is either extinction or transmutation.

Of Pain. Pain that is past bearing, brings an 33 end ; pain that lasts, can be borne. The understanding in abstraction maintains its calm, and the Inner Self is unimpaired. As for the parts injured by the pain, let them (as best they can) state their own case.

Of Glory and the vainglorious. Look at their 34 understandings, what they are, what they shun, what they seek. And remember that as drift hides drift of piling sand, so too in life what comes after soon hides what went before.

From Plato. "'*Think you the man of lofty* 35 *understanding, whose vision ranges over all time and all being, can think great things of man's life ?*'—'*Impossible.*'—'*Such an one then will attach no very great importance to death.*'—'*Death ! no indeed.*'"[1]

From Antisthenes. "*Well - doing, ill-report* 36 —*a king's portion.*"

[1] Plato, *Republic*, vi. 486 A.

87　　Shame on it—for feature and gesture and exterior adornment to obey the bidding of the understanding, and for the understanding not to rule its own gesture and adornment.

88　　　　Fret not at circumstance, which recks not of it. [1]

89　　　　To the immortal gods and us give joy.

40　　　　Lives are reaped like ears of corn,
　　　　One is spared, another shorn. [2]

41　　　　Though I and both my sons be spurned of God,
　　　　There is be sure a reason.

42　　　　Right on my side and justice. [3]

43　　*" No wailing with the wailers, and no fever-throbs."*

44　　From Plato.　*" To such an one I should justly reply—There, friend, you are mistaken ; a man who is worth anything at all should not reckon the chances of life or death, but simply ask himself, in regard to any action, Is it right or is it wrong ? a good man's action or a bad ? "* [4]

45　　*" The truth is, gentlemen, it stands thus. Wherever a man's post is, whether selected by*

---

[1] Euripides, *Bellerophon* (Fr. 298).
[2] Euripides, *Hypsipyle* (Fr. 752).
[3] Aristophanes, *Acharnians*, v. 661.
[4] Plato, *Apology* 28 B.

*himself or assigned by his commander, there, as I
believe, it is his duty to stand fast in the hour of
danger, recking nothing of death or anything else
in comparison with dishonour."* [1]

   " O my friend, I would have you see that the 46
*noble and the good is possibly something quite
different from saving and being saved; the true
man will take little account of a few years more
or less of life; that he will leave to God, not
hugging life, but believing that, as the women say,
no man can escape the hour of destiny; and he
will turn his thoughts to consider how he can best
spend the term of life appointed him to live."* [2]

   " Survey the courses of the stars, and join their 47
heavenly race." Constantly realise the mutual
transformations of the elements. For such
imaginings purge away the soils of this earth-
life.

   A fine thought of Plato's. So likewise in 48
discoursing of men, we should, *"as from some
eminence, survey earth and its herds,"* — camps,
farms, marriages, severances, births, deaths, the
babel of the law - courts, wastes of wilderness,
motley barbarians, festivals, dirges, fairs, all the

   [1] Plato, *Apology* 28 E.   [2] Plato, *Gorgias* 512 D E.

H

pell-mell of life and the order wrought out of opposites.

49   Review the past, its changing powers and dynasties, and you can forecast the future too. The same forms will in every case repeat themselves ; the march of things keeps steady time. To witness human life for forty years, or forty thousand, is all one.   What more will you see ?

50   Growths of earth return to earth ;
                Seeds that spring of heavenly birth,
                To heavenly realms anon revert—[1]

yes, by dissolution of the atomic combinations, and consequent scattering of the impassive elements.

51   By meat and drink and sorcery
                Divert the sluice of destiny ![2]

          •   •   •   •   •

                God sends the breeze ; then murmur not,
                Undaunted face the apportioned lot."

52   " *More knock-me-down* "[3] I grant, but not more social-minded, more self-respecting, more

---

[1] Euripides, *Chrysippus* (Fr. 833).

[2] Euripides, *Supplices*, v. 1110-1.

[3] The word belongs to the Dorian vernacular, and recalls at once the Spartan apophthegm dear to Stoic teachers.   Plutarch thus gives it, *Apoph. Lac.* 236 E.   A young Spartan was vanquished at Olympia. 'So your antagonist,' said some one, 'proved the better man.'—' Better, nay ! but more knock-me-down.'

disciplined to circumstance, more charitable to
the oversights of neighbours.

Where an act can be performed in accord- 53
ance with that reason which men share with gods,
have no fear.　Where service may be rendered by
action that keeps the even way and tenor of your
appointed being, you need apprehend no harm.

Everywhere, always, thus much is in your 54
power, god-fearing contentment with your present
hap, just dealing in your present circle, and
absorption in the present impression, that none
intrude uncertified.

Look not aside to other men's Selves, but fix 55
your eyes straight on the goal, to which nature
guides you——nature at large by circumstance,
your own nature by the acts required of you.
Everything must act according to its constitution : and by constitution all other things exist
for sake of those with reason, just as in every
other case the lower exist for sake of the higher,
and things with reason for sake of one another.
In man's constitution the primary element is the
social ; the second, that it is proof against the
bodily affections ; for the motions of reason and
mind are self-determinant, and refuse subordin-

ation to the motions of sense or impulse, both which are animal in kind. The intellectual claim primacy, and will not be brought into subjection ; and justly so, for their function is to use all the rest. Thirdly, the constitution of man's reason includes circumspection and immunity from error. Let but the Inner Self hold fast to these and keep a straight course, and it comes by its own.

56   As one dead, and who has heretofore not found life, resolve to live out what is left in nature's way, as a gift of grace.

57   Love that which comes to pass inwoven in the web, that and nothing else. What could better suit your need ?

58   At each cross hap keep before your eyes those who had the same to bear, who consequently were vexed and aggrieved and full of complaining. Where are they now ? nowhere. Why follow their example then, instead of leaving others' moods to those who sway or are swayed by them, and devoting yourself solely to making what use you can of the mishap ? Then you will put it to good use ; you will make it your working material. Aim only and care only in each action to stand self-approved. In both respects remember that

that on which action is based is in itself in-different.[1]

Dig within. Within is the fountain of good ; 59 ever dig, and it will ever well forth water.

Keep the body as well as the face in control, 60 and avoid contortions, either when in motion or at rest. Just as in the face understanding exhibits itself by preserving intelligence and comeliness, we must make the same demand of the body as a whole. It needs no practised artifice to ensure this much.

Life is more like wrestling than dancing ; it 61 must be ready to keep its feet against all onsets however unexpected.

Always be clear whose approbation it is you 62 wish to secure, and what their inner principles are. Then you will not find fault with unintended blunders ; neither will you need credentials from them, when you look into the well-springs of their views and impulses.

"*No soul*," says the philosopher,[2] "*wilfully* 63 *misses truth* ;" no nor justice either, nor wisdom, nor charity, nor any other excellence. It is

[1] The whole is doubtful interpretation, and in parts corrupt.
[2] Plato, as twice quoted by Epictetus, *Arr.* 1, 28, 2 and 22.

essential to remember this continually ; it will make you gentler with every one.

64   In sickness or pain remind yourself that it cannot demean or vitiate your pilot understanding ; it does not impair it on the universal or the social side.   In most cases you may find support in the saying of Epicurus, that "pain cannot be past bearing or everlasting, if only you bear in mind its limits, and do not let fancy supplement them." Remember too that many things which surprise us out of patience are really in the same category as pain——heaviness for instance, feverishness, or want of appetite.   Whenever any of these makes you discontent, say to yourself that you are giving in to pain.

65   Do not you feel towards the inhuman, as human beings too often do to one another.

66   How do we know that Telauges was not morally superior to Socrates ?   It proves nothing that Socrates died a more notable death, or was a more proficient dialectician, or showed more endurance on a frosty night, or had the spirit to resist when ordered to arrest Leon, or that he 'perked his head'[1] in the streets.   On all this

[1] Cf. Plato, *Symp.* 221 B, from Aristophanes, *Clouds* 362.

one may have one's doubts, even assuming it true ; the one important consideration is, what sort of soul had Socrates ? could he rest content with being just to men, and holy towards the gods ? did he on the one hand resent men's evil-doing or fall in bondage to another's ignorance ? did he on the other accept the portion assigned, not as something counter to nature or too grievous to be borne ? and did he keep the affections of the mind distinct from the affections of the flesh ?

In commingling mind with the other elements of the compound, nature did not forbid it power of self-determination, and supremacy within its own domain. A man may easily enough be godlike, yet never be recognised as such. Ever remember this, and also that true happiness lies in a very few things. Do not, because dialectic and physics lie beyond your ken, despair on that account of freedom, self-respect, unselfishness, and tractability to god.

Live life out unrebelliously in perfect peace, though the whole world bawl its wishes at you, yes though wild beasts tear limb by limb this material integument of flesh. Amid it all nothing can prevent your understanding from possessing

itself in calm, in true judgment upon each besetting claim, and in ready use of all material
at its disposal.   So that judgment may say to
circumstance, ' This is what you intrinsically are,
though you may get credit for being something
different ' : and use may say to opportunity, ' You
are what I was looking for.   For whatever comes
to hand is material for the practice of rational
and social virtue, in a word of that art which is
proper to man or god.'   All that befalls is so
much assimilative material for god or man, never
novel or impracticable, but familiar and apt for use.

69   Herein is the way of perfection—to live out
each day as one's last, with no fever, no torpor,
and no acting a part.

70   The immortal gods do not lose patience at
having to bear age after age with the froward
generations of men ; but still show for them all
manner of concern.   Shall you, whose end is in
a moment, lose heart ? you, who are one of the
froward ?

71   It is absurd, not to fly from one's own evil-
doing, which is possible, but to fly from others',
which is impossible.

72   Whatever the rational and social faculty finds

devoid of mind or social aim, it reasonably accounts inferior to itself.

You have done a kindness, another has 73 received it ; why be as the foolish and hanker after something more, the credit for the kindness, or the recompense ?

No one tires of service rendered. Service is 74 action after nature's way. Do not tire then of service gained by service given.

The impulse of Nature made for a world of 75 order. All that now happens follows in the train of consequence ; else you must deny reason to the sovereign ends which guide the impulse of the World-soul. This thought will oftentimes minister calm.

BOOK VIII

AEQUANIMITAS.—*Antoninus*

ONE good corrective to vainglory is to remember
that you cannot claim to have lived your entire
life, nor even from youth up, as a philosopher.
To many another it is no secret, and no secret
to yourself, how far you fall short of philosophy.
Having touched pitch, it is hard for you still to
win the title of philosopher : and your position
militates against it. Now that your eyes are
really open to what the facts are, never mind
what others think of you ; be self-content, if only
for life's remainder, just so long as nature wills
you to live on. You have but to apprehend
that will, and let nothing else distract you :
you have tried much, and in misguided ways,
and nowhere have you found the happy life ;
not in systems, nor wealth, nor fame, nor self-

indulgence, nowhere.   Where then is happiness?
in doing that which man's nature craves.   How
do it? by holding principles, from which come
endeavours and actions.   What principles? principles touching good and bad — to wit, that
nothing is good for a man, which ˑdoes not make
him just, temperate, brave, free; nothing evil,
that does not produce the opposite results.

Of every action ask yourself, What does it 2
mean for me? shall I repent of it?   A little while
and I am dead, and there is an end of all.
Why crave for more, if only the work I am
about is worthy of a being intellectual, social-
minded, and on a par with god?

Alexander, Cæsar, Pompey, what are they 3
compared with Diogenes, Heraclitus, Socrates?
The latter saw into things and what things were
made of, and their Inner Selves were at one; as
for the former, how much foresight did they
possess, and in how much were they slaves!

Protest——till you burst!   Men will go on all 4
the same.

First and foremost, keep unperturbed.   For 5
all things follow the law of Nature: and in a
little while you will vanish and be nought, even

as are Hadrian and Augustus.   Secondly, face
facts open-eyed, bearing in mind that it is your
duty to be a man and to be good ; what man's
nature demands, that do without swerving ; so
speak, as seems to you most just ; only be it
considerately, modestly, and with sincerity.

It is Nature's work to shift and to transpose, to
remove thence and to carry thither.   All is change ;
yet need we not fear any novelty ; all is the
wonted round ; nay even the apportionments equal.

Every nature finds content in pursuing the
tenor of its way : and the reasoning nature
moves on its own way, when in impressions it
yields assent to nothing false or insecure ; when
it directs impulse towards social action only ;
when it confines inclination and avoidance to
things within our power ; and when it welcomes
every apportionment of universal nature.   For of
this it is a part, as the nature of the leaf is part
of the nature of the plant ; only that leaf-nature
is part of nature without sense or reason and
liable to contravention, while man-nature is part
of nature that is above contravention, possessed
of mind, and just ; seeing that it apportions to
successive men, equally and by scale of worth,

their participation in time, being, cause, action, and circumstance.   Only do not look for exact equality in every case between individual and individual, but in comparing the sum totals of collective wholes.

Know everything [1] you cannot ; but check 8 arrogance you can, rise superior to pleasures or pains you can, spurn reputation you can, keep your temper with the stupid and the ingrate, yea even care for them, you can.

For the future let none hear you reviling court- 9 life, nor you [2] yourself.

Repentance is self-reproach at having let slip 10 something of use.   Now all good must be of use, and the good man's object in life ; but no good man would ever repent of having let a pleasure slip ; pleasure therefore is neither of use, nor good.

Of any particular thing ask, What is it in 11 itself, and by its constitution ? what in substance

---

[1] A slight and plausible correction for the MS. 'read.' See *Appendix*.

[2] Some manuscripts omit 'you' and read merely 'your own,' but perhaps in order to save the grammar. The variation is of some importance, as with 'you' retained the antithesis is not between Court-life and his own, but between grumbling before others, and grumbling to himself.   With 'you' omitted, the Court must be contrasted with the Camp.

and in matter ? what in respect of cause ? what is it doing in the world ? and how long does it subsist ?

12   When you are drowsy and waking comes hard, remind yourself that social action belongs to your constitution and to human nature, while sleep is a function shared by unreasoning animals. And that which belongs to the individual nature, is more proper and organic to it, and likewise more congenial.

13   To every impression apply, if possible, the tests of objective character, of subjective effect, and of logical relation.

14   Whomsoever you meet, say straightway to yourself—What are the man's principles of good and bad ? for if he holds such and such principles regarding pleasure and pain and their respective causes, about fame and shame, or life and death, I shall not be surprised or shocked at his doing such and such things ; I shall remember that he cannot do otherwise.

15   Think of being shocked at the fig-tree bearing figs ! you have just as little right, remember, to be shocked at the world bearing the produce proper to it. Shame on the physician or the pilot who is shocked at a case of fever, or a contrary wind.

Remember that to change your course and to 16
accept correction is no surrender of freedom. Your
action follows your own impulse and judgment,
and keeps the course which your own mind sets.

If the fault rests with you, why do it? if with 17
another, with what do you find fault? the atoms,
or the gods? Either is idiotcy. Find fault with
nobody. If you can, set the doer right; if that
is impossible, at least set the thing right; if
even that cannot be, to what purpose is your
fault-finding? For everything must have some
purpose.

That which dies does not drop out of the 18
universe. Here it bides, and here too it changes
and is dispersed into its elements, the rudiments
of the universe and of yourself. And they too
change, and murmur not.

Everything—horse, vine, or what not—exists 19
for some end. Marvel not that even the Sun
says, 'I have a work to do,' and so too the
other gods. What then is yours? Pleasure? Is
the thought tolerable?

Nature takes concern in everything, in its 20
cessation no less than its first beginning or con-
tinuance. It is like one casting a ball. What

good pray is it to the ball to rise, what harm to drop, or even to lie fallen? what good to the bubble to hold together, or what harm to burst? so likewise with a candle.

21   Turn a thing inside out, and see what it is like; or what it becomes like when old or diseased or in decay.   Short-lived are praiser and praised alike, remembrancer and ʹremembered: and that too only in a corner of one continent, and even there all are not in accord with one another, or even with themselves: and even the whole earth is but a point.

22   Attend to what you have in hand—whether material object, or principle, or action, or thing signified.

Rightly served; you prefer becoming good to-morrow to being good to-day.

23   Acting—let me refer all to the service of men: bearing—let me take what comes, referring all to the gods, and to the universal source, from which all things that come to pass concatenate.

24   Think of bathing and its accessories—oil, sweat, filth, foul water, and all things nauseating.   So is it with every part of life, and each material thing.

25   First Verus, then Lucilla; first Maximus, then

Secunda ; first Diotimos, then Epitynchanos ; first Faustina, then Antoninus. And so always. First Hadrian, then Celer. The keen wits that were, the prophets, or the magnates, where are they now ? keen wits like Charax, Demetrius the Platonist, Eudaimon and the like. All lived their little day, all long since dead ; some denied even brief remembrance, some passed into a tale ; or fading ere now out of tales. Think on these things, and remember that either your mortal compound must be dispersed into its atoms, or else the breath of life must be extinguished, or be transmuted and enter a new order. ____

Man's mirth is to do man's proper work ; and 26 it is proper to man to wish well to his kind, to rise superior to the motions of sense, to distinguish impressions that are plausible, and to survey at large Nature and her processes.

Man has three relations : first to the physical 27 organ, his material shell : secondly, to the divine cause, from which proceed all things for all ; thirdly, to those with whom he has to do.

Pain is either an evil for the body—and if so, 28 let body state its case ; or for the soul—but the soul can maintain its own unclouded calm, and refuse to view it as evil. For every judgment or impulse or inclination or avoidance is within, and nothing evil can force entrance there.

29   Efface impressions, reiterating to yourself—It rests now with me, that within this soul of mine there be no vice, nor desire, nor any perturbation at all ; perceiving the true nature of all things, I use each at its proper worth. Remember this prerogative is yours by nature.

30   Alike in Senate and in individual intercourse, let your language be dignified, but not elaborate ; your words all sound.

31   Look at the court of Augustus—wife, daughter, offspring, elders, sister, Agrippa, kinsmen, intimates, friends, Areius, Maecenas, physicians, priests —the whole circle dead. Pass again to other instances, to the death not of an individual, but of a stock, such as the Pompeii, and to the superscription graven upon tombs—LAST OF HIS LINE : reflect how hard his forefathers strained, to leave behind them a successor ; and how after all there needs must be a last ; and here finally the extinction of a long line.

32   In every single action try to make life a whole : if each, so far as it can, contributes its part, be

satisfied ; and that, no man can hinder.—' Some outer obstacle,' you say, 'will interfere.'—' Nay, but nothing can touch the justice, wisdom, reasonableness of the intention.'—' But may not some form of action be prevented ? '—' Possibly ; but by welcoming that prevention, and with a good grace adopting the alternative, you at once substitute a course that will fit into its place in the whole we have in view.'

Modestly take, cheerfully resign. 33

Have you ever seen a dismembered hand, or 34 foot, or decapitated head, lying severed from the body to which it belonged ?   Such does a man, so far as he can, make himself, when he refuses to accept what befalls, and isolates himself, or when he pursues self-seeking action.   You are cast out from the unity of nature, of which you are an organic part ; you dismember your own self.   But here is this beautiful provision, that it is in your power to re-enter the unity.   No other part of the whole doth god privilege, when once severed and dismembered, to reunite.   But consider the goodness of god, with which he has honoured man : he has put it in his power never to be sundered at all from the whole ; and if sundered, then to rejoin it once more, and coalesce, and resume his contributory place.

85   Each rational being shares (speaking generally) the attributes of rational nature at large, among others the following : as rational nature continually modifies each form of obstruction or resistance, subordinates it to the scheme of destiny, and so incorporates it with itself, so too can the rational being convert each hindrance into material for himself, and use it to further his endeavour.

36   Do not let the impression of life as a whole confound you. Do not focus in one all the train of possible and painful consequences ; but as each trouble comes, say to yourself—What is there here too hard to bear or to endure? and you will be ashamed to avow it so. And yet again remember, that you have not to bear up against the future or the past, but always against the present only. And even that you minimise, when you strictly circumscribe it to itself, and repudiate moral inability to hold out merely against that.

37   Does Pantheia or does Pergamus still sit beside the bier of Verus ? Chabrias or Diotimos by Hadrian's ? Folly ! And suppose they did,

would the dead be conscious of it ? or if conscious, glad ? or if glad, would the mourners live on for ever ? must they not in the order of things first turn into old men and women, and then die ? and when they died, what could their lovers do next ? All comes to stench and refuse at last.

If you have sharp eyes, see and discern the 38 inly wise.

In the constitution of the reasoning being I 39 perceive no virtue in mutiny against justice ; in mutiny against pleasure I see self-control.

Take away your own view of what you regard 40 as painful, and you stand unassailable. ' But of what *you* is this true ? '—' Of reason.'—' But reason and I are not the same.'—' Very good : then spare reason the pain of giving itself pain ; and if some other part of you is amiss, let it keep that view to itself.'

A contravention of sense is an injury to the 41 life-nature ; so likewise is a contravention of impulse ; and similarly with any other form of contravention or injury to the natural constitution. In the same way any contravention of mind is an injury to the mind-nature. Apply all this to yourself. Are you affected by pain or pleasure ?

Sensation must see to that. Has impulse or endeavour suffered some check? Well, if it was without reservation, you therein did reason a wrong; accept the universal limitation, and forthwith the injury or contravention vanishes. But the freehold of the mind none other may contravene; fire cannot touch it, nor steel, nor tyrant, nor slander, nor any other thing; so long as it abides " poised as a sphere self-orbed."

42   What right have I to vex myself, when I never yet wilfully vexed another?

43   To every man his own good cheer. Be mine —health in the Inner Self; estranged from no man, and from no vicissitude of men, let me look on everything and accept everything with charitable eye, and use each according to its worth.

44   Harvest the present. Those who prefer pursuit of after-fame do not reflect that posterity will be men just like those who gall them now; and that they too will be but mortal. And after all what matters to you the rattle of their voices, or the kind of views they entertain about you?

45   Take me and cast me where you will. There I shall still have my deity within serene, content so long as it can feel and act after the ordering of

its own constitution.   Is change of place any good
reason for my soul injuring and debasing itself by
cringing, or craving, or cowering, or flinching?
What indeed is worth that?

Nothing can befall a man that is not incidental 46
to men ; nor a cow, to cows ; nor a vine, to vines ;
nor a stone, that is not proper to stones.   Why
chafe then at the occurrence of that which is
customary and natural to each?   Nature brings
nothing that you cannot bear.

If you are pained by anything without, it is 47
not the thing agitates you, but your own judgment
concerning the thing ; and this it is in your own
power to efface.   If the pain comes from inward
state and disposition, who hinders you from correct-
ing the principle at fault?   If however the pain
consists in not taking some action which you perceive to be wholesome, why not act rather than
prolong the pain?—'But some obstacle stronger
than yourself bars the way.'—'Then grieve not ;
the responsibility for inaction does not lie with
you.'—'But life is not worth living, with the act
undone.' — ' If so, take kindly leave of life,
serenely owning the obstacle and dying even as
he dies who succeeds.'

48   Remember that your Inner Self is inexpugnable, when once it rallies to itself and consistently declines to act against its will, even though the defiance may be irrational. How much more then, when its judgment is rational and made with circumspection? Therefore the mind free from passions is a citadel; man has no stronger fortress to which he can fly for refuge and remain impregnable. Ignorant is he, who has not seen this; unhappy he, who, having seen, yet flies not to the refuge.

49   Do not draw inferences in excess of that which the primary impressions announce. They announce, 'So and so is speaking ill of you;' yes, but they do not add that you are thereby injured: or, 'I see my child is sick;' yes, but that there is danger, I do not see. Always keep strictly to the first impressions, without adding comments of your own, and you are unaffected. Or rather, add from within the recognition that all is part of the world-order.

50   The gourd is bitter: drop it then! There are brambles in the path: then turn aside! It is enough. Do not go on to argue, Why pray have these things a place in the world? The natural

philosopher will laugh at you, just as a carpenter
or cobbler would laugh, if you began finding fault
because you saw chips or parings lying about
their shop. And yet they have a place for the
rubbish ; but Nature has nothing outside herself.
Herein is the marvel of her handiwork, that thus
self-circumscribed she yet transmutes into herself
every content that seems corrupt and old and useless, and from the same materials recreates afresh :
so as to avoid the need of fresh substance from
without, or of some place for her refuse. Her
own space, her own material, and her own handiwork suffice.

In action, not dilatory ; in intercourse, not 51
indiscriminate ; in impressions, not rambling ; your
soul neither numb with constraint, nor fevered
with transports ; your life, undriven.

Say men kill you, quarter you, pursue you with
execrations : what has that to do with your understanding remaining pure, lucid, temperate, just ?
It is as though a man stood beside some sweet
transparent fountain, abusing it, and it ceased not
to well forth draughts of pure water ; nay though
he cast in mud and filth, it will speedily disperse
them and wash them forth and take no stain.

How then can you create a living fountain within ?
imbue yourself in freedom every hour, with charity,
simplicity and self respect.

52   He who knows not the world-order, knows not
his own place therein.   And he who knows not
for what end he exists, knows not himself nor the
world.   He who fails in either knowledge, cannot
so much as say for what he himself exists.   What
think you then of him, who seeks or shuns the
clatter of men, who understand not where or what
they are ?

53   Would you have the praises of him who thrice
an hour execrates himself?   Would you satisfy
the man who cannot satisfy himself?   And can a
man satisfy himself, who repents of nigh everything he does ?

54   You breathe the air that encompasses you :
think likewise with the all-encompassing mind.
Mind-power is no less all-pervading and diffused
for him who can draw therefrom, than the atmosphere for respiration.

55   Evil-doing does not hurt the universe at large :
evil to one part does not hurt another.   It is
hurtful to the evil-doer only, and release from it is
within his reach as soon as he so wills.

To my moral will my neighbour's will is as 56
completely unrelated, as his breath is or his flesh.
Be we ever so much made for one another, our
Inner Selves have each their own sovereign rights :
otherwise my neighbour's evil might become my
evil, which is not god's good pleasure, lest another
have power to undo me.

We see the sun everywhere diffused and all- 57
pervading, yet unexhausted.   For its diffusion is
by extension, and its rays (*aktines*) are so called
from *ekteinesthai* to extend.   The nature of a ray
you may see, if you watch sunlight admitted
through a chink into a darkened room : for it
extends straight on, and supports itself on any solid
object which encounters it and disparts it from the
air beyond ; there it remains, and does not slip or
fall.   Such too should be the effusion and diffusion
of the understanding, never exhausting but ever
extending itself, not impinging furiously and
violently upon the hindrances which it encounters ;
yet never failing or falling, but resting there and
illuminating that which receives it.   That which
refuses to transmit it, will but deprive itself of
light.

He who fears death, fears either loss of sensa- 58

tion or change of sensation. But if sensation ceases, you will feel no evil ; if sensation is changed in kind, you will be a changed creature, and will not cease to live.

59 Men exist for one another. Teach them then, or bear with them.

60 There is motion and motion—the motion of the arrow, and the motion of mind. Yet mind, even when it works cautiously and plays around some problem, is none the less moving straight on, towards its appointed end.

61 Enter into every man's Inner Self: and let every other man enter into thine.

BOOK IX

DUCUNT VOLENTEM FATA, NOLENTEM TRAHUNT.—*Seneca*

To be unjust is to sin. By Nature rational [1]
beings have been constituted for one another's
sake, each to help each according to its worth,
and in no wise to hurt : and he who transgresses
the will of Nature, sins—to wit, against the
primal deity.

And to lie is to sin against the same godhead.
For Nature is the nature of all things that are ;
and things that are have union with all things
from the beginning. Truth is indeed one name
for Nature, the first cause of all things true. The
wilful liar sins in that he deceives and does un-
justly ; the unwitting, in that he is at variance
with Nature, disordering and combating the order
of the Universe. For he who goes counter to the

truth is at civil war within ; he has neglected the faculties provided by Nature, and cannot any longer distinguish false from true.

Again, to seek pleasures as good, or to shun pains as evil, is to sin. For it inevitably leads to complaining against Nature for unfair awards to the virtuous and to the vile, seeing that the vile are oftentimes in pleasure and come by things pleasurable, while the virtuous are overtaken by pain and things painful. Moreover, he who fears pain will some time fear that which will form part of the world-order ; and therein he sins. And he who seeks after pleasures will not abstain from unjust doing ; which is palpably an act of sin. Where Nature makes no difference——and were she not indifferent, she would not bring both to pass——those who would fain walk with Nature should conform their wills to like indifference. Not to be indifferent to pain or pleasure, death or life, evil report or good report, all which Nature treats indifferently, is plainly to be guilty of sin. By Nature treating them indifferently, I mean that they befall indifferently all whose existence is consequent upon the original impulse of providence, which gave the origin and first momentum to the cosmic ordering of things, by selecting certain germs of future existences, and assigning to them productive capacities of realisation, change, and phenomenal succession.

The truly gentle would pass from among men 2 untainted by falsehood, insincerity, luxury, or pride : and next best is, to grow disgusted with these things before one breathes one's last. Or can it be, that you are resolved to cleave fast to evil, and that even experience does not prevail upon you to shun the pestilence ? For corruption of the understanding is a pestilence more deadly far than any distemper or phase of the surrounding atmosphere.[1] That is death to animals, as animals ; but this to men, as men.

Contemn not death, but give it welcome ; is 3 not death too a part of nature's will ? As youth and age, as growth and prime, as the coming of teeth and beard and grey hairs, as begetting and pregnancy and bearing of children, as all other operations of nature, even all that 'life in its seasons brings to pass,' even such is dissolution. Therefore the rational man should not treat death with impatience or repugnance or disdain, but

1 Lit. *pneuma*, on which see Introd. p. liv pp.

wait for it as one of nature's operations. Just as now you wait for the offspring to issue from your wife's womb, so expect the hour when your atom of soul will slip its mortal case. If your heart asks for some simple and effective reassurance, the best solace against death is correct appreciation of the material things from which you are to part, and of the moral natures with which your soul will then cease to inter-mingle. Far be it from you to take offence at them ; nay rather, care for them and deal gently with them ; yet remember, that you are parting with men whose principles are not your principles. The one thing, if any, which could hold you back and chain you still to life, would be companionship with kindred spirits. As it is, amid the besetting worry and jangle of life, you cry, ' Come quickly, death, for fear I too forget myself ! '

He who sins, sins against himself ; he who does wrong, wrongs himself, making himself evil.

Wrong comes often of not doing as well as doing.

Certitude in present view, unselfishness in present act, present contentment with all that

overtakes you from without——have these, and it
suffices you.

Efface impression ; stay impulse ; quench in- 7
clination ; be master of your Inner Self.

The soul distributed among the irrational 8
animals is one, and so too is the soul instinct with
mind, that is portioned out among the rational ;
just as earth is one in all things earthy, and the
light one by which we see, and the air one which
we breathe, even all that have sight and breath
of life.

Things that share a common element feel the 9
impulse of kind towards kind. The earthy ever
gravitates towards earth, the aqueous seeks its
own level, and so too the aerial ; nothing short
of force can dispart them. Fire ascends attracted
by the elemental fire ; so ready is it always to
combine for ignition, that every solid, in proportion to its dryness, readily ignites, the infusion of
that which hinders ignition being smaller. So
too everything which participates in the common
mind-nature feels the like impulse towards kind ;
nay more so——for the higher the nature, the
readier the impulse to combination and fusion
with its counterpart. For observe ; among the

K

irrational animals, bees swarm, cattle herd, birds nest together, all owning forms of love. For at this stage soul is present, and on this higher plane of being a mutual attraction asserts itself, which is not present in plants or stones or sticks. Again among rational beings there are societies and friendships, homes and communities, and in war compacts and armistices. In the still higher orders of being, even among distant bodies there exists unity of a kind, as among the stars ; so that ascent in the scale of being induces sympathetic action in spite of distance. See what we come to then. None but things possessed of mind ignore the mutual impulse of attraction ; here only does the natural gravitation disappear. Yes, but even in the act of evasion, men are caught and overtaken ; nature prevails. Watch, and you will see : sooner will you find some particle of earth detached from other earth, than man isolated from man.

10   Man bears fruit, so does god, so does the world, all in their own season. That custom has appropriated the term to the vine or the like, matters not. Reason too bears fruit, alike for the world and for itself ; and from it spring fruits of like kind with reason itself.

Convert men, if you can: if you cannot, 11
charity, remember, has been given you for this
end. See! the gods too have charity for such,
helping them to divers things, health, wealth and
reputation; so good are they. You too can do
the same; who hinders you?

Work hard, not making a martyr of yourself, 12
and not seeking pity or applause: seek one thing
only, action or inaction, as social law demands.

To-day I got clear of trouble; say rather, I 13
cleared trouble out; the trouble was not without
but within, a matter of views.

All things are alike—familiar, fleeting, foul: 14
everything as it was in the days of the dead and
buried.

Facts stand outside us, just as they are, 15
knowing nothing and stating nothing about
themselves. What is it states the case for them?
the Inner Self.

For a rational and social being good and evil 16
lie not in physical affection but in moral action,
just as virtue and vice lie not in an affection, but
in action.

To the thrown stone it is no ill to drop, nor 17
good to rise.

18   Penetrate to men's Inner Selves, and you will see what judges you fear, and how they judge themselves.

19   Everything is in change. You yourself are undergoing continuous variation, and piecemeal destruction. So is the world at large.

20   Another's error—let it lie.

21   In cessation of action, in surcease of impulse or of judgment, in what may be termed their death, there is no evil. Retraverse the stages of growth, childhood, boyhood, youth, age—each one of them a change, a death. Is there anything to be afraid of? Or retraverse the periods of life, first under your grandfather, then under your mother, then your father. Gather up all the many phases and changes and cessations of experience, and then ask yourself, Is there anything to be afraid of? No more is there in the cessation, the surcease, the change from life itself.

22   Press straight to the Inner Self—your own, the world's, your neighbour's. Your own, that you may make of it a true vessel of justice; the world's, that you may bear in mind of what you are a part; your neighbour's, that you may under-

stand whether it is ignorance or knowledge, and may take into account the bond of brotherhood.

You are part of a social whole, a factor necessary to complete the sum ; therefore your every action should help to complete the social life. Any action of yours that does not tend, directly or remotely, to this social end, dislocates life and infringes its unity. It is an act of sedition, and like some separatist doing what he can to break away from civic accord.

Children's squabbles, a stage farce, and "*poor breath carrying a corpse*" ! is not phantom-land more palpable and solid ?

Get to the cause and its quality ; isolate it from the material embodiment and survey it ; then delimit the full span for which the individuality in question can subsist.

" *Woes unnumbered you have borne*"—because you are not content to let your Inner Self follow the law of its own being. Hold ! enough !

When others censure, or resent, or make an outcry over this or that, go near and penetrate into their souls, and see what manner of men they are. You will see there is no need for straining to commend yourself to their good opinion. Yet kindliness remains a duty; love is nature's claim. And see! the gods aid them in all manner of ways, by dream and by oracle, yes even to gain the ends on which they are bent.

28   Up and down, to and fro, moves the world's round, from age to age. Either the World-mind imparts each individual impulse—in which case, accept the impulse it imparts: or else it gave the impulse once for all, with all its long entail of consequence. It comes to this—either a concourse of atoms, or an appointment of destiny.[1] In fine, either god works, and all is well; or, if all is random, be not you too a part of the random.

Anon earth will cover us all; then earth in its turn will change; then the resultant of the change; then the resultant of the resultant, and so *ad infinitum*. The billows of change and variation roll apace, and he who ponders them will feel

29 contempt for all things mortal. The universal cause is like a winter torrent; it sweeps all before it.

How cheap in sooth are these pygmies of

[1] The restoration is conjectural.

politics, these sage doctrinaires in statecraft!
Drivellers every one. Well, man, what then?
This and this only : do what nature here and now
demands. Endeavour the best you may ; do not
look round for your cue to some one else. Do not
hope for Utopia ; suffice it, if the smallest thing
makes head : to compass that one issue, believe,
is no small feat. Which of them all changes one
moral principle? And without change of principles, what hope for them but bondage and
growling and lip-profession? Go to, with your
Alexander and Philip and Demetrius of Phalerum ;
whether they saw the will of Nature, and schooled
themselves accordingly, is their affair ; but because
they strutted their parts, no one has condemned
me to follow suit. Simplicity and modesty are
the work of philosophy ; do not lead me away into
self-conceit.

"*As from some eminence survey the countless* 30
herds" of men—their thronging festivals, their
voyages of storm and voyages of calm, the
chequered phases of their appearance, action,
disappearance ; or imagine again the life of ages
past, the life of generations to come, the life now
living among savage tribes ; how many have never

heard your name, how many will at once forget it! how many who perhaps applaud you now, will very soon revile! how valueless in sooth is memory, or fame, or all else put together!

31   To vicissitudes caused from without, be imperturbable: in actions whose cause lies with yourself, be just—in other words, let impulse and act make social action their one end, and so fulfil the law of nature.

32   The agitations that beset you are superfluous, and depend wholly upon judgments of your own. You can get rid of them, and in so doing will indeed live at large, by embracing the whole universe in your view and comprehending all eternity and imagining the swiftness of change in each particular, seeing how brief is the passage from birth to dissolution, birth with its unfathomable before, dissolution with its infinite hereafter.

33   All that you see will soon have perished, and those who have watched them perishing will soon perish themselves: the longest-lived will be at one with the babe who dies untimely.

34   Look at their Inner Selves, the things they push for, the titles to their liking and respect. Conceive their souls stripped naked—and then,

fancy their censure hurting, or their plaudits doing any good !

Loss is another word [1] for change ; and change is the joy of Nature. By Nature all things are ordered well, all were of the same form from the beginning, all will be like to everlasting. Why then say that all things have been, that all things ever will be evil, that among all the gods no power has ever been devised to set them right but that the world is doomed to labour under interminable ills ?

Decay is in the material substance of all things —water, dust, bones, and stench ! What is marble but knobs of earth ? gold or silver but sediment ? raiment but tags of hair ? purple but shell - fish blood ? and so on throughout. Yes even the pneumatic current is in the same case, ever changing from this to that.

Enough of moans, and murmurs, and monkey-chatter ! Why perturb yourself ? There is nothing new, to excite you so. The cause, is it ? Look the cause then in the face. Or the material substance ? Then look that in the face. Cause, or

---

[1] The word-play of the original—ἀποβολή, μεταβολή—cannot be reproduced.

substance—it can be nothing else. Only, as in god's sight, be yourself from this day forth more simple-hearted and good. It is the same whether you witness it a hundred years or three.

38   If he did wrong, with him lies the evil. Suppose after all he did not!

39   Either all things spring from a single source possessed of mind, and combine and fit together as for a single body, and in that case the part has no right to quarrel with the good of the whole : or else, it is a concourse of atoms, a welter ending in dispersion. Why then perturb yourself?

Say to your Inner Self, Are you dead, perished, false to yourself? like a beast, do you but join the herd and chew the cud?

40   The gods either have power, or they have not. If they have not, why pray at all? If they have, why not pray for deliverance from the fear, or the desire, or the pain, which the thing causes, rather than for the withholding or the giving of the particular thing? Assuredly, if they can help men at all, this is the way of help. But perhaps you will say, The gods have put all that in my own power. Then is it not better to exercise your power and remain free, rather than to be set

on what is not in your own power, and become a
slave and cringer? And who told you that the
gods do not assist us even to what is in our own
power? Begin there with your prayers, and you
will see. Instead of 'Oh! to enjoy her caresses!'
—pray you against lusting after the enjoyment.
Instead of 'Rid me of my enemy!'—pray you
against desire for the riddance. Instead of 'Spare
my little one!'—pray you that your fears may be
at rest. Be this the direction of your prayers,
and watch what comes.

Says Epicurus—'When I was sick, I did not 41
converse about my bodily ailments, nor discuss
such matters with my visitors; but continued to
dwell upon the principles of natural philosophy,
and more particularly how the understanding,
while participating in such disturbances of the
flesh, yet remains in unperturbed possession of
its proper good. And I would not,' he adds,
'give the doctors a chance of blustering and
making ado, but let life go on cheerily and
well.' Imitate Epicurus—in sickness, if you are
sick, or in any other visitation. To be loyal to
philosophy under whatsoever circumstances, and
not join the babel of the silly and the ignorant,

is a motto for all schools alike. Stick only to the work in hand, and to the tool you have for doing it.

42   When some piece of shamelessness offends you, ask yourself, Can the world go on without shameless people?——Certainly not!——Then do not ask for the impossible. Here you see is one of the shameless, whom the world cannot get on without. Similarly in any case of foul play or breach of faith or any other wrong, fall back on the same thought. When once you remember that the genus cannot be abolished, you will be more charitable to the individual. Another helpful plan is, at once to realise what virtue Nature has given to man to cope with the wrong. For she provides antidotes, such as gentleness to cope with the graceless, and other salves for other irritants. You can always try to convert the misguided; for indeed every wrongdoer is really misguided and missing his proper mark. Besides what harm has he done to you? for look——none of the objects of your ire has done anything that can inflict injury upon your understanding; yet there, and there only, can evil or hurt to you find realisation. What is there wrong, pray, or shocking, in the

clown acting the clown ? See that the fault does
not lie rather at your own door, for not expecting
him to go wrong thus. Reason supplied you with
faculties enabling you to expect that he would go
wrong thus ; you forgot, and then are surprised
at his having done so. When you complain of
some breach of faith or gratitude, take heed first
and foremost to yourself. Obviously the fault lies
with yourself, if you had faith that a man of that
disposition would keep faith, or if in doing a kindness you did not do it upon principle, nor upon
the assumption that the kind act was to be its
own reward. What more do you want in return
for a service done ? Is it not enough to have
acted up to nature, without asking wages for it ?
Does the eye demand a recompense for seeing, or
the feet for walking ? Just as this is the end for
which they exist, and just as they find their reward
in realising the law of their being, so too man is
made for kindness, and whenever he does an act
of kindness or otherwise helps forward the common
good, he thereby fulfils the law of his being and
comes by his own.

BOOK X

* ASPICE · RESPICE · PROSPICE

1 WILT thou one day, O my soul, be good and simple, all one, all naked, clearer to sight than this thy material shell? Wilt thou taste one day of fond and satisfied contentment? Wilt thou one day be full and without lack, craving naught and coveting naught, neither things with breath nor things without, for indulgence of self-pleasing? neither time, for prolongation of enjoyment? nor region place or clime, nor sweet society of fellow-men? Wilt thou be content with thine actual estate? happy in all thou hast? convinced that all things are thine, that all is well with thee, that all comes from the gods, that all must be well which is their good pleasure, and which they bring to pass for the salvation of the living whole, good just and beautiful, from which all things have

their being their unity and their scope, and into
which they are received at dissolution for the production of new forms of being like themselves?
Wilt thou be such one day, my soul, having
attained such fellowship with gods and men, as to
make no more complaint at all, nor be found of
them in any fault?

Take heed to what your personal nature craves, 2
knowing that you are solely at nature's disposition;
comply with it and do it, unless it involves injury
to your animal nature. But correspondently,
give heed to each craving of the animal nature
and accept it in full, unless it involves injury to
your nature as a rational being: and the rational
is *ipso facto* social. Apply these *criteria* to life,
and do so without fuss.

Whatever befalls, one of two things is true: 3
either you have strength to bear it, or you have
not. If what befalls is within your strength, do
not lose patience, but use your strength to bear
it: if it is beyond your strength, again lose
not patience: in destroying you it will cease to
exist. Yet remember that you have strength
to bear everything, which your own view of
the case can render endurable and bearable,

if once regarded as a part of interest or else of
duty.

4   If a man mistakes, reason with him kindly and
point out his misconception.   If you fail, blame
yourself, or no one.

5   Whatever befalls was fore-prepared for you
from all time ; the woof of causation was from all
eternity weaving the realisation of your being, and
that which should befall it.

6   Be the world atoms, or be it nature's growth,
stand assured—first, that I am a part of the whole,
at nature's disposition ; secondly, that I am related
to all the parts of like kind with myself.   First
then, inasmuch as I am a part, I shall not be discontent with any portion assigned me from the
whole : for nothing is hurtful to the part which
is good for the whole.   The whole contains nothing
which is not for its own good ; this is true of
all nature's growths, with this addition in the case
of the world-nature, that there is no external cause
compelling it to generate anything hurtful to itself.
Thus in the thought that I am a part of such a
whole, I shall be content with all that comes to
pass.   And, secondly, in so far as I own my relation to the parts of like kind with myself, I shall

do nothing for self-seeking, but shall feel concern for all such parts, directing every endeavour towards the common good, and diverting it from the contrary. So long as I pursue this course, life must perforce flow smooth, smooth as the ideal life of one ever occupied in the well-being of his fellow-citizens, and accepting gladly whatever the city assigns him as his part.

The parts of the whole, which are comprehended in the growth and nature of the world-order, must necessarily perish——signifying thereby variation of form. Now if such variation is inherently an evil and a necessity for the parts, how can the whole escape deterioration, seeing that the parts are prone to variation, and so constituted as to perish in a variety of ways? Did nature, we ask, purposely intend the injury of things which are part of herself, and make them liable, nay necessarily incident, to injury? or were such results unforeseen by nature? Neither supposition is credible. But suppose, dropping the term Nature, we explain them as the natural course of things, see the absurdity; we first speak of change as natural to the parts of the universe, and then in the same breath express surprise or resent-

L

ment as though at some unnatural procedure, while
all the time dissolution is merely into the original
elements of composition.   For dissolution means
either dispersion of the elements of which I was
compounded, or else a change from solid into earthy
and from pneumatic into aerial, this being the
mode of re-assumption into the universal reason,
whether its destiny be cyclic conflagration or alternations of eternal renovation.   And do not regard
the solid or the pneumatic elements as a natal
part of being ; they are but accretions of yesterday
or the day before, derived from food and respiration.   The change affects that which is received
from without, not the original offspring of the
mother's womb.   But even admitting that you are
intimately bound up with that by your individuality,
that does not affect the present argument.

You claim for yourself the attributes good,
modest, true, open-minded, even-minded, high-
minded : take care not to belie them.   And should
you forfeit them, make haste to reclaim them.   The
open mind, remember, should import discriminating
observation and attention ; the even mind un-
forced acceptance of the apportionments of Nature ;
the high mind sovereignty of the intelligence over

the physical currents, smooth or rough, over vainglory, death, or any other trial. Keep true to
these attributes, without pining for recognition of
the same by others, and a changed man you will
enter upon a changed life. To go on being what
you have been hitherto, to lead a life still so distracted and polluted, were stupidity and cowardice
indeed, worthy of the mangled gladiators who,
torn and disfigured, cry out to be remanded till
the morrow, to be flung once more to the same
fangs and claws. Enter your claim then to
these few attributes. And if stand fast in them
you can, stand fast—as one translated indeed to
Islands of the Blessed. But if you find yourself
falling away and beaten in the fight, be a man and
get away to some quiet corner, where you can still
hold on, or in the last resort take leave of life,
not angrily but simply, freely, modestly, achieving
at least this much in life, brave leaving of it.
Towards bearing these attributes in mind, it will
greatly assist you to keep in mind the gods, to
remember that they desire not flattery, but rather
that all reasoning beings should come unto their likeness, and be as the fig-tree doing fig-tree's work, the
dog the dog's, the bee the bee's, and man the man's.

9   A stage-play, a fight, a scramble, a stupor, or
a bondage——such is life ! and each day will help to
efface the sacred principles, which you divest of
philosophic regard or allegiance.   It is your duty
to keep sight and action so alert, as to satisfy each
call, to effectualise each perception, and to maintain the full courage of conviction in reserve, but
unsuppressed.   Ah ! when will you find fruition in
simple-heartedness? in dignity ? in that understanding which apprehends each thing's true being, its
position in the world, its term of existence, and
its composition, and which can say to whom it of
right belongs, and who can either give it or take
away ?

10   The spider is proud of catching a fly——so is
one man of catching a hare, another of netting
a sprat, another boars, or bears, or Sarmatians.
Tested by philosophic principles, are they not
brigands, every one ?

11   Habituate yourself to the perception of all-pervading change ; dwell on it continually, and order
your thoughts accordingly ; nothing more elevates
the mind, and emancipates it from the body.   He
who realises that at any moment he may be called
on to leave the world and to depart from among

men, commits himself without reserve to justice in
all his actions, to Nature in all that befalls.   To
what will be said or thought of him, to what will
be done against him, he does not give a thought ;
but is content with two things only—to be just in
his dealings and glad at his apportioned lot.   Free
of all hurry and distractions, he has but one wish
—to run the straight course of law, following on
in the straight course of god.

What need for misgivings, when you can see 12
what ought to be done ?   If all is clear, go forward
—considerately, but without swerving ; if not,
pause and take the best advice ; if new resistance
meets you, follow the lights of reason and its
faculties, holding fast to what is plainly just ;
success is victory indeed, where in good truth
' default is no defeat.'   Alacrity without hurry, a
bright mien and a steady mind—this is the faithful
follower of reason.

Ask yourself as your waking thought, Can it 13
make any difference to me whether another does
what is just and right ?   None whatever.   When
you hear men blustering praise or blame of others,
do not forget what they themselves are in bed and
in board, the things they do, the things they shun,

the things they seek, their thefts and rapines done not with hands and feet, but with the most precious organ we possess, even that whereby, if we so will, we attain to faith and honour and truth and law and a good god within.

14   To nature the all-giver and all-taker the schooled and self-respecting mind says—'Give what thou wilt, and take back what thou wilt'— not in any tone of bravado, but solely of obedience and goodwill.

15   The residue of life is short. Live as on a mountain. It matters not whether here or there ; everywhere you are a citizen of the city of the world. Let men see and witness a true man, a life conformed to nature. If they cannot bear him, let them make away with him. Better that, than life on their terms.

16   No more mere talk of what the good man should be. Be it !

17   Embrace in your regard all time and all being— and see that by the side of being, all individual things are but a grain of millet, by that of time as the turn of a screw.

18   Get a clear understanding of all material things —picture each one of them in dissolution, in

change, and in decay, either by process of dispersion, or by its own appointed mode of death.

Eating, sleeping, breeding, excreting—only 1
look at them : look at their lasciviousness and
wantonness, their rages and their outbursts of abuse!
A while back, to how many did they bow the
knee, and for what ends! A little while, and
what will be their plight!

For each is best, what Nature brings : and best 2
too at the time, when Nature brings it.

Earth is in love with rain, and holy æther loves.[1]   2

Yes, the world-order is in love with fashioning
whatever is to be. To the world-order I profess
'Thy love is mine.' Is there not a truth implicit
in the familiar 'as it listeth.'[2]

Either—You live on where you are ; to that 2
you are well used : or—You move off, and so
doing have your wish : or—You die, and your

---

[1] Euripides.

[2] The double meaning of the Greek φιλεῖ, 'loves,' and 'is
wont,' has no exact counterpart in English. The adaptation is
suggested by a passage of kindred spirit. 'Who took as the type
of the true man, the wind?—the wind that blows where it *likes ;*
and of which no man need ask whence or whither ; he may be
sure that it is going where it is needed to keep Nature's balance
true. Were not the wind's law, law enough for us ? '—Hinton,
The Place of the Physician.

service is finished.   There is no other alternative.
So be of good cheer.

23   Take for your axiom the old truth—the field [1]
is where you make it ; life here is just the same
as life within the field, or on the mountain, or the
shore, or where you will.   In Plato's own phrase
—"*encompassed in his mountain fold, milking his
herds.*"

24   What of my Inner Self? what am I making
of it at this minute? to what use am I putting it?
is it empty of mind? divorced and dissociated
from the bond of fellowship? is it so ingrown
and engrossed in flesh, as to share each shift and
change?

25   The slave who makes away from his master is
a runaway ; but law is our master ; and whoever
breaks away from law is a runaway.   But vexation, anger, or fear mean refusal of something,
past present or to come, ordained by the sovereign
disposer, even Law,[2] who allots [2] to every man his
appointed work.   So then to be vexed or angry
or afeard, is to make oneself a runaway.

---

[1] In Marcus Aurelius the ' field ' signifies the place of seclusion
and retirement, as in IV. § 3.   The phrase of Plato is from
Theætetus, 174 DE.

[2] The Greek plays on the common derivation of νόμος—νέμειν.

The man drops seed into the womb and goes 26
his way, and thereupon a new cause takes up the
work and perfects the babe. What a flower of
what a seed! Or again, one passes food through
the gullet, and thereupon a new cause takes up
the work, and makes of it sensation, impulse, in a
word life and all forms of vital strength. Consider all that passes within the veil, and perceive
the power implied, just as we perceive the upward
and downward force of gravitation not with the
outward eye, yet no less palpably.

Let imagination remind you how all the varied 27
present does but repeat the past, and rehearse the
future. From your own experience, or from the
page of history, picture to yourself the same
dramas, the self-same scenes reproduced : the court
of Hadrian, the court of Antoninus, the court of
Philip, Alexander, Crœsus ; the same stock *rôles*,
only with change of actors.

He who feels umbrage or discontent at any- 28
thing is like a sacrificial pig, which kicks and
squeals. And he who sits silent and solitary on
his couch, bemoaning our bonds, is in the same
case. To the reasonable being and to him only
is it vouchsafed to go freely hand in hand with all

that comes ; the bare act of going with it none
can avoid.

29   Point by point, get clear upon every single act
you do, and ask yourself, ' Need loss of this make
me afraid of death ? '

30   When offended at a fault in some one else,
divert your thoughts to the reflection, What is the
parallel fault in me ?   Is it attachment to money ?
or pleasure ? or reputation ? as the case may be.
Dwelling on this, anger forgets itself and makes
way for the thought—' He cannot help himself—
what else can he do ?   If it is not so, enable
him, if you can, to help himself.'

31   Let sight of Satyron, Eutyches, or Hymen,
call up the thought of some Socratic ; Euphrates
that of Eutychion or Silvanus ; Alciphron that
of Tropæophorus ; Xenophon that of Crito· or
Severus ; a look at yourself, that of some Cæsar
of the past ; and similarly with every other case,
suggesting the thought, Where are they all now ?
Nowhere—or nobody knows where.   In this way
you will come to look on all things human as
smoke and nothingness : especially if you bear in
mind, that the thing once changed can never be
itself again to all eternity.   Why fret yourself

then ? Why not be content decently to weather out your little span ? What have you to fear, what form of matter or condition ? What are they all, but exercises for reason, scientifically and philosophically facing the facts of life ? Persevere then, till you make them part of your own being, just as the healthy stomach assimilates its food, or a quick fire turns everything you throw on into flame and light.

Let no man have it in his power to say of 32 you with truth, that you lack simplicity or good-ness ; make it a lie, for any one to think thus of you. It is within your power : for who can hinder you from being good and simple ? You have but to decide to live no longer, if you can-not be such ; for in that case reason itself does not dictate it.

Given the material, what can produce the 33 soundest result in action or in speech ? that, whatever it be, is in your power to do or say : and no excuses, please, about being hindered. You will never cease growling, till it comes as natural to you to use all the available materials for fulfilling the law of your being, as it is for pleasure-seekers to choose luxury : every opening for giving our nature play we should view as a form of enjoyment.   And the opening is always there.   The cylinder indeed cannot always enjoy its proper motion ; neither can water, nor fire, nor things which are at the disposition of the lower organic nature or of irrational soul : in their case lets and obstacles abound.   But mind and reason have the power of finding a way at will through every impediment.   Picture the facility with which reason will find itself a way, as that by which fire ascends, or a stone drops, or a cylinder rolls downhill——it leaves nothing more to crave for. Remaining interferences either affect the body only, which is a dead thing, or else, apart from the assumptions and admissions of reason itself, have no power to crush or to inflict any injury what- soever ; otherwise the person exposed to them would thereby be injured.   For observe——in the case of all other forms of being, any injury be- falling them implies deterioration of the object ; but in this case the man is one may say bettered and improved, by making good use of circum- stances.   Nothing in fine can hurt the true citizen, which does not hurt the city ; and nothing can hurt the city, which does not first hurt Law.   But

misadventures so-called hurt not the Law : therefore they hurt not city, nor yet citizen.

When once true principles have bitten in, 34
even the shortest and most trite of precepts serves
as a safeguard against the spirit of brooding or
fear.   For instance—

> As wind-shed leaves on the sod. . . .
> Such are the children of men.[1]

As autumn leaves thy little ones! and as leaves
too the crowd who shout their heartening plaudits
or heap their curses, or in secret cavil and gibe ;
as leaves too, even those who will succeed to
fame hereafter!   These all, and the like of them,
are but—

> Blossoming buds of the spring-time,

which the wind scatters, and a new foliage
clothes another wood.   Transitoriness is written
upon them all ; and yet you seek or shun, as
though they would last for ever.   A little while,
and you will close your eyes : and anon the dirge
will sound for him who bore your bier.

The healthy eye should see all that comes in 35
sight, and not say, 'I want things green'—
the confession of weak eyes.   Healthy hearing,

[1] Homer, *Il.* vi. 147-8.

healthy smell should be prepared for every sound and every scent; and the healthy stomach too for all kinds of food, no less than the molar for everything which it was made to grind. So too the healthy understanding should be prepared for all that befalls. The mind which cries ' Save my little ones ' or ' Let every one applaud whatever I do,' is the eye that wants things green, or the tooth that wants them soft.

No one is so fortunate, but that beside his death-bed there will stand some welcoming the coming blow. He was virtuous, say, and wise. Well, at the last will not one and another say in his heart, ' Now let us breathe again, free of master pedagogue ? True, he was never hard on any of us, but I always felt that he was tacitly condemning us.' Such is the reward of the virtuous. But in our case how many other reasons there are, to swell the throng of those who would be quit of us ! Realise this as death draws on, and solace your departure with the reflection——I am leaving a life, in which my own associates, for whom I have so striven, prayed and thought, themselves wish for my removal, hoping that they will perchance gain something in freedom thereby. Why then should one cling to longer sojourn here? Yet do not therefore leave them with any lack of charity; keep true to your own wont, friendly well-wishing and serene, here too not dissociating yourself from others. As in euthanasia the soul slips quietly from the body, so let your departure be. Of these elements nature joined and compounded you: now she dissolves the union. Be it dissolved: I part from what was mine—yet unresisting, unrebelliously; just one step more in nature's course.

Whatever is done, and whoever does it, so far 37 as may be, make it a habit to ask the further question, To what does the man's action tend? And begin with yourself, testing yourself first of all.

That which pulls the strings, remember, is the 38 power concealed within; there is the mandate, the life, there, one may say, the man. Never confound it with the mere containing shell, and the various appended organs. They may be compared to tools, with this difference, that the connexion is organic. Indeed, apart from the inner cause which dictates action or inaction, the parts are of no more use, than the weaver's shuttle, the writer's pen, or the coachman's whip.

BOOK XI

Ζεῦ φύcεωc ἀρχηγέ, νόμου μετὰ πάντα κυβερνῶν
πάντα νομιcτί
                                            Cleanthes

1 THE properties of rational soul—it views itself,
determines itself, makes itself what it wills, bears
and itself reaps its own fruit——while in the
vegetable or animal world the fruit is reaped by
others—and, finally, attains its proper end at the
point where life reaches its term. In a dance or
a play or such like, an interruption leaves the
action incomplete : but not so with the soul ; at
every point and wheresoever arrested, she leaves
her task fulfilled and self-complete, and can say
' I have come by my own.' Furthermore soul
ranges the universe, alike the world of form and
the world of void, and reaches forth into eternity,
and encompasses and comprehends the cyclic
regeneration of the universe, and perceives that

our fathers had no fuller vision, neither will our
children behold any new thing, but that the man
of any understanding who has come to two-score
years has in effect beheld all the uniform past and
the uniform to come.   And yet another property of
rational soul is love of neighbours, truth, self-respect,
and that supreme self-reverence which is likewise
an attribute of Law.   And this implies that the
law of Reason is coincident with the law of justice.

You will be disenchanted of the delights of 2
song and dance and the pancratium, if once you
decompose the melody into its constituent notes,
and ask yourself one by one, ' Is this the spell I
own ? '   You will turn from each in disgust.   Or
analyse dancing in the same way into successions
of motion and rest ; or do the same with the
pancratium.   In short, setting aside virtue and
virtuous acts, you have but to press analysis to
the component parts and you are disenchanted.
Apply the process to life too as a whole.

O for the soul ready, when the hour of dis- 3
solution comes, for extinction or dispersion or
survival ! [1]   But such readiness must proceed from
inward conviction, not come of mere perversity,

---

[1] Compare iv. § 21, p. 40.

M

like the Christians', but of a temper rational and grave, and—if it is to convince others—unostentatious.

Have I acted unselfishly? Good, I have my reward. Be this your ever-present stay; and weary not.

What is your business? to be good. How can you succeed in this but by philosophic views, first of Nature, then of man's own constitution.

Tragedy, the first form of drama, drew its lessons from experience, partly as true to the facts of existence, and partly to take the sting, upon the larger stage of life, from things which appeal to the emotions on the stage. For there you see the fulfilment of the just denouement; and also that there is strength to bear even in the agony of *O Cithæron, Cithæron!*[1] And the dramatists give us words of help, such as the exquisite

> Though I and both my sons be spurned of God,
> There is be sure a reason.

Or again

> Fret not at circumstance.

---

[1] The cry of Oedipus the King (Soph. *Oed. T.* 1391) after the terrible disclosure. For the quotations following, compare vii. 38, 40, 41.

Or
Lives are reaped like ears of corn—

and the like. After tragedy came the old comedy,
reprimanding like a schoolmaster, and in its
bluff outspoken way usefully rebuking pride;
somewhat in the style of like deliverances by
Diogenes.. Next understand the meaning of middle
comedy, and finally of the new comedy, noting to
what ends it was applied and how it gradually
degenerated into mere mimic diversion. That
some good things occur even here, every one
knows; but what was the main object and aim of
that school of poetry and drama?

Palpably, no condition of life is so well suited 7
for philosophy, as that in which chance puts
you.

A branch lopped from its neighbour branch, 8
is inevitably lopped also from the main trunk.
So too a man, isolated from one of his fellow-
beings, is ' severed from the general fellowship.
Another's hand lops the branch; but it is a
man's own act when hatred or estrangement
separates him from his neighbour, and he wots
not that he thereby cuts himself off from
the great world society. But, thanks be to

Zeus who knits the bond of fellowship, it is in
our power to coalesce once more with our neighbour, and recomplete the whole.   Yet constant
repetition of the severance makes reunion and
restoration difficult for the separatist.   The branch
which is part of the original growth and has
shared the continuous life of the tree, is not the
same as one that has been lopped off and rein-
grafted, as the gardeners know well.   So then—
One at core, if not in creed.

9   Those who put obstacles in the way of your
following the law of Reason cannot divert you
from sound action ; so likewise let them not give
your charity a check.   Make sure of both—of
stedfastness in judgment and action, but also of
gentleness towards those who try to baulk or
otherwise annoy you.   To lose your temper with
them is no less weakness, than to abstain from
action or to be cowed into giving in.   Both are
alike deserters from the ranks—both he who
succumbs, and he who is estranged from his
natural brother and friend.

10   Nature is never inferior to art ; for the arts are
but imitations of nature.   If so, nature in its most
perfect and comprehensive form cannot fall short

of true artist workmanship. But all the arts use .
the lower for the higher ; and so too does nature.
Thus we get at the origin of justice, which is the
basis of all the other virtues ; for we are not true
to justice, if we strive for things secondary, or if
we allow ourselves to be imposed upon, or draw
hasty and fallible conclusions.

The things it so perturbs you to seek or shun, 11
do not come to you ; rather, you go to them.
Only let your judgment of them hold its peace,
and they on their side will remain stationary, and
no one will see you either seeking them or
shunning.

The soul becomes a " self-rounded sphere," when 12
it neither strains outward, nor contracts inward by
self-constriction and compression, but shines with
the light, by which it sees all truth without and
truth within.

Will any contemn me ? See he to that. It 13
is for me to see that neither by act nor word I
merit contempt. Or hate me ? Again, his affair.
Mine is to be in charity and kindliness with every
one, ready to show this very man his misconception, not in a carping spirit or with a parade of
forbearance, but honestly and in good part, like old

Phocion,[1] if indeed he meant what he said. That is the right inward temper, and before the eye of god man should not ever cherish resentment or indignation. How can it be an evil for you, to follow the present authorisation of your own nature, and to accept the seasonable course of Nature? Have you not been set here as an instrument for the advantage of the universe?

14   Mutual fawning for mutual contempt, mutual abasement for mutual mastery.

15   ' To be simple, sir, in all my dealings, that is my resolve!' What a hollow spurious ring it has! Tut, man, no need of professions. Truth will speak for itself; it should be written upon your forehead : it rings in the voice, it looks out of the eyes, just as in the lover's expression the beloved reads all. Goodness, true and simple, should be like musk, so redolent that, will-he nill-he, every one who draws near perceives its fragrance. But the affectation of simpleness is a dagger in the sleeve :[2] 'wolf-friendship' is the depth of meanness ; beyond everything, shun that.

[1] Referring probably to Phocion's charge to his son, before drinking the hemlock, ' to bear no ill-will against the Athenians.'

[2] Literally, ' a crooked stick,' referring to the Greek proverb, ' Nothing can make a crooked stick straight.'

Goodness, simplicity and kindness, look out of the eyes, and there is no mistaking.

The perfecting of life is a power residing in 16 the soul, realised by indifference towards things indifferent. The indifference will be attained by contemplating everything in its elements, and also as a whole, and by remembering that nothing can imbue us with a particular view about itself or enforce an entrance ; things are stationary, it is we who originate judgments regarding them, and as it were inscribe them upon our minds, when we need inscribe nothing, or can efface any inscription transcribed there unawares. The call upon self-discipline will not be long, only till life is done with. Why make a grievance and wish things otherwise ? If they are in accordance with nature, rejoice therein and find all easy ; if not, then seek what is in accord with your own nature, and press towards it through good repute or ill. The quest after one's own good is its own excuse.

Consider from whence each thing has come, of 17 what materials it is composed, into what it is changing, what it will be like when changed, and that no harm can come to it.

Heads of Philosophy

First. My relation towards men. We are made for one another : or——another point of view ——I have been set at their head, as the ram heads the flock, or the bull the herd : or, going back to the beginning——If not atoms, then nature disposing all ; if so, things lower exist for the higher, and the higher for one another.

Second. What are men like in board, in bed, and so on ? above all, what principles do they hold binding ? and how far does pride enter into their actual conduct ?

Third. If others are doing right, you have no call to feel sore ; if wrong, it is not wilful, but comes of ignorance. Just as " *No soul wilfully misses truth,*"[1] none wilfully disallows another's due ; are not men distressed if called unjust, or ungracious, or grasping, or in any other way unneighbourly ?

Fourth. You are like others, and often do wrong yourself. Even if you abstain from some forms of wrong, all the same you have the bent for wrongdoing, though cowardice or desire for

[1] See vii. 63.

popularity, or some other low motive keeps you from wrong of that kind.

Fifth. You cannot even be sure if they are doing wrong ; for many actions depend upon some secondary end.   In short one has much to learn, before one can make sure and certain about another's action.

Sixth. When sorely provoked and out of patience, remember that man's life is but for a moment ; a little while, and we all lie stretched in death.

Seventh. Men's actions — resting with *them* and their Inner Selves—cannot agitate us, but our own views regarding them.   Get rid of these, let judgment forego its indignation, and therewith anger departs.   How achieve this ? by reflecting that they cannot demean you.   For if anything except what morally demeans is bad, you too must plead guilty to all sorts of wrongdoing, from brigandage [1] onwards.

Eighth. How much more unconscionable are our anger and vexation at the acts, than the acts which make us angry and vexed !

Ninth. Kindness is invincible if only it is

[1] x. 10 explains the reference.

honest, not fawning or insincere. What can
the most aggressive do, if you keep persistently
kind, and as occasion offers gently remonstrate,
and seize the moment, when he is bent on mischief,
for trying quietly to convert him to a better frame
of mind. 'Not so, my son, we are made for other
ends ; you cannot hurt me, you hurt yourself, my
son.' Then point him gently to the general law
of things, that neither do the bees act so, nor any
of the gregarious animals ; but avoid any touch of
irony or fault-finding, and be affectionate and conciliatory in tone ; not in schoolmaster style, or to
show off before others, but quietly in his own ear,
even if others are standing by.

Bear these nine heads in mind, gifts as it
were of the nine Muses. While you still live,
before it is too late, begin to be a man ! Be on
your guard against flattering as well as against
petulance ; both come of self-seeking, and both
do harm. In fits of anger remind yourself that
true manliness is not passion, but gentleness
and courtesy, the more masculine as well as the
more human : this it is, and not irritation or
discontentment, that implies strength and nerve
and manhood ; the absence of passion gives the

measure of its power. Anger, like grief, is a mark of weakness ; both mean being wounded, and wincing. ,

Tenth and lastly—a gift, so please you, from Apollo leader of the Choir. Not to expect the worthless to do wrong, is idiotcy : it is asking an impossibility. To allow them to wrong others, and to claim exemption for yourself, is graceless and tyrannical.

There are four moods to which your Inner Self 19 is liable, against which you must constantly be upon the watch, and as soon as detected suppress with the appropriate comment. Either, this is a needless fancy : or, this is anti-social : or, this does not come from your own heart—and not to speak from one's heart is a moral inconsequence. Or, fourthly, you will never forgive yourself ; for such a feeling implies subjection and abasement of the diviner element in you to the perishable and less honourable portion, the body and its coarser apprehensions.

By nature breath and all the igneous element 20 in your composition ascend ; yet in obedience to the order of things, they accept subordination and keep their place in the compound. Conversely,

all the earthy and watery elements in you tend to
descend; yet by steady levitation they retain a
position which is not theirs by nature. Thus the
elements, we see, obey the law of things, and
persistently retain their appointed place, until the
signal for dissolution sounds their release. Fie on
it, that your mind-element alone should disobey
and resent the post assigned; though no violence
is laid upon it, nothing but what is in accordance
with its nature; yet it breaks away impatiently.
For motions of injustice, intemperance, anger,
vexation, fear, are simply a rebellion against
nature. When our Inner Self chafes against anything that happens, in so doing it quits its post.
It is made for holiness and god-fearing, no less
than for justice. These too are included in the
thought of world-communion, nay are prior even
to the dues of justice.

21   Where the life has no unity of aim, the man
cannot live life at unity with himself. Nor is it
enough to say this, unless you go on to add what
the true aim should be. In the idea of goods at
large, as popularly understood, there is no unity,
but only in goods of a certain kind, namely social
goods; similarly for unity of aim, the basis of the

aim must be social and unselfish. Direct all your inward endeavours to this end, and you will give unity to all your actions, and be always consistent with yourself.

Think of the mountain-mouse[1] and the town- 22
mouse, and the poor beast's scurry and scare!

Socrates called popular beliefs Bug-bears for 23
children.

The Spartans at their festivals, for their guests 24
set seats in the shade, for themselves sat where they could.

Socrates declined the invitation of Archelaus 25
son of Perdiccas, "*to avoid*" he said "*death with ignominy*"——to wit, receiving favours he could not return.

Among the statutes of the Ephesians was an 26
injunction, to meditate continually on some ancient model of virtue.

The Pythagoreans bid us every morning lift our 27
eyes to heaven, to meditate upon the heavenly bodies pursuing their everlasting round——their order, their purity, their nakedness. For no star wears a veil.

[1] Marcus habitually uses 'mountain' to signify unperturbed withdrawal from the world, and the adjective here echoes x. 15, 23, and opening of iv. 2.

28   Think of Socrates with the sheepskin round his loins, when Xanthippe had marched off with his cloak, and what he said to his friends who modestly beat a retreat when they saw him in such a guise.

29   In reading and in writing you cannot give rules till you have obeyed them.   Much more in life.

30   Slave that thou art, reason is not for thee !

31   And my dear heart laughed within.[1]

32   Virtue they'll taunt and with hard words revile.[2]

33   To look for figs in winter is fool's work ; so is it to look for a child, when the time is past.

34   As you fondle your little one, says Epictetus, murmur to yourself 'To-morrow perchance it will die.'—'Ominous, is it ? '—'Nothing is ominous,' said the sage, 'that signifies an act of nature.   Is 35 it ominous to harvest the ripe ears ? '   The green grape, the cluster, the raisin, change following change, not into nothingness but to the not yet realised.

36   "*No man can rob us of our will*," says Epictetus.[3]

37   Epictetus urged the need of a sound grammar

---

[1] Homer, *Od.* ix. 413.   [2] Hesiod, *Works and Days*, v. 184.
[3] Arrian, Epict. I. xi. 37, III. xxii. 105.

of assent ; and in dealing with the impulses, to take good heed to keep them subject to reservation, unselfish, and in due proportion to their object : always to refrain inclination, and to limit avoidance to things within our own control. . 38

"It is no trifle at stake," he said—*" it means, are you in your senses, or are you not ? "*

' What would you have ?' Socrates used to say, 39 ' rational men's souls, or irrational? '—'Rational.'— ' Souls healthy or souls depraved ? '—' Healthy.' ' Then why not seek for them ? '—' Because we have them already.'—' Then why fight and be at variance ? '

BOOK XII

Animula vagula blandula,
Hospes comesque corporis,
Quae nunc abibis in loca?—*Hadrian*

1 ALL the good things to which you pray sooner
or later to attain may be yours at once, if
only you will not stand in your own way; if
only, leaving the past alone and committing the
.future to the hand of providence, you will direct
the present and that only, in the way of holiness and justice: of holiness, that you may be
glad in your apportioned lot, nature's assignment,
it for you and you for it; of justice, that
you may freely and without subterfuge speak
truth and follow law and treat things at their
worth, knowing no contravention from evil in
another, nor from false view within, nor from
sound nor yet sensation of this fleshly shell: for

the part affected must look to that. If then, now
that you near your end, leaving all else alone,
you will reverence only your Inner Self and the
god within, if you will fear not life some time
coming to an end, but never beginning life at all
in accord with nature's law, then indeed you will
be a man, worthy of the universe that begat you,
and no more a stranger to your fatherland, ever
in amaze at the unexpectedness of what each day
brings forth, and hanging upon this event or that.

God sees men's Inner Selves stripped of their 2
material shells and husks and impurities. Mind
to mind, his mental being touches only the like
elements in us derivative and immanent from him.
By accustoming yourself to the same habit, you
will save yourself most part of the distracting
strain. For he who looks not to his shell of
flesh, will assuredly not make ado over raiment
and house and reputation, intent on the mere
trappings and stagings.

You consist of three parts — body, breath, 3
mind. The first two are yours, to the extent of
requiring your care: the third only is properly
your own. Now if you separate from your true
self—your understanding—all that others do or

N

say, all that you have yourself done or said, all that perturbs you for the future, all that belongs to your material shell or vital breath and lies outside your own control, all finally that sweeps past you in the swirl of circumstance, if thus exempting and clearing your mind - faculty from the play of destiny, you enable it to live free and unrestricted, doing what is just, willing what befalls, and saying what is true—if, I say, you thus separate from your Inner Self the outer ties and attachments, the influences of time past and time to come, and so make yourself in the language of Empedocles

A rounded sphere, poised in rotating rest ;

and train yourself to live in what alone is life— the present, then you will be able, for life's remainder and till death, to live on constant to the deity within, unperturbed, ingenuous, serene.

How strange it is, that every one loves himself above all others, yet attaches less weight to his own view of himself, than to that of other men. Suppose, for instance, some god or some wise teacher stood at a man's elbow and bade him utter aloud each thought that came into his heart or mind, he could not endure it for a single day. So much more deference do we pay to what our neighbours think of us, than to our own selves.

How is it that the gods, who ordered all things 5 well and lovingly, overlooked this one thing; that some men, elect in virtue, having kept close covenant with the divine, and enjoyed intimate communion therewith by holy acts and sacred ministries, should not, when once dead, renew their being, but be utterly extinguished? If it indeed be so, be sure, had it been better otherwise, the gods would have had it so. Were it right, it would be likewise possible; were it according to nature, nature would have brought it to pass. From its not being so, if as a fact it is not so, be assured it ought not so to be. Do you not see that in hazarding such questions you arraign the justice of god? nay we could not thus reason with the gods, but for their perfectness and justice. And from this it follows that they would never have allowed any unjust or unreasonable neglect of parts of the great order.

Practise even where you despair of success. 6 Want of practice makes the left hand helpless in all else, but in handling the bridle it is more efficient than the right : that comes of practice.

7   Think what a man should be in body and soul, when death overtakes him : think of the shortness of life, of the unfathomable eternity behind and before, of the weakness of all things material.

8   Strip off the husks, and look at the underlying causes ; look at the tendencies of action ; at pain, pleasure, death, reputation ; at man, his own disquieter ; see how every contravention comes from within, not from without ; how the view taken is everything.

9   In applying principles to action be like the boxer [1] not the swordsman. The swordsman lays by his sword and takes it up again ; but the boxer's hand is always there, he has nothing to do but to clench it.

10   Look at things as they are, discriminating matter, cause, and tendency.

11   How great is man's prerogative—to do nothing but what god approves, and to accept all that god assigns.

12   In the order of nature, we must not find

---

[1] Strictly "pancratiast"—a mixture of boxing and wrestling.

fault with gods who *do no wrong, witting or unwitting; nor yet with men, whose wrong is done unwittingly. Therefore find fault with none.

How silly and how strange, to be amazed at 13 anything in life!

Either fixed necessity and an inviolable order, 14 or a merciful providence, or a random and un- governed medley. If an inviolable necessity, why resist? If a providence, waiting to be merciful, make yourself worthy of the divine aid. If a chaos uncontrolled, be thankful that amid the wild waters you have within yourself an Inner governing mind. If the waves sweep you away, let them sweep flesh, breath and poor mortality; the mind they shall never sweep.

Shall the flame of a lamp give light till it is 15 extinguished, and not lose its radiance; and shall the truth within you and justice and wisdom con- sent to premature extinction?

He gives me the impression of wrongdoing, 16 but after all how do I know, whether it is wrong? or supposing it was, that he did not upbraid him- self for it—like the mourner defacing his own visage? He who would not have the vile do

wrong, is like one who would not have the fig-tree
bear juice in her figs, or infants squall, or the
horse neigh, or anything else that is in the order
of things.   What else can result, his bent being
what it is?   If it aggrieves you, amend it.

17   If it is not your duty, do not do it : if it is not
true, do not say it.   .

18   Be it your endeavour always to look at the
whole, and see what the actual thing is that produces the impression, and resolve it by analysis
into cause, matter, tendency, and duration of time
within which it must cease to exist.

19   It is time to recognise that you have within
you something higher and more divine than that
which produces the affections of sense, or just
pulls the strings within.   How is it with my
understanding, at this moment? fear? suspicion?
desire? or what?

20   First, do nothing at random, or unpurposed.
Secondly, direct all action to some social end.

21   A little while and your place will know you
no more : so too with everything you now see,
and every one with whom you live.   All things
change and pass and perish, that others may
succeed.

The view taken is everything ; and that rests 22
with yourself.   Disown the view, at will ; and
behold, the headland rounded, there is calm, still
waters and a waveless bay.

No action whatsoever is the worse for ceasing, 23
when the time for cessation comes : neither is the
author of the action, merely because his action
ceases.   So too with the sum of all our actions,
which is life—when the time for cessation comes,
it is none the worse merely because it ceases ; nor
do we impute evil to him, who at the right time
brings the sequence to an end.   Nature sets the
right time and the limit ; sometimes the individual
nature with its bidding of old age, but in any case
Nature at large, who by constant changes of the
parts keeps the whole universe ever fresh and
vigorous : and that which is of advantage to the
universe is ever good and lovely.   To the individual then cessation of life is no evil, for there
is nothing in it demeaning, seeing that it lies
outside our own control and comes not of self-
seeking : and it is a good, in that to the universe
it is seasonable, serviceable, and subserving other
ends.   Thus man becomes a vessel of god, at one
with god in tendency and in intent.

24   Three maxims to fall back upon.

I. In action, do nothing at random, or at variance with the ways of justice: all outward circumstance, remember, is either chance or providence; you cannot quarrel with chance, and you cannot, arraign providence.

II. Think what everything is from the seminal germ to its quickening with soul, and from soul-quickening to the yielding up of soul; think of what it is compounded and into what it is dissolved.

III. Supposing that translated to some higher region you could look down upon the world of man, and discern its manifold variety, and embrace within your vision his vast environment of things in air and things in heaven, remember that, however often so translated, you will see always the same sights, all uniform, all transitory. What food is here for pride?

25   Reject the view — and straightway, you are whole.   Who hinders the rejection?

26   Impatience at anything means that you forget —That all things follow the law of Nature; that the fault lies at another's door; that everything which happens, ever did, ever will, ever does in

every case so happen : further, that you forget man's brotherhood with all mankind, not by blood or physical descent, but by community in mind : and yet again that each man's mind is god, an efflux of deity ; that nothing is strictly a man's own, but even his child, his body, his very soul, have come from god ; that the view taken is everything ; and that every one can live, or lose, the present alone.

Dwell in retrospect on those who gave resent- 27 ment rein, who knew the transports of big ambitions, failures, feuds, and every change and chance. Then reflect, Where are they all now ? Smoke, ashes, and a tale, or less than a tale. Recall each instance of the kind—Fabius Catulinus on his farm, Lucius Lupus in his gardens, Stertinius at Baiæ, Tiberius at Capreæ, Velius Rufus, or any other such fanciful endeavour! how paltry all such striving! how far more philosophical simply to use the material supplied to make oneself just and wise and a follower of gods! The pride which masks as modesty is the most perverse of all.

To those who press the question, 'Where have 28 you seen the gods, whence your conviction of their existence, that you worship them as you do ? '

I reply——first, they are visible even to the bodily eye : secondly, neither have I set eyes upon my soul, and yet I do it reverence. So is it with the gods ; from my continual experience of their power, I have the conviction that they exist, and yield respect.

29   This is the way of salvation——to look throughly into everything and see what it really is, alike in matter and in cause ; with your whole heart to do what is just and say what is true : and one thing more, to find life's fruition in heaping good on good so close, that not a chink is left between.

30   The light of the sun is one, even though disparted by walls, hills, or a hundred other things : its common substance is one, though disparted by any number of individual bodies. So too soul is one, though disparted among any number of natures and individualities. And soul possessed of mind is one, though we think of it as distributed in parts. All the other constituents of the various wholes——breath, material elements, and so forth—— possess neither sense nor mutual relationship ; yet even they are held in union by the unifying element and identity of gravitation. But thought tends specifically towards its counterpart, and

combines with it, and the instinct of community
declines disunion.

Why hanker for continuous existence? is it 31
for sensation, desire, growth? or again, for speech,
utterance, thought? which of these seems worth
the craving? If each and all of these are of
small regard, address yourself to the final quest,
the following of reason and of god. Reverence
for them cannot be reconciled with repining at the
losses death entails.

What a jot of infinite unfathomable time is 32
assigned to any one of us! In a moment it
vanishes into eternity. What a morsel of the
sum of being! or of the sum of soul! on what a
grain of the whole earth you crawl! Mindful of
all this, regard one thing only as of moment, to
do what your own nature directs, to bear what
universal nature brings.

How goes it with your Inner Self? *that* is 33
everything. All else, in your control or out of it,
is dust of the dead and smoke.

The best quickener to contempt of death is 34
this—that even those who account pleasure good
and pain evil, contemn it notwithstanding.

For the man, to whom good means solely that 35

which comes in season, to whom it is all one whether he follows the law of Reason in few acts or in many, to whom it matters not whether his outlook on the world be long or short——for that man death has no terrors.

Man, you have been a citizen of the great world city. Five years or fifty, what matters it? To every man his due, as law allots. Why then protest? No tyrant gives you your dismissal, no unjust judge, but nature who gave you the admission. It is like the prætor discharging some player whom he has engaged.——'But the five acts are not complete; I have played but three.'——Good: life's drama, look you, is complete in three. The completeness is in his hands, who first authorised your composition, and now your dissolution; neither was your work. Serenely take your leave; serene as he who gives you the discharge.

APPENDIX

SELECTED emendations of the text, adopted in the translation and not found in printed editions. The line-numbering is from the Tauchnitz text.

BOOK I

§ 14, *l.* 7   For ἀμελές or ὁμαλές, read ἐμμελές

§ 16, *l.* 12   For ἀπολειφθέντων, read ἀποληφθέντων

14   Read ἐπίμονον ὧν ἂν ἄλλος τις προαπέστη τῆς ἐρεύνης, ἀρκεσθείς . .

41   Omit ἐκτός

48   Omit τὸ τὰ πάτρια φυλάσσειν

57   For ἀνθρώποις, read ἄλλοις, taken for $\overline{ανοις}$

59   For οὐκ ἐν ἀωρεῖ, read οὐκ ἦν ἀωρὶ

§ 17, *l.* 53   For καὶ τούτου ἐν Καιήτῃ ὥσπερ χρήσῃ, read καὶ τὸ τοῦ ἐν Καιήτῃ "ὥσπερ χρήσῃ"

BOOK II

§ 2, *end*   For ὑποδύεσθαι, read ἀποδύρεσθαι

§ 4, *end*   For οἰχήσεται καὶ οἰχήσῃ καὶ αὖθις οὐχ ἥξεται, read οἰχήσεται καὶ αὖθις οὐκ ἔξεσται

§ 6, *opening* For ὕβριζε, ὕβριζε αὐτήν, ὦ ψυχή· read
ὑβρίζῃ; μὴ ὕβριζε cεαυτήν, ὦ ψυχή·
and in following line εἶc for the εὖ, οὐ,
or βραχύc variants

§ 16, *l.* 5 For ἐν μέρει, read ἐνώcει

Book III

§ 2, *l.* 18 For ἡδέωc πωc διαcυνίcταcθαι, read ἡδέωc
πωc ἰδίᾳ cυνίcταcθαι

§ 4, *ll.* 3-4 For ἤτοι γὰρ ἄλλου ἔργου cτέρῃ τουτέcτι
φανταζόμενοc, read τί γὰρ ἄλλου ἔργου
cτέρῃ οὕτωc ἔτι φανταζόμενοc κτλ.

§ 5, *l.* 9 For ἐν δὲ τὸ φαιδρόν, read ἐν δὲ τούτῳ τὸ
φαιδρόν

§ 8, *l.* 2 For μεμολυcμένον, read μεμωλυcμένον

§ 12, *l.* 7 For ἡρωϊκῇ, read εὐροϊκῇ

Book IV

§ 3, *l.* 12 For αὐτήν, ἁὐτήν, or λύπην, read αὐλήν
ll. 23-24 Read ἀλλὰ τὰ cωματικά cου ἅψεται;
ἔτι ἐννοήcαc . .

§ 5, *l.* 2 Read cύγκριcιc ἐκ τοιούτων cτοιχείων,
λύcιc εἰc ταὐτά

§ 16, *l.* 1 After θεόc, insert θεοῖc

§ 18, *l.* 1 For ἀcχολίαν, read εὐcχολίαν

§ 19, *end* I have modified punctuation, and as final
words read παρίηc γὰρ νῦν ἀκαίρωc τὴν
φυcικὴν δόcιν, ἄλλου τινὸc ἐχόμενοc
λόγου λοιπόν

§ 21, *l.* 4 For πρὸc ἥντινα ἐπιδιαμονήν, read ἐπὶ
ποcήν τινα διαμονήν

§ 24, *l.* 2 After ἄμεινον, insert μόνον

§ 27, *opening* Read ἤτοι κόσμος διατεταγμένος, ἢ κυκεὼν συμπεφορημένος. ἀλλὰ μὴν κόσμος· ἢ ἐν coὶ μέν . . . ;

§ 30 Repunctuated ; with ἄλλως (for ἄλλος) attached to βιβλίου clause

§ 33, *l.* 4 For Λεοννάτος, read Δέντατος

§ 40, *l.* 2 For ἐπέχον, read ἀπέχον, or better ἐφέπον

§ 46, *end* Read ὅτι οὐ δεῖ παῖδας τοκέων ὦν [or ὥς], τουτέςτι κατὰ ψιλόν, καθότι παρειλήφαμεν

§ 51, *l.* 4 For cτρατείας, read cτραγγείας

BOOK V

§ 5, *l.* 7 For μεγαλεῖον, read ἀμεγαλεῖον

§ 6 Besides small amendments—φύcει for φηcί— I have at various points re-arranged

§ 26, *l.* 5 For τὴν ἑτέραν cυμπάθειαν, read τὴν μερῶν cυμπάθειαν

BOOK VI

§ 13, *l.* 13 For ἱcτορίαν, read τορείαν

§ 45, *l.* 4 Insert ἢ before ἐπὶ τῶν μέσων

BOOK VII

§ 2, *opening* Read ἴδε τὰ δόγματα· πῶς γὰρ ἄλλως . . .

§ 16, *l.* 8 For οὐ γὰρ ἕξεις, read οὐ παρέλξεις

§ 31, *l.* 4 For ἔτι εἰ δαίμονα τὰ cτοιχεῖα, read εἴτε δαιμόνια, εἴτε cτοιχεῖα, ἀρκεῖ δὴ μεμνῆcθαι

§ 56, *l.* 1 Insert μὴ before μέχρι νῦν βεβιωκότα

§ 66, *l.* 7 For ἐπιστήσειεν, read ἀπιστήσειεν

§ 67, *opening* Supply τὸν νοῦν (with Schultz) from end of preceding section

Book VIII

§ 8, *opening* πάντα γινώςκειν for ἀναγινώςκειν seems probable

§ 21, *l.* 2 For νοςᾶςαν δέ, πορνεῦςαν, read νοςᾶςαν [δ'] ἢ ἀποπυᾶςαν

§ 35, *l.* 4 For ἐπιπεριτρέπει, read ἔτι περιτρέπει

§ 38 Read βλέπε κρίνων φύςει ςοφωτάτους

§ 41, *end* Read οὐχ ὁτιοῦν ἅπτεται, ὅταν γένηται ςφαῖρος κυκλοτερὴς μονίη

§ 51, *end* Read πῶς οὖν πηγὴν ἀέννaον ἕξεις; εἰςδύου ςεαυτόν κτλ.

§ 57, *l.* 7 For ὥςπερ διαιρεῖται read ἐπερείδεται

Book IX

§ 1, *l.* 36 Read ἀντὶ τοῦ ςυμβαίνειν ἐπίςης τοῖς ἐπι- γινομένοις, omitting κατὰ τὸ ἑξῆς and γινομένοις καί

§ 3, *l.* 9 For ὁλοςχερῶς, read δυςχερῶς

§ 28, *l.* 4 Provisionally read ἢ ἅπαξ ὥρμηςε, τὰ δὲ λοιπὰ κατ' ἐπακολούθηςιν κατεκτείνει· τρόπον γάρ τινα ἄτομοι ἢ ἡ εἱμαρμένη

Book X

§ 7, *end* For ςε λίαν προςπλέκει, read ςὺ λίαν προςπλέκῃ

§ 9, *l.* 3 For ὁ φυςιολογητός, read οὐ φυςιολογητῶς

APPENDIX

§ 12, *l.* 8 Read ἤ γε ἀπόπτωσις ἀπότευγμ' οὐκ ἔστιν (for ἀπὸ τούτου ἐστίν)

§ 19, *l.* 2 For ἀνδρονομούμενοι, read ἀνδρογυνού- μενοι

BOOK XI

§ 6 In first clause, for ὅτι . . . μὴ ἄχθεσθε, read ὥστε . . . μὴ ἄχθεσθαι

§ 12, *l.* 2 For σπείρηται, read συσπειρᾶται.

§ 15, *l.* 3 Read αὐτὸ φανήσεται· ἐπὶ τοῦ μετώπου γεγράφθαι ὀφείλει· εὐθὺς ἡ φωνὴ τοιοῦ- τον ἠχεῖ· εὐθὺς ἐν τοῖς ὄμμασιν ἐξέχει

§ 16, *l.* 10 Read τί μέντοι δύσκολον οὐκ ἄλλως ἔχειν ταῦτα ;

BOOK XII

§ 2, *end* For ἀσχολήσεται, read εὐσχολήσεται
§ 30, *l.* 8 For τὸ νοοῦν of Edd., read τὸ ἐνοῦν
§ 31, *l.* 2 For τὸ λήγειν, read τὸ λέγειν

THE END

Printed by R. & R. CLARK, LIMITED, *Edinburgh.*

MACMILLAN AND CO.'S PUBLICATIONS.

THE FOURTH BOOK OF THE
MEDITATIONS OF MARCUS AURELIUS ANTONINUS.

A Revised Text with Translation and Commentary, aod an Appendix
on the Relations of the Emperor with Cornelius Fronto.

By HASTINGS CROSSLEY, M.A., Hon. D.Lit. Queen's University;
Sometime Scholar of Trinity College, Dublin; Professor of Greek
in Queen's College, Belfast. 8vo. 6s.

ESSAYS IN CRITICISM. By MATTHEW ARNOLD, D.C.L.,
formerly Professor of Poetry in the University of Oxford, and Fellow of
Oriel College. First Series (contains Essay on MARCUS AURELIUS). Second
Series. Globe 8vo. 5s. each. [*Eversley Series.*

PLATO AND PLATONISM. A Series of Lectures. By WALTER
H. PATER, M.A., Fellow of Brasenose College, Oxford. Extra Crown 8vo.
8s. 6d.

SEEKERS AFTER GOD. THE LIVES OF MARCUS AURELIUS,
SENECA, and EPICTETUS. By FREDERIC W. FARRAR, D.D., F.R.S., late
Fellow of Trinity College, Cambridge; Archdeacon and Canon of West-
minster, Chaplain in Ordinary to the Queen. Crown 8vo. 3s. 6d.

THE REPUBLIC OF PLATO. Translated by J. LL. DAVIES,
M.A., and D. J. VAUGHAN. Pott 8vo. 2s. 6d. net. [*Golden Treasury Series.*

THE TRIAL AND 'DEATH OF SOCRATES. Being the
Euthyphron, Apology, Crito, and Phaedo of Plato. Translated by F. J.
CHURCH. Pott 8vo. 2s. 6d. net. [*Golden Treasury Series.*

PHAEDRUS, LYSIS, AND PROTAGORAS. A new transla-
tion by J. WRIGHT, M.A. Pott 8vo. 2s. 6d. net. [*Golden Treasury Series.*

MACMILLAN AND CO., LTD., LONDON.

CPSIA information can be obtained
at www.ICGtesting.com
Printed in the USA
LVOW10s1828210118

563422LV00011B/846/P